Lana J. Manganiello

CAREERS IN BUSINESS LAW

Forging Your Path to Success

AMERICAN BAR ASSOCIATION
Business Law Section

Cover design by Catherine Zaccarine.

Printed in the United States of America.

28 27 26 25 24 5 4 3 2 1

ISBN: 978-1-63905-534-0

Table of Contents

Prologue

Shaping the Future of Law

The legal profession is undergoing a profound transformation. Over the past three decades, every aspect of law has evolved at an unprecedented pace. The methods by which clients seek legal assistance, the laws that govern our society, the delivery of legal services, the criteria for entering the legal profession, and even the structure of legal businesses and education—all have shifted dramatically. Today, the legal landscape is richer in opportunities than ever before, presenting a myriad of paths for those aspiring to make their mark.

For those aiming to achieve success in the legal field, the journey ahead requires a departure from traditional routes. The most accomplished lawyers of today followed paths that are no longer available. The future belongs to those who can envision a career that aligns with their aspirations and are prepared to carve out their own unique trajectory. This challenge is not only exciting but also crucial. Lawyers play a pivotal role in driving forward advancements in technology, business, and social movements. Their influence is central to the progress of our society.

It is important to acknowledge that the legal profession, in its current state, has its flaws. However, this book aims to provide guidance on how to navigate and succeed within this evolving system. By thriving both personally and professionally, you can contribute to the betterment of the profession and, by extension, society as a whole.

The need for intelligent, empathetic individuals to take on this challenge cannot be overstated. The future of law is ripe for innovation, and the next generation of legal professionals will need to be trailblazers. This book offers insights into achieving success in the modern legal environment and leveraging that success to effect a positive change within the profession.

As we stand at the cusp of further changes, the possibilities for shaping the future of law are limitless. This book is a call to action for those ready to explore these new horizons and make a lasting impact. The legal profession is evolving, and with it, the opportunity to redefine success and contribute to a more just and equitable society.

Introduction

This book is conceived as a comprehensive guide for those within the legal profession who are either embarking on a career in business law, considering a transition into a new specialization within the field, or contemplating a career shift within its broad spectrum. It is designed to serve law students, seasoned attorneys, and professionals at various stages of their careers, offering information, insights, and actionable strategies aimed at facilitating a successful and fulfilling career in business law.

The realm of business law is characterized by its dynamic nature, presenting a wide array of opportunities and challenges that demand a strategic approach, keen insight, and a forward-thinking mindset. This guide endeavors to equip readers with the knowledge and tools necessary to navigate this complex landscape, emphasizing career choices that are not only strategically sound but also aligned with personal aspirations and values.

Central to this book is the provision of practical advice and actionable steps that attorneys can employ to prepare themselves for a thriving career in business law. This includes developing a deep understanding of the field, identifying niche areas of specialization, leveraging technology and innovation, and building a robust professional network. The guidance offered herein is designed to be evergreen, ensuring its relevance and applicability in the face of the legal profession's ongoing evolution.

The narratives and profiles featured in this book highlight individuals who have made significant strides in business law, often against the backdrop of historical underrepresentation and adversity. These include women, people of color, and individuals from marginalized backgrounds, whose experiences and achievements illuminate the diverse pathways to success within the legal profession. Although the focus is on early and mid-career professionals who exemplify the future of the field, the insights gleaned from their journeys are universally applicable, offering valuable lessons for readers at any career stage.

By showcasing these pioneering individuals, the book aims to inspire readers to be intentional and proactive in their career planning, demonstrating that success in business law is attainable through dedication, innovation, and a commitment to excellence. Their stories serve as a testament to the potential for achieving professional fulfillment and impact, regardless of one's starting point or the obstacles encountered along the way.

As you proceed through the chapters that follow, you are encouraged to approach your career in business law with both ambition and mindfulness, recognizing that the path to success is as individual as you are. This book is your guide to navigating the complexities of the legal profession, empowering you to carve out a career that is not only successful but also deeply rewarding and aligned with your vision for the future.

Career Foundations and Choices

Choosing the Right Path: Exploring Career Choices, Including Law School Selection, Practice Areas, and Early Career Decisions

Self-Assessment and Career Reflection in Business Law

Embarking on a career in business law requires more than just a solid grasp of legal doctrines; it demands a profound introspection to understand one's own abilities, preferences, and values. This chapter aims to guide aspiring business lawyers through the essential process of self-assessment and career reflection, laying the foundation for a successful and fulfilling legal career.

The Foundation of Self-Assessment in Legal Careers

At its core, self-assessment is pivotal for anyone aiming to carve out a successful path in the legal field. It serves as the cornerstone of legal professionalism, enabling lawyers to navigate the myriad opportunities within business law effectively. Identifying one's strengths, weaknesses, and interests is particularly critical in this area, as it directly influences the choice of specialization. Whether it is an analytical mind suited to financial regulation or a talent for negotiation in corporate deals, understanding these intrinsic abilities guides lawyers toward their ideal niche.

Tools for Self-Discovery

The journey toward self-discovery employs various tools and methodologies designed to uncover personal traits and competencies:

- **Personality Assessments:** Tools like the Myers–Briggs Type Indicator and the Holland Code test offer insights into personality traits that align with specific legal roles.
- **Personal SWOT (Strengths, Weaknesses, Opportunities, and Threats) Analysis:** This method helps identify competitive advantages and areas for development, especially valuable for those considering niche specializations within business law.

- **Career Journals and Reflection:** Keeping a record of daily experiences and reflections can reveal patterns in motivations and challenges, providing clarity on work preferences.
- **Informational Interviews and Shadowing:** Engaging with seasoned professionals through interviews or shadowing opportunities offers practical insights and helps in identifying areas of interest.

Aligning Career Choices with Personal Values: The congruence between career choices and personal values is fundamental to achieving job satisfaction. For business lawyers, this may mean choosing practice areas that harmonize with their ethical beliefs, such as promoting corporate responsibility or focusing on environmental law to reflect personal interests in sustainability.

Understanding Personal Working Styles: Recognizing one's preferred working style is crucial in selecting a suitable specialization. Some may thrive in the dynamic environment of litigation or mergers and acquisitions, while others may prefer the detailed focus required in compliance or contract drafting. Identifying these preferences early on helps in avoiding burnout and ensuring career longevity.

Goal Setting and Career Planning: Effective self-assessment culminates in the ability to set realistic, achievable career goals. A lawyer passionate about advocacy might aim to become a prominent figure in consumer rights law, whereas one skilled in mediation could strive for excellence in dispute resolution. These goals inform the career planning process, providing a roadmap for professional growth.

Adaptation and Lifelong Learning: The legal profession, particularly business law, is characterized by constant evolution. Committing to lifelong learning is essential, ensuring lawyers stay abreast of legal, business, and technological trends. This commitment extends beyond legal expertise to encompass business acumen, tech proficiency, and soft skills development.

Proactive Career Management: Managing one's career proactively is about staying informed of industry trends, emerging legal areas, and shifting client demands. It involves seeking growth opportunities through education, networking, and mentorship, ensuring lawyers remain adaptable and capable of delivering exceptional service.

Specialty and Further Education: Choosing a focus within business law should be an informed decision, reflective of an individual's strengths and interests. Pursuing further education or specialized training can enhance expertise in a chosen field, addressing any skill gaps. For instance, a lawyer drawn to international business law may benefit from courses in international relations, while someone interested in tech start-ups could explore certifications in data privacy.

Self-assessment and career reflection are indispensable for navigating the complexities of business law successfully. They enable lawyers to make informed decisions, adapt to the legal landscape's evolving nature, and align their careers with their values and interests. Understanding oneself equips lawyers to tackle the challenges and seize the opportunities of a career in business law, paving the way for professional success and personal fulfillment.

Business Law Areas of Focus

Scope of Business Law

Business Law encompasses a broad range of legal services designed to support businesses in their operational, transactional, and regulatory needs. In the context of this discussion, "business law" refers to the practice of law with a focus on clients that are businesses themselves. Lawyers in this field provide the counsel and support that businesses require to navigate the legal landscape, ensuring they not only remain compliant with laws and regulations but also thrive in their respective industries. This includes everything from start-up legal considerations, mergers and acquisitions, contract negotiations, and intellectual property rights, to dispute resolution and litigation.

The Dynamic Nature of Business Law

The realm of business law is dynamic, reflecting the evolving nature of business itself. Legal practitioners in this field must be versatile, adapting to the changing trends, emerging markets, and technological advancements that influence their clients' operations. For attorneys aspiring to specialize in business law, understanding this area as a foundational field offers the opportunity to align their legal expertise with the strategic goals of businesses, crafting solutions that propel clients toward success.

Role of Specialists

In essence, specializing in business law is not just about mastering the statutes and regulations; it's about becoming an integral part of the business ecosystem, providing the legal scaffolding that supports businesses in their growth and innovation endeavors. Whether it's helping a start-up navigate its formation, aiding a company in protecting its intellectual property, or guiding a corporation through a complex international merger, business law specialists are key players in the economic landscape, ensuring their clients' business ventures are both legally sound and strategically poised for success.

Considerations for Various Practice Areas in Business Law

As we delve into this multifaceted domain, it's crucial to understand the nuances of each area of practice, how they affect the broader marketplace, and what they demand from legal professionals.

This section provides a brief overview of various practice areas within business law, highlighting the distinct challenges and opportunities they present.

Antitrust and Competition Law

Antitrust and Competition Law is essential for maintaining fair competition in the marketplace, preventing monopolies, and regulating anticompetitive practices. Lawyers specializing in this field work to ensure that businesses comply with antitrust laws, representing them in investigations and litigation related to competition issues. Their expertise helps businesses navigate complex regulatory environments, ensuring competitive practices that benefit consumers and the economy.

- **Workflow:** Steady, with fluctuations based on regulatory investigations and litigation.
- **Urgency:** High in the face of government investigations or court proceedings.
- **Types of Clients:** Businesses of all sizes across various industries potentially affected by antitrust and competition regulations.
- **Law Firms:** Firms with strong antitrust and competition law practices, including both specialized boutiques and large, full-service firms.

Banking and Finance Law

Banking and Finance Law regulates the operations of banks, credit extension, and financial services. Lawyers in this domain are engaged in loan transactions, regulatory compliance, asset finance, and restructuring, providing critical advice on navigating the legal and regulatory landscape. Their role facilitates the execution of financial transactions and compliance with regulatory standards.

- **Workflow:** The workflow is steady, punctuated by peaks of project-based work centered on the negotiation and closing of financing deals, regulatory filings, and restructuring negotiations.
- **Urgency:** High urgency is often a hallmark of this field, especially during deal negotiations and closings, where timely legal advice and action can be critical to the success of financial transactions.

- **Types of Clients:** This specialization caters to a diverse clientele, including banks, nonbank financial institutions, borrowers, and other entities engaged in the borrowing, lending, and regulation of money.
- **Law Firms:** Banking and Finance Law is practiced in firms with dedicated banking and financial services departments as well as in specialized finance law firms, offering expertise in the complexities of finance law and regulation.

Bankruptcy and Restructuring Law

Bankruptcy and Restructuring Law addresses the legal and financial challenges facing businesses in distress, guiding them through the process of restructuring operations, renegotiating debts, and, when necessary, navigating bankruptcy proceedings. Attorneys in this specialty provide critical support for filing bankruptcy, developing strategies for creditor negotiations, and implementing restructuring plans to revive financial stability. Their work is vital in steering distressed businesses toward recovery, preserving value for stakeholders, and ensuring compliance with legal frameworks governing insolvency and restructuring.

- **Workflow:** The workflow may be steady but is prone to spikes during economic downturns or when companies face significant financial challenges, requiring specialized legal intervention to address complex financial and operational issues.
- **Urgency:** High urgency is common, especially in crisis situations where rapid legal and financial actions are necessary to protect the interests of the company, its creditors, and other stakeholders in a distressed situation.
- **Types of Clients:** Clients include financially distressed businesses, creditors looking to recover debts, and bankruptcy trustees responsible for overseeing the bankruptcy process and asset distribution.
- **Law Firms:** Practiced in law firms with strong litigation and corporate departments, capable of handling the multifaceted aspects of bankruptcy cases and corporate restructuring efforts.

Commercial Law

Commercial Law governs the rights, relations, and conduct of individuals and businesses engaged in commerce, merchandising, trade, and sales. It encompasses a variety of legal issues, including the contractual agreements, sales transactions, and the legal implications of domestic and international trade. Lawyers specializing in commercial law advise on transaction structures, draft and review contracts, and assist in resolving disputes that arise in the course of business operations.

- **Workflow:** Steady, with variations depending on the volume and complexity of commercial transactions.
- **Urgency:** Varies, with particular deadlines driven by transaction needs or dispute resolutions.
- **Types of Clients:** Wide-ranging, including businesses of all sizes engaging in commercial transactions, from small enterprises to multinational corporations.
- **Law Firms:** Practiced in both specialized commercial law boutiques and full-service firms with dedicated commercial law departments.

Construction Law

Construction Law covers all legal aspects related to construction projects, from the initial contract negotiation through to dispute resolution and ensuring compliance with safety and building regulations. Lawyers specializing in construction law represent project owners, contractors, and professionals in the construction industry, providing advice on contracts, helping to resolve disputes, and ensuring projects comply with all applicable laws and regulations.

- **Workflow:** Project-based, aligning with the life cycle of construction projects, which includes planning, execution, and completion phases.
- **Urgency:** Varies, with heightened periods during contract negotiations, when addressing compliance issues, or while resolving disputes.
- **Types of Clients:** Construction companies, project owners, developers, contractors, and construction professionals, each facing unique legal challenges related to construction projects.
- **Law Firms:** Specialized construction law boutiques and full-service firms with construction law departments, offering expertise across the spectrum of legal issues in the construction industry.

Consumer Protection Law

Consumer Protection Law is dedicated to safeguarding consumer rights, addressing issues related to product liability, and ensuring fair trading practices. Lawyers in this field represent businesses in ensuring compliance with consumer protection laws, defending against consumer lawsuits, and advising on fair marketing and sales practices.

- **Workflow:** Steady, with spikes related to consumer complaints, regulatory inquiries, and litigation.
- **Urgency:** High during litigation or in response to regulatory investigations.

- **Types of Clients:** Retailers, manufacturers, service providers, and any business directly interacting with consumers.
- **Law Firms:** Firms specializing in consumer protection law and full-service firms with strong consumer law practices.

Corporate Finance Law

Corporate Finance Law focuses on the legal aspects of funding business operations and managing financial risks. This includes advising on capital raising (through debt and equity), complying with regulatory requirements, executing transactions, and managing corporate financial structures. Lawyers in this field play a crucial role in facilitating mergers and acquisitions, initial public offerings (IPOs), and private equity and venture capital investments.

- **Workflow:** Project-based, with heightened activity during funding rounds, M&A transactions, and when navigating regulatory changes.
- **Urgency:** High, especially during transactional closings and when meeting regulatory compliance deadlines.
- **Types of Clients:** Businesses seeking to raise capital, investors, and financial institutions involved in corporate finance transactions.
- **Law Firms:** Large, full-service law firms with international reach and boutique firms specializing in corporate finance.

Corporate Law

Corporate Law is pivotal in guiding businesses through the complexities of corporate governance, compliance, entity formation, and shareholder relations. Lawyers specializing in this area provide essential advisory services, ensuring that businesses operate within legal frameworks while pursuing their strategic objectives. Their expertise supports the life cycle of a corporation, from inception through growth phases, including mergers and acquisitions, to routine compliance and governance.

- **Workflow:** Consistent, characterized by ongoing advisory services and support for corporate transactions and events. Corporate lawyers are integral to the planning and execution of strategic business moves, providing stability and foresight in corporate operations.
- **Urgency:** Ranges from moderate to high, influenced by corporate milestones, governance issues, or legal compliance deadlines. The need for swift, accurate legal advice becomes particularly acute during pivotal corporate events such as mergers, acquisitions, or public offerings.

- **Types of Clients:** Encompasses a wide array of businesses, from nascent start-ups seeking to establish their legal foundations to established multinational corporations navigating complex global regulations.
- **Law Firms:** Practiced within both full-service law firms that offer a broad spectrum of legal services and specialized corporate law boutiques that focus on corporate legal matters, providing tailored advice and support to businesses in all stages of their development.

Entertainment and Media Law

Entertainment and Media Law covers the legal aspects of the entertainment industry, including film, television, music, and digital media. Lawyers in this field draft and negotiate contracts, protect intellectual property rights, and litigate disputes. They work closely with artists, production companies, and media outlets to ensure that creative content is produced, distributed, and monetized in compliance with applicable laws and agreements.

- **Workflow:** Project-based, closely aligned with the cycles of production, publication, and distribution in the entertainment and media industries.
- **Urgency:** Varies, often high during contract negotiations, copyright and trademark disputes, and other time-sensitive legal matters affecting the production and distribution of entertainment and media content.
- **Types of Clients:** Production companies, artists, entertainers, publishers, and digital media companies, all requiring specialized legal support to navigate the unique legal landscape of the entertainment and media sectors.
- **Law Firms:** Found in entertainment-focused boutique law firms and in the entertainment departments of larger, full-service law firms, offering expertise in the complex intersection of law and creative content.

Environmental Law

Environmental Law is dedicated to the protection of the environment and natural resources, addressing compliance with environmental regulations, litigating environmental disputes, and advising clients on sustainable business practices. This field is vital for ensuring that businesses and other entities operate in a manner that is environmentally responsible and compliant with complex regulatory frameworks.

- **Workflow:** The workflow in Environmental Law can vary, being project-based for environmental impact assessments and more steady for ongoing regulatory compliance and advisory services.

- **Urgency:** High urgency is common in litigation scenarios or when facing compliance deadlines, necessitating quick and strategic legal responses to environmental issues.
- **Types of Clients:** Includes a wide range of industries subject to environmental regulations, nonprofit organizations focused on environmental protection, and government agencies overseeing natural resources and environmental quality.
- **Law Firms:** Found within specialized environmental law boutiques known for their deep understanding of environmental regulations and in the environmental practices of larger firms with strong regulatory and litigation capabilities.

Financial Services Regulation

Financial Services Regulation entails advising businesses on compliance with the complex web of banking laws, financial regulations, and securities laws. This field is critical for financial institutions and companies offering financial products and services, ensuring they operate within the legal frameworks established by regulatory bodies. Lawyers in this area navigate the intricacies of regulatory compliance, represent clients in dealings with regulators, and provide guidance on the development and marketing of financial products.

- **Workflow:** Steady, with variations based on changes in financial regulations and the introduction of new financial products.
- **Urgency:** High, particularly when responding to regulatory inquiries or compliance audits, to avoid penalties and ensure ongoing operational integrity.
- **Types of Clients:** Banks, financial institutions, investment firms, and any business involved in the offering of financial services or products.
- **Law Firms:** Firms with specialized practices in financial services regulation, including both boutique law firms and large, full-service firms with dedicated financial regulatory departments.

Franchising Law

Franchising Law focuses on the legal aspects of franchising, including the creation, operation, and expansion of franchise systems. Attorneys in this specialty draft franchise agreements, ensure compliance with franchise laws, and resolve disputes between franchisors and franchisees. Their work supports the growth and management of franchise businesses, safeguarding the interests of both franchisors and franchisees through legal counsel and representation.

- **Workflow:** Consistent, involving ongoing support for franchise operations, agreement negotiations, and legal compliance, with a focus on supporting the growth and governance of franchise systems.
- **Urgency:** Moderate, with peaks during the negotiation of franchise agreements, the resolution of disputes, and compliance with franchise law, necessitating knowledgeable and strategic legal advice.
- **Types of Clients:** Franchisors and franchisees, ranging from small businesses to international brands, all seeking to navigate the franchising landscape successfully.
- **Law Firms:** Specialized in franchising law firms and commercial law firms with a focus on franchising, offering expertise in the nuanced area of franchise law and practice.

Healthcare Law

Healthcare Law involves navigating the complex regulatory frameworks that govern the healthcare industry. Attorneys in this field ensure compliance with healthcare laws and regulations, advise on healthcare transactions, and represent clients in litigation and disputes, including those related to patient privacy and healthcare fraud. Their expertise is crucial in guiding healthcare providers, insurance companies, and other stakeholders through the legal challenges unique to the healthcare sector.

- **Workflow:** Steady, with a focus on regulatory and compliance advice, transactional support, and occasional litigation.
- **Urgency:** High for regulatory investigations, compliance audits, and disputes, requiring timely and precise legal guidance to navigate complex healthcare regulations.
- **Types of Clients:** Hospitals, healthcare providers, insurance companies, and other entities within the healthcare sector, each facing unique regulatory and legal challenges.
- **Law Firms:** Practiced in healthcare-specific law firms as well as in full-service firms with dedicated healthcare departments, providing a wide range of legal services tailored to the healthcare industry.

Intellectual Property (IP) Law

Intellectual Property Law is dedicated to protecting and managing the rights associated with creative and innovative works. IP Lawyers are instrumental in filing for patents and trademarks, defending intellectual property in litigation, drafting licensing agreements, and advising on IP strategy. This specialty is crucial for any entity looking to protect its innovations, creative works, or brand identity.

- **Workflow:** Steady, with consistent attention to portfolio management and active enforcement against infringement.
- **Urgency:** High urgency for litigation and for meeting filing deadlines, ensuring timely protection of IP rights.
- **Types of Clients:** A wide array of clients, including technology companies, inventors, artists, and any business possessing valuable intellectual property.
- **Law Firms:** Found within specialized IP law firms and in the intellectual property departments of large, full-service firms that offer comprehensive IP services.

International Business Law

International Business Law covers the legal aspects of international trade and business operations, focusing on cross-border transactions, international trade regulations, and global corporate structuring. Lawyers in this area advise businesses on navigating the complexities of operating in multiple jurisdictions, ensuring compliance with international laws and regulations, and structuring international transactions to maximize business success.

- **Workflow:** Project-based, with significant work around cross-border transactions and international expansions.
- **Urgency:** Varies with the complexity of international deals and the need for compliance in diverse legal systems.
- **Types of Clients:** Multinational corporations, businesses engaged in international trade, and companies looking to expand into global markets.
- **Law Firms:** Large firms with international reach and boutique firms specializing in international trade and business law.

International Trade Law

International Trade Law governs the legal aspects of cross-border commerce, dealing with the rules and regulations that apply to international business transactions. This includes advising on customs regulations, trade agreements, export and import controls, and resolving disputes under international trade law frameworks. Lawyers in this area help businesses navigate the complexities of trading across borders, ensuring compliance with international laws and treaties.

- **Workflow:** Project-based, influenced by the initiation of trade agreements, negotiations, and compliance audits.

- **Urgency:** Varies, with critical periods during trade negotiations, customs disputes, and when adapting to new trade regulations.
- **Types of Clients:** Importers, exporters, multinational corporations, and businesses engaged in international trade.
- **Law Firms:** Firms with a strong international presence and boutique practices specializing in international trade and customs law.

Labor and Employment Law

Labor and Employment Law focuses on the relationship between employers and employees, encompassing everything from employment contracts to compliance with labor regulations. Lawyers in this field provide advisory services, assist with dispute resolution, and represent clients in litigation and regulatory investigations. Their work ensures fair and legal treatment of workers while supporting employers in maintaining compliant and productive workplaces.

- **Workflow:** Generally steady, with regular advisory services and potential spikes due to litigation or disputes.
- **Urgency:** The urgency can vary, becoming particularly high during disputes, litigation, or when responding to regulatory investigations.
- **Types of Clients:** Broad, including employers across all industries and sectors, as well as employee associations and unions.
- **Law Firms:** Practiced in boutique firms specializing in labor and employment law, as well as in the labor and employment departments of larger, full-service firms.

Mergers and Acquisitions (M&A)

Mergers and Acquisitions (M&A) Law involves the complex, strategic process of combining, acquiring, or selling businesses to drive growth, expand market reach, or enhance operational efficiencies. M&A attorneys are integral to this process, providing expert advice on negotiating, drafting, and reviewing transaction documents; conducting thorough due diligence; and ensuring compliance with regulatory requirements. Their role is pivotal in navigating the intricacies of M&A transactions, aligning legal strategies with business objectives to facilitate successful deal closures.

- **Workflow:** Project-based and often cyclical, with activity intensifying around financial quarters and when strategic opportunities arise, demanding a focused and strategic approach to deal execution.
- **Urgency:** High, due to tight deadlines for deal closure that require efficient coordination, meticulous due diligence, and effective negotiation to secure optimal outcomes for clients.

- **Types of Clients:** A diverse range of clients, including corporations, private equity firms, and investment banks, each engaging in M&A activities to achieve specific strategic goals.
- **Law Firms:** Practiced within large, international law firms and boutique firms specializing in M&A, offering depth of expertise and a global perspective on complex transactions.

Partnership Disputes Law

Partnership Disputes Law deals with the conflicts that arise between business partners or within joint ventures. This area of law aims to resolve disputes through negotiation, arbitration, or litigation, depending on the nature and severity of the disagreement. Lawyers specializing in partnership disputes assist in interpreting partnership agreements, mediating conflicts, and, when necessary, litigating to resolve disputes and protect their clients' rights and interests in the partnership.

- **Workflow:** Steady, with periods of intensification as disputes move toward resolution, whether through negotiation, arbitration, or litigation. Lawyers must be prepared to escalate their approaches based on the development of the dispute.
- **Urgency:** High when disputes escalate to litigation or arbitration, necessitating decisive legal action to resolve conflicts and safeguard the interests of the involved parties.
- **Types of Clients:** Business partners and joint ventures facing internal conflicts or disputes over the terms of the partnership agreement, operational management, or the division of assets and liabilities.
- **Law Firms:** Found in litigation firms and in full-service firms with strong dispute resolution departments, where attorneys are skilled in the nuances of partnership law and adept at navigating the complex dynamics of business disputes.

Privacy and Data Protection Law

Privacy and Data Protection Law focuses on advising businesses on compliance with data protection regulations and cybersecurity laws. Lawyers in this field help companies manage personal data responsibly, navigate data breach incidents, and comply with privacy laws to protect consumer information and avoid legal penalties.

- **Workflow:** Steady, with increasing demand due to the growing importance of data protection.
- **Urgency:** High, especially in the aftermath of data breaches or when adapting to new privacy regulations.

- **Types of Clients:** Businesses across all sectors that collect, use, or manage personal data.
- **Law Firms:** Specialized privacy and data protection boutiques and full-service firms with dedicated cybersecurity and privacy practices.

Real Estate Law

Real Estate Law encompasses the legal aspects of buying, selling, and managing property. This includes handling property transactions, drafting leasing agreements, advising on zoning and land use, and negotiating financing agreements. Lawyers in this field play a crucial role in ensuring that real estate dealings are conducted in accordance with the law, protecting the interests of their clients throughout the process.

- **Workflow:** Project-based, closely following the ups and downs of the real estate market. Activity levels can vary significantly, with peak periods often centered on the closing of major deals.
- **Urgency:** Generally moderate, but urgency can spike around the closing of transactions or when addressing zoning and land use disputes, requiring prompt and effective legal action.
- **Types of Clients:** A diverse client base, including real estate developers, investment trusts, commercial tenants, and private property owners, each with unique legal needs related to property.
- **Law Firms:** Practiced within real estate–focused boutique law firms as well as in the real estate departments of larger, full-service firms that offer a broad range of property-related legal services.

Securities Law

Securities Law specializes in the regulatory framework governing financial securities, including stocks, bonds, and derivatives. Attorneys in this field ensure the transparency, fairness, and integrity of financial markets by guiding clients through securities offerings, mergers and acquisitions, regulatory compliance, and corporate governance. Their expertise is vital in managing interactions with regulatory bodies like the SEC and ensuring adherence to all financial disclosure and reporting requirements.

- **Workflow:** The workflow is steady, punctuated by peaks of project-based work centered on the negotiation and closing of financing deals, regulatory filings, and restructuring negotiations.
- **Urgency:** High urgency is often a hallmark of this field, especially during deal negotiations and closings, where timely legal advice and action can be critical to the success of financial transactions.

- **Types of Clients:** This specialization caters to a diverse clientele, including banks, nonbank financial institutions, borrowers, and other entities engaged in the borrowing, lending, and regulation of money.
- **Law Firms:** Banking and Finance Law is practiced in firms with dedicated banking and financial services departments as well as in specialized finance law firms, offering expertise in the complexities of finance law and regulation.

Tax Law

Tax Law focuses on the rules, policies, and laws that oversee the tax process. A tax attorney's responsibilities extend beyond advising on tax planning and compliance. They represent clients in disputes with tax authorities, offering defense strategies in audits and litigation. In addition, they provide insightful guidance on the tax implications of various business transactions and personal investments. This includes navigating complex tax codes, structuring transactions to be tax-efficient, and ensuring compliance with state, federal, and international tax laws, thereby safeguarding clients from potential legal and financial penalties.

- **Workflow:** Generally consistent, with noticeable peaks during tax filing seasons and at the year's end when businesses and individuals plan for taxes. Tax lawyers often work long hours during these periods to accommodate the increased demand for their services.
- **Urgency:** Particularly high around tax filing deadlines and in situations involving audits by tax authorities. Timeliness and accuracy in filing and responding to audits are critical to avoid penalties and maximize client benefits.
- **Types of Clients:** Includes businesses of all sizes and sectors, nonprofit organizations, and, occasionally, high-net-worth individuals seeking sophisticated tax planning and compliance advice.
- **Law Firms:** A mix of specialized tax law boutiques that offer deep expertise in tax matters and larger, full-service firms with dedicated tax departments providing comprehensive legal services.

Technology Law

Technology Law addresses the legal challenges associated with the development, distribution, and use of technology. This includes issues related to software licensing, data security, digital commerce, and protection of intellectual property online. As technology continues to evolve rapidly, lawyers in this field must stay abreast of the latest legal developments affecting the tech industry and advise clients accordingly.

- **Workflow:** Steady, with spikes related to product launches, IP litigation, or regulatory changes affecting technology use.
- **Urgency:** High for compliance with fast-changing technology laws and regulations, and during IP disputes.
- **Types of Clients:** Tech start-ups, software companies, e-commerce platforms, and businesses using technology in their operations.
- **Law Firms:** Specialized technology law firms and full-service firms with dedicated technology law practices, capable of navigating the intersection of law and technology.

Beyond the Specialties: A World of Evolving and Emerging Legal Fields

Although we have explored a significant array of business law specialties, it's important to recognize that the legal landscape is continually evolving, giving rise to new areas of expertise and specialization. Beyond the domains we've discussed, numerous other specialties are gaining prominence, driven by technological advancements, regulatory changes, and shifting market dynamics. This constant evolution reflects the adaptive nature of the legal profession and highlights the endless possibilities for legal practitioners to find their niche in uncharted territories or emerging fields. As business law continues to adapt to new challenges and opportunities, so too will the opportunities for lawyers to specialize and excel in novel and impactful ways.

Analyzing Market Trends in Different Practice Areas

Overview of the Evolution in Legal Services

Over the past fifty years, the legal services sector, especially in business law, has witnessed transformative changes. This evolution has been driven by several key factors, ranging from technological advancements to shifts in global economic structures.

In the 1970s and 1980s, law firms began growing in size and geographical reach, primarily driven by the expanding needs of corporate clients. This era saw the rise of the "mega law firm," with firms expanding beyond local and national boundaries to establish a global presence. The focus was heavily on corporate, finance, and litigation services, reflecting the business landscape of the time.

The 1990s introduced significant technological advancements, revolutionizing how legal work was conducted. The advent of the internet and digital communication tools began to reshape the traditional lawyer–client interaction, making information more accessible and communication more instantaneous.

The early 2000s witnessed a further shift with the increasing importance of intellectual property law, spurred by the tech boom and the growing digital economy. Law firms started to place greater emphasis on IP law and related practices, recognizing the growing value of intangible assets in business.

The 2008 global financial crisis marked another turning point, leading to increased regulatory scrutiny over businesses. This period saw a surge in demand for legal expertise in compliance, financial regulation, and corporate governance. Law firms responded by bolstering their regulatory practices and focusing more on risk management services for their clients.

In the last decade, the legal industry has been profoundly affected by the digital revolution. The rise of legal tech start-ups, artificial intelligence (AI), and automation tools has started to change the way legal services are delivered. These technologies have introduced efficiencies in traditional legal processes such as document review, due diligence, and even some aspects of legal research, fundamentally altering the workflow within law firms.

Factors Influencing Current Trends

Economic Factors

- **Globalization Example:** The formation of the European Union and subsequent legal frameworks exemplify the complexities of cross-border trade, necessitating legal expertise in multinational regulatory compliance.
- **Market Volatility Example:** The 2020 pandemic-induced economic downturn saw businesses grappling with contractual obligations under force majeure clauses, highlighting the need for legal navigators in times of uncertainty.

Technological Factors

- **Digitalization Example:** The General Data Protection Regulation's (GDPR) implementation in 2018 underscored the challenges and complexities surrounding data privacy, affecting businesses globally and reshaping the focus of legal practices.
- **Legal Tech Example:** The introduction of AI-based tools such as ROSS Intelligence for legal research demonstrates how technology is streamlining traditional legal processes, setting new benchmarks for efficiency.

Societal Factors

- **CSR and ESG Criteria Example:** The landmark case of Juliana v. United States, where plaintiffs (youth activists) sued the government over climate change, showcases the growing legal intersections between corporate responsibility, environmental law, and societal expectations.

- **Diversity and Inclusion Example:** The American Bar Association's Resolution 113, urging law firms to enhance diversity within their practice, reflects the broader societal push toward inclusive legal practices and the profession's response to these demands.

Projecting Future Growth and Opportunities in Business Law

Emerging Fields in Business Law

- **Fintech Example:** The rapid adoption of blockchain technology by financial institutions, exemplified by JP Morgan's launch of the JPM Coin, highlights the burgeoning need for legal expertise in fintech innovations.
- **AI Example:** The ethical and legal debates surrounding autonomous vehicles, such as those developed by Tesla, underscore the complex liability and regulatory issues at the intersection of AI and law.
- **Privacy and Data Protection Example:** Facebook's Cambridge Analytica scandal has catapulted data privacy laws into the spotlight, demonstrating the critical role of legal experts in navigating the intricacies of information governance and privacy protections.
- **Green Energy Example:** The international Paris Agreement on climate change has spurred legal demand in green energy projects, requiring expertise in environmental regulations, clean technology patents, and sustainability initiatives.

Interdisciplinary Opportunities

- **Law and Technology Interface:** Lawyers advising on cybersecurity measures for e-commerce platforms, such as Shopify, exemplify the growing importance of understanding both legal and technological landscapes.
- **CSR and Law:** Legal advisors working with companies like Patagonia on embedding sustainability and ethical labor practices into their business models highlight the integration of CSR into legal advisement.
- **International Relations and Law:** Legal experts navigating the complexities of Brexit for multinational corporations illustrate the critical interplay between international relations and business law.
- **Healthcare Law and Bioethics:** The legal challenges posed by gene-editing technologies, such as Clustered Regularly Interspaced Short Palindromic Repeats (CRISPR), spotlight the need for legal professionals at the crossroads of healthcare innovation, ethics, and regulation, as CRISPR enables precise DNA modifications with potential applications in treating genetic

disorders but also raises complex ethical and legal issues regarding genetic privacy, off-target effects, and the implications of germline editing.

Understanding Globalization in the Business World

The Rise of Global Business

Globalization has fundamentally reshaped the business landscape, heralding the rise of multinational corporations and increasing the frequency of cross-border transactions. This evolution encompasses businesses expanding into new markets, navigating international mergers and acquisitions, and addressing the intricacies of diverse legal systems and cultural norms. The global business environment demands a sophisticated understanding of how legal practices intersect with international operations and strategies.

Impact on Legal Practice

Legal Complexities of International Trade

Globalization has introduced significant complexities into legal practice, particularly in areas like international trade. Legal professionals must adeptly navigate a maze of international trade agreements, customs laws, and export–import regulations, ensuring compliance and strategic advantage for their clients.

Cross-Border Transactions

The legal intricacies of cross-border transactions require a nuanced understanding of multiple legal jurisdictions. Business lawyers need comprehensive knowledge of international law, foreign investment regulations, and the varying legal frameworks across countries to manage these complex deals effectively.

Compliance with International Laws

Compliance with international laws and regulations is paramount. This includes adherence to anti-corruption laws such as the Foreign Corrupt Practices Act (FCPA) and the U.K. Bribery Act, data protection regulations such as the GDPR, and international tax laws that ensure businesses navigate the global regulatory environment responsibly.

Litigation and Dispute Resolution

International litigation and dispute resolution present unique challenges, from the enforcement of judgments across borders to the intricacies of international arbitration. Lawyers must be adept at handling these nuances to effectively represent their clients in the global arena.

Developing Global Legal Skills

Cultivating Cultural Competence

To thrive in the global business environment, lawyers must develop cultural competence. This includes an appreciation for diverse business practices, negotiation styles, and legal expectations, ensuring respectful and effective international interactions.

Language Skills

Multilingualism offers a significant advantage in global legal practice, enhancing communication with international clients and aiding the understanding of foreign legal documents and proceedings.

Building International Networks

Establishing a robust international professional network is invaluable for referrals, gaining insights into local legal practices, and fostering collaborative opportunities across borders.

Adapting to Global Legal Trends

Staying Informed on Global Developments

Keeping abreast of global economic and political developments is crucial, as they can profoundly affect international business law practices and strategies.

Specializing in International Law

There are tangible benefits to specializing in international business law. This specialization can include a focus on international arbitration, trade law, and navigating the complexities of cross-border mergers and acquisitions.

Integrating Market Realities with Career Aspirations

Balancing Idealism with Pragmatism in Business Law

As they journey through their professional lives, lawyers specializing in business law often encounter the challenge of aligning their idealistic visions for their careers with the practical realities of the market. Achieving a balance between these aspects is key to ensuring both satisfaction and longevity in the legal field.

The Dream vs. Market Demand

The path into law is frequently embarked upon with specific ambitions or preferred areas of specialization in mind, fueled by a combination of passion, interest, and a commitment to societal impact. Yet, the actual conditions of the legal market necessitate a consideration of several critical factors, including market demand, job availability, and the landscape of emerging legal fields.

- **Understanding Market Demand:** A fundamental aspect of navigating one's legal career involves a deep dive into the current trends and demands within the legal market, identifying growth sectors and recognizing areas saturated with legal practitioners.
- **Evaluating Personal Aspirations:** It is equally important for lawyers to introspectively examine their own professional desires, considering their motivations for gravitating toward certain legal domains and how these align with their capabilities, ethical values, and long-term objectives.

Strategies for Balancing Idealism and Pragmatism

- **Flexibility and Openness:** Maintaining an openness to various facets of business law, particularly in the initial stages of one's career, can uncover previously unconsidered interests and opportunities that resonate with both personal goals and market needs.
- **Continuous Learning and Adaptation:** Keeping abreast of the evolving legal landscape and proactively enhancing one's skill set can enable a strategic pivot toward specializations that offer personal fulfillment while remaining in demand.
- **Seeking Mentorship and Advice:** Leveraging the wisdom and experiences of mentors and industry veterans can shed light on effective strategies for aligning individual aspirations with the practical demands of the legal market.
- **Building a Diverse Skill Set:** Cultivating a broad array of skills applicable across different areas of business law not only increases marketability but also provides the flexibility needed to navigate market fluctuations while pursuing personal interests.
- **Integrating Passion with Practicality:** It's possible to weave one's passions into more pragmatic, market-driven specializations. For instance, a lawyer

with a strong inclination toward environmental advocacy may carve a niche in corporate sustainability and environmental compliance within the broader spectrum of business law.

Long-Term Career Planning in Business Law: Navigating a Dynamic Field

In the fast-paced and ever-evolving realm of business law, carving out a sustainable and rewarding career trajectory necessitates strategic foresight, adaptability, and a thorough understanding of the market landscape. This chapter delves into the crucial elements of successful long-term career planning within the business law sector, providing practical guidance and real-life illustrations to support both budding and seasoned legal professionals.

Understanding the Market: The Cornerstone of Career Planning

- **Analyzing Current Trends:** Begin with a comprehensive analysis of the current landscape of business law, identifying growth sectors and high-demand areas such as technology and environmental law. For instance, the burgeoning start-up ecosystem may highlight the need for expertise in venture capital law.
- **Anticipating Future Developments:** Look beyond the immediate to anticipate where the legal market is headed. Keeping an eye on economic and technological trends can help forecast future demands, such as the potential need for expertise in cryptocurrency regulations due to advancements in blockchain technology.

Crafting a Flexible Career Plan

- **Setting Achievable Goals:** Differentiate between immediate objectives and your vision for the future. Short-term goals might include acquiring specific skills or gaining experience in a certain area, whereas long-term ambitions could aim at senior positions or recognition as a subject matter expert.
- **Adapting to Change:** The legal sector's landscape can shift dramatically, underscoring the importance of flexibility in your career strategy. This could mean exploring diverse specializations or assuming varied roles as new opportunities emerge, such as a corporate lawyer transitioning to privacy law amid growing concerns over data protection.
- **Committing to Lifelong Learning:** Staying current in a continuously evolving field requires ongoing education. This can be achieved through specialized training, attending workshops, and keeping up with the latest legal publications.

- **Networking Effectively:** Building a robust professional network is crucial for staying informed about industry trends and opportunities. Participation in legal conferences, professional associations, and online forums can broaden your circle of contacts and knowledge.

Strategies for Sustained Growth in Business Law

- **Diversifying Your Skill Set:** Lawyers with a broad skill set are more adaptable and appealing to potential clients or employers. For example, expertise in corporate law can be complemented with skills in mediation and negotiation.
- **Balancing Specialization with Flexibility:** Although deep expertise in a specific area of business law can be beneficial, maintaining a wide-ranging knowledge base allows for greater agility in responding to market shifts.
- **Developing a Personal Brand:** Your unique skills and experiences can form the basis of a powerful personal brand. Engaging in legal publications, speaking engagements, and contributing to industry discussions can elevate your professional standing.
- **Embracing Mentorship and Sponsorship:** Guidance from experienced mentors can be invaluable, as can sponsorship from influential individuals within your network, opening doors to new opportunities and career advancement.
- **Innovating and Taking Risks:** Stay open to innovation and be prepared to take calculated risks, whether by adopting new legal technologies or exploring nontraditional career paths.
- **Active Community Engagement:** Involvement in legal communities and contributing to professional discussions not only enhances your profile but also keeps you connected with the latest developments in the field.

Empowering Legal Professionals: Insights from Alé Dalton

Partner, Bradley

Alé Dalton stands out in the legal profession not only for her expertise in healthcare law but also for her deep commitment to community service and professional development. With an educational background that includes graduating cum laude from the University of Tennessee College of Law and magna cum laude from Lipscomb University, Alé has carved a niche for herself by focusing on transactional, operational, and regulatory matters within the healthcare industry. Her practice is particularly noted for providing counsel during mergers and acquisitions, a testament to her adeptness at navigating the complexities of a highly regulated sector.

Beyond her legal practice, Alé's journey is marked by her dedication to filling the legal service gaps in her community. Her active involvement in staffing community legal clinics and participation in pro bono programs underscores her belief in the power of law as a tool for social good. Furthermore, her leadership roles within her firm, including serving as the vice chair of the Lawyers of Color Resource Group and as a liaison for the Women's Initiative, highlight her commitment to fostering an inclusive professional environment.

Alé's story is also one of breaking barriers and paving the way for others. As a first-generation student, lawyer, and American originally from Colombia, she leverages her unique experiences to mentor other first-generation students, demonstrating the importance of representation and support within the legal field.

Building Social Networks and Community Engagement

Alé Dalton emphasizes the significance of building robust professional networks and actively engaging within the legal community. For her, platforms such as Twitter and LinkedIn are not just social media spaces but vital tools for fostering professional relationships and mentoring the next generation of legal professionals. Alé shares, "Law Twitter and LinkedIn were the places where these aspiring lawyers found me. I just started connecting, tweeting, and also following and liking and engaging with content from other folks." This approach features the importance she places on being accessible and supportive, especially to those who seek her guidance.

Her strategy for engaging with the legal community online is both simple and effective. Alé focuses on sharing her experiences as an associate, offering advice that has helped her navigate her career successfully. "I focused on sharing my experience as an associate and giving tips that have helped me to do things well," she explains. This sharing of insights and best practices not only aids others in their professional journey but also establishes Alé as a resourceful and approachable figure within the legal field.

Ale's commitment to mentoring goes beyond just professional advice. She actively makes herself available to talk with first-generation or diverse aspiring associates and law students, recognizing the impact such conversations can have. Her dedication to giving back to the community, stemming from her own experiences as a first-generation professional, showcases her belief in the transformative power of mentorship and community support in shaping the careers of emerging legal professionals. Through her active involvement and intentional efforts on social media, Ale Dalton not only builds her network but also contributes significantly to the development and encouragement of aspiring lawyers.

Leadership and Development within the Law Firm

Alé's career trajectory in the legal profession is as much about her prowess in healthcare law as it is about her passion for leadership and development within her law firm. Her journey reflects a keen interest in roles that merge legal expertise with functions such as professional development and mentoring. For Alé, the draw toward partnership at her firm wasn't just about the prestige or the financial benefits that come with the role. "I love the idea of working in a large law firm because of the resources you have," she says, highlighting the advantages of being part of a well-established firm. However, it is the non-billable aspects of the job—developing people, leadership, mentoring—that truly resonate with her. "My dream job is something like a managing partner of a firm. I love the developing people and leadership side of the legal profession," Alé shares, emphasizing her inclination toward nurturing talent and fostering a supportive environment for professional growth.

Alé recognizes that the landscape of law firms is changing, with an increasing emphasis on roles that contribute to the firm's growth beyond traditional client work. At her firm, partners are expected to be dedicated to client work, but there is a clear emphasis on leadership and people development. "Our partners work hard, but there's a greater emphasis on non-billable activities, such as developing and mentoring others, rather than just meeting high billable hours," she explains. This shift toward valuing contributions that enhance the firm's culture and employee development is something that Alé finds particularly appealing. Her belief is that while she is a competent lawyer, her strengths lie more significantly in the realms of development, leadership, and mentoring.

The Power of Authenticity and Kindness

Alé believes strongly in the power of authenticity and kindness in the legal profession, a stance that not only defines her approach to her career but also shapes her interactions with colleagues and clients. Reflecting on her upbringing and personal values, Ale shares, “I grew up cleaning houses with my mom, so my snootiness baseline is zero.” This humble beginning has grounded her in a sense of genuine kindness and approachability that she considers almost a “superpower” in her career. Contrary to the often aggressive stereotype associated with lawyers, Ale's demeanor challenges this notion and advocates for a more inclusive and supportive legal community.

Her philosophy extends beyond mere personal conduct; it influences her professional relationships and the way she handles transactions and negotiations. “Just being nice to people has gone a really long way,” she notes, explaining how this approach has positively impacted her work, especially in healthcare law. Her kindness and authenticity have not only facilitated smoother interactions but also been pivotal in building trust with clients and colleagues. Ale recounts instances where her approachability and genuine care have led clients to express a preference for working with her, highlighting the significant impact of personal demeanor on professional success.

Alé's perspective on authenticity and kindness as integral to legal practice offers a refreshing view on how lawyers can navigate their careers. She encourages her peers to embrace their true selves, whether they are naturally outgoing or more reserved. “You don't have to be something that you're not. But if you are nice or have a sunny disposition, you can be that and do well in the law firm world,” she asserts. This encouragement to be authentic serves as a powerful reminder that success in the legal profession doesn't require fitting into a rigid mold. Instead, Alé's career exemplifies how embracing one's unique qualities can create a more diverse, understanding, and effective legal community. ”

Selecting a Law School and Area of Focus

Criteria for Choosing a Law School

Choosing the right law school is a decision that sets the foundation for your future career in law. It is essential to consider various factors to ensure that your choice aligns with your career aspirations and personal circumstances.

Location: The Strategic Importance of Geography

- **Legal Market Access:** The location of your law school can significantly influence your access to specific legal markets. For instance, schools in metropolitan areas such as New York or San Francisco are often in close proximity to major law firms and corporate headquarters, offering ample opportunities for internships and networking. Even large law firms often hire from local law schools, so choosing a school that is in the region or city where you ultimately want to work has its advantages. Plus you will be building your network while in law school with local connections, and those will have more leverage locally.
- **Regional Law Practices:** Some legal markets may have a strong focus on specific practice areas. For example, a law school in Texas might offer more insight into oil and gas law, while a school in Silicon Valley might be better suited for technology law.
- **Lifestyle Considerations:** Besides professional aspects, consider the lifestyle, cost of living, and cultural environment of the school's location. Where you study can also affect your quality of life during law school.

Reputation: Weighing Prestige Against Practicality

- **Career Opportunities:** Top-tier law schools often boast high employment rates and opportunities at prestigious firms. However, the competition can be fierce, both in gaining admission and excelling in a highly competitive environment.
- **Cost Considerations:** Higher reputation often comes with higher tuition. Evaluate the return on investment (ROI) and consider how student debt might impact your postgraduation choices.
- **Beyond Rankings:** While reputation is important, it's not the only factor. Many successful lawyers come from a wide range of law schools. Sometimes, a less prestigious school can offer more personalized attention, scholarships, or unique opportunities that align better with your goals.

Alumni Network: The Power of Connections

- **Mentorship Opportunities:** Alumni can be valuable mentors, offering guidance, career advice, and insights into the legal profession. They can also help you navigate the early stages of your career.
- **Job Prospects:** A strong alumni network can open doors to job opportunities. Law schools often have alumni events, which are excellent for networking and job hunting.

- **Long-Term Professional Relationships:** The relationships you build with alumni can last throughout your career, offering support and opportunities for collaboration.

Specialty Programs: Aligning with Your Interests

- **Focused Learning:** If you have a clear idea of your preferred specialization, look for schools with strong programs in that area. This could be environmental law, human rights, corporate law, or any other specific field.
- **Faculty and Resources:** Consider the faculty's expertise in your area of interest and the resources the school offers, such as specialized clinics, research opportunities, and external partnerships.
- **Career Placement:** Investigate the school's track record for placing graduates in your chosen field. Some schools may have stronger connections or a better reputation in certain specializations.

Selecting the right law school requires a balance of professional goals, personal circumstances, and long-term career aspirations. It is a decision that should be made after careful consideration of all these factors, ensuring that your choice sets you up for a successful and fulfilling legal career.

Deciding on a Specialization or Maintaining Flexibility in Course Selections

The choice between specializing early or keeping your options open during law school is a critical one. Your approach can shape your career trajectory, so it is important to weigh the benefits and potential limitations of each path.

Specialization: The Targeted Approach

- **Early Expertise:** Specializing in a particular area, such as tax law, environmental law, or intellectual property, can provide you with in-depth knowledge and skills. This targeted approach can make you a more attractive candidate to employers looking for expertise in these areas.
- **Career Direction:** If you have a strong interest in a specific legal field, specializing early allows you to align your law school experience with your career goals. This focus can provide clarity and purpose throughout your studies.
- **Networking and Opportunities:** Specializing can help you build a targeted professional network from the start. You'll have opportunities to connect with faculty, alumni, and practitioners in your chosen field, which can open doors to internships, clerkships, and job offers.

Challenges of Early Specialization

- **Limited Exposure:** By focusing narrowly, you might miss out on a broader understanding of the law and how different fields intersect.
- **Changing Interests:** Your interests might evolve over time, and early specialization can limit your flexibility to pivot to new areas.

Maintaining Flexibility: The Exploratory Path

- **Broad Foundation:** Keeping your course selections varied allows you to gain a well-rounded understanding of different legal fields. This broad base can be advantageous, especially in roles that require a generalist's perspective.
- **Discovering Your Passion:** Law school is a time for exploration. By remaining open to different courses, you might discover a passion for an area of law you hadn't previously considered.
- **Adaptability:** A diverse legal education can equip you with a wide range of skills, making you adaptable in a rapidly changing legal market. This can be particularly valuable if you end up pursuing opportunities outside of traditional law firm roles.

Challenges of Maintaining Flexibility

- **Delayed Specialization:** You may graduate without a clear area of expertise, which can be a disadvantage when competing for specialized roles.
- **Overwhelming Choices:** Without a clear focus, the vast array of courses and opportunities in law school can be overwhelming.

Making the Decision

- **Self-Reflection:** Consider your interests, strengths, and career aspirations. Are you passionate about a specific area of law, or are you still exploring your options?
- **Market Trends:** Research the demand for various legal specialties. Some fields might offer more opportunities or be more aligned with future market trends.
- **Seek Advice:** Talk to faculty, practicing lawyers, and alumni to get insights into different specializations and career paths.
- **Consider Internships:** Internships can provide practical experience and insight into different areas of law, aiding your decision-making process.

Whether you choose to specialize early or keep your options open, the key is to make an informed decision that aligns with your personal and professional goals. Remember, law school is not just about acquiring knowledge; it is also about understanding yourself and your place in the legal world.

Early Career Decisions and Strategies

Joining a Law Firm: Navigating Size, Specialization, and Culture

Understanding Firm Size Dynamics

- **Large Firms:** Large law firms, often referred to as "Big Law," typically offer extensive resources, structured training programs, and the opportunity to work on high-profile cases. They are known for their rigorous work environment and often provide substantial compensation. However, they can also be highly competitive, with a demanding workload and sometimes less opportunity for early substantive work.
- **Midsize Firms:** Midsize firms strike a balance between the extensive resources of large firms and the personalized approach of smaller firms. They often offer a diverse range of legal services but with a more manageable client base. Midsize firms can provide a good mix of structured training along with opportunities for early responsibility.
- **Small Firms:** Small firms or boutique firms often specialize in specific areas of law. They provide a more intimate working environment where junior lawyers can gain hands-on experience relatively quickly. These firms might offer more work–life balance and can be ideal for those looking to avoid the high-pressure environment of larger firms.

Aligning Practice Area Focus with Firm Size

- **Specialization and Firm Size:** Your chosen specialization might influence the size of the firm you join. For instance, fields like mergers and acquisitions or international trade law are often the domain of larger firms due to their resources and global reach. On the other hand, practice areas like family law, immigration, or criminal defense are more commonly found in small or midsized firms.
- **Clientele and Opportunities:** Large firms typically cater to institutional clients and can offer experiences in complex, high-stakes legal matters. Small and midsized firms may offer more direct client interaction and involvement in local or more specialized legal issues.

Researching Culture and Environment

- **Firm Culture:** Firm culture encompasses values, work environment, and the approach to work–life balance. A firm's culture can significantly impact your job satisfaction and professional development. Researching and understanding a firm's culture, perhaps through discussions with current or former employees, can provide valuable insights.

- **Mentorship and Support:** Look for firms that emphasize mentorship and support for junior lawyers. A nurturing environment can greatly enhance learning and professional growth.
- **Diversity and Inclusion:** Consider the firm's commitment to diversity and inclusion. A diverse and inclusive environment not only fosters a broader perspective on legal issues but also contributes to a more positive and supportive workplace.
- **Work Style Compatibility:** Assess whether the firm's working style aligns with your personal preferences. Some firms may encourage teamwork and collaboration, whereas others may value individual initiative and autonomy.

Choosing the right law firm requires careful consideration of the firm's size, the alignment of your practice area focus with the firm's clientele and expertise, and the firm's culture and environment. Balancing these factors can help you find a firm where you can thrive professionally while also aligning with your personal values and career aspirations.

Pursuing In-House Roles: Navigating Industry-Specific Challenges and Work–Life Balance

Embracing Diverse Legal Challenges in the Corporate Environment

- **Varied Legal Responsibilities:** In-house roles often require lawyers to handle a wide array of legal matters. Unlike a law firm that might focus on specific legal services, in-house lawyers deal with everything from drafting and negotiating contracts to managing litigation, overseeing compliance, and advising on corporate governance. This diversity offers a comprehensive view of legal issues within a business context.
- **Proactive Legal Management:** In-house counsel plays a crucial role in proactive legal risk management. They need to anticipate potential legal issues and address them before they escalate, requiring a keen sense of business acumen combined with legal expertise.

Gaining Industry-Specific Experience

- **Sector-Specific Insights:** For lawyers interested in particular industries, such as technology, health care, or finance, in-house roles offer an opportunity to delve deeply into sector-specific legal challenges. These positions provide a unique perspective on how legal decisions impact business operations and strategy.

- **Building Relevant Experience:** To transition successfully into an in-house role, gaining relevant experience is key. This can be achieved through specialized law firm practice, industry-focused legal projects, or networking with professionals in the desired industry. Engaging in continuing education or obtaining certifications relevant to the industry can also be beneficial. For instance, lawyers aiming for in-house roles in tech companies might focus on intellectual property law or data privacy regulations.
- **Learning from In-House Attorneys:** Conversations with in-house attorneys, as seen in the thread discussions, reveal the importance of understanding the business side of the legal profession. These professionals emphasize the need for lawyers to be not just legal experts but also strategic partners to the business.

Considering Work–Life Balance and Career Growth

- **Work–Life Balance:** In-house roles are often perceived to offer a better work–life balance compared with the demanding schedules of law firms. While the workload can still be significant, the direct alignment with a single organization often allows for more predictable hours and less of the "client-driven" urgency typical in law firms.
- **Career Progression:** It is important to note that in-house roles typically don't include the structured apprenticeship and training model found in law firms. Therefore, these positions are generally more suited for lawyers who have already gained substantial experience and expertise. New lawyers interested in going in-house should plan strategically, focusing on gaining relevant experience and skills in their early career.
- **Networking and Mentoring:** Building a strong professional network and seeking mentors within the industry can be invaluable for transitioning to an in-house role. Engaging in industry events, legal forums, and corporate law associations can provide connections and insights into in-house opportunities.

In summary, pursuing an in-house legal role involves understanding the varied legal challenges of the corporate environment, gaining industry-specific experience, and balancing career growth with personal life. While offering a different set of opportunities and challenges compared with law firm roles, in-house positions can be highly rewarding for those with a keen interest in aligning legal expertise with business strategy.

Exploring Government Positions in Business Law

Government roles in business law offer a unique blend of public service, comprehensive training, and diverse career opportunities. For lawyers interested in public policy, regulatory frameworks, or public interest law, these positions can be both challenging and rewarding.

Public Service in Business Law

- **Variety of Government Roles:** Government positions for lawyers in business law are varied. They can range from working in regulatory agencies, such as the Securities and Exchange Commission (SEC) or the Federal Trade Commission (FTC), to roles in departments focusing on commerce, trade, or economic development. Each of these roles involves a deep dive into the specific regulatory and legal frameworks governing business practices and policies.
- **Regulatory and Compliance Expertise:** Lawyers in these roles often deal with regulatory compliance, ensuring that businesses adhere to laws and regulations. They might also be involved in drafting and interpreting legislation that impacts the business environment, providing a unique perspective on how laws are created and enforced.
- **Public Policy and Advocacy:** For those interested in shaping public policy, government positions offer a platform to influence the legal landscape of business. This can include advocating for consumer protection, fair trade practices, or economic policies that foster business growth.

Building a Foundation in Law

- **Hands-On Experience:** Government roles often provide substantial hands-on experience, allowing lawyers to take on significant responsibilities early in their careers. This can include leading investigations, participating in policy development, or representing the government in legal proceedings.
- **Comprehensive Training:** Many government positions offer robust training programs, equipping lawyers with a broad understanding of legal processes, administrative law, and regulatory frameworks. This training can be invaluable, laying a strong foundation for a versatile legal career.

Career Advancement and Transition to Private Sector

- **Career Growth within Government:** A career in government can lead to senior roles within the public sector, such as becoming a chief legal advisor for a government agency or advancing to policy-making positions.
- **Leveraging Experience for Private Sector Roles:** The skills and experience gained in government positions are highly transferable to the private sector. Lawyers can leverage their expertise in regulatory compliance, public

policy, and administrative law to move into in-house roles in corporations or specialized positions in law firms.

- **Networking and Reputation:** Building a strong professional network and reputation while in a government role can open doors to future opportunities. Participation in high-profile cases, involvement in significant policy developments, or collaborations with private sector entities can enhance a lawyer's portfolio, making them attractive to future employers.
- **Transition Strategies:** To transition successfully, lawyers should focus on areas of business law that are in demand in the private sector, such as compliance, regulatory affairs, or government relations. Maintaining connections with former colleagues in the private sector and staying abreast of industry trends can also facilitate a smoother transition.

In conclusion, government positions in business law offer a unique opportunity to engage in public service, acquire a diverse set of legal skills, and lay a solid foundation for a dynamic legal career. Whether aiming for career advancement within the government or transitioning to the private sector, these roles provide lawyers with critical experiences and skills that are highly valued across the legal landscape.

Compensation and Impact: Navigating Early Career Choices in Law

When choosing an initial path in a legal career, two significant factors often come into play: compensation and the desire to make an impact. These elements can vary greatly depending on whether one chooses private practice, government roles, or different sizes of law firms, and even the chosen area of specialization. Understanding these dynamics can help guide early career decisions, especially for those balancing the need to pay off law school debt with a desire to contribute positively to society.

Compensation in Different Legal Paths

Private Practice

- **Large Law Firms:** Generally offer the highest starting salaries, which can be crucial for lawyers with significant law school debt. Compensation often comes with expectations of long hours and high performance.
- **Midsize and Small Firms:** Tend to offer lower salaries compared with large firms but can provide more hands-on experience and a better work–life balance.
- **Specialization Impact:** Specializations such as corporate law, intellectual property, and mergers and acquisitions, typically found in larger firms, often command higher salaries.

Government Positions

- **Lower Starting Salaries:** Government roles usually offer lower starting salaries than private practice. However, they often come with benefits like student loan forgiveness programs, job stability, and a structured work schedule.
- **Long-Term Financial Considerations:** While the initial compensation may be lower, government positions can lead to lucrative opportunities in the private sector later on, leveraging the experience and connections gained.

In-House Roles

- **Varied Compensation:** In-house counsel positions can offer competitive salaries, especially in large corporations. Compensation often aligns with industry standards and the company's size.
- **Consideration of Industry:** Salaries in in-house roles can vary greatly depending on the industry and the company's financial health.

Impact and Making a Difference

Private Practice

- **Large Firms:** Opportunities to work on high-profile cases and influence significant legal developments. Pro bono programs can offer avenues to make a social impact.
- **Smaller Firms:** May provide more direct community involvement and opportunities to work closely with clients on impactful cases.

Government Positions

- **Public Service and Policy Influence:** A direct path to contribute to public policy, regulatory frameworks, and societal change. Lawyers can play a key role in shaping laws and regulations that impact communities.
- **Advocacy and Public Interest Law:** Opportunities to work in areas such as civil rights, environmental law, and consumer protection, where the focus is on serving the public interest and advocating for societal change.

In-House Roles

- **Corporate Social Responsibility (CSR):** In-house lawyers can influence corporate policies and practices, steering companies toward ethical, socially responsible, and sustainable business methods.
- **Impact on Business Practices:** By advising on compliance, risk management, and ethical business practices, in-house counsel can have a significant impact on how businesses operate and contribute to society.

Balancing Compensation and Impact

- **Personal Priorities:** It is crucial to weigh personal values and financial needs. For some, the priority may be to pay off student debt rapidly, which makes higher-paying positions more attractive. Others might prioritize making an immediate social impact, even if it means accepting a lower salary initially.
- **Career Trajectory Considerations:** Consider the long-term trajectory of your career. For example, starting in a government role might offer less compensation initially but can lead to lucrative opportunities later. Similarly, gaining experience in a large firm can provide the financial means and skills to transition into impactful roles in the future.
- **Finding a Middle Ground:** There are ways to balance both compensation and impact. For instance, working in a private practice while engaging in pro bono work, or choosing in-house roles in companies known for their CSR initiatives, can offer a compromise between financial gain and making a difference.

Choosing an initial path in law involves a complex interplay between the desire for financial security, career prioritization, and the aspiration to contribute positively to society. Understanding the compensation and impact potential of various legal paths can help guide this decision-making process. It is important to reflect on personal priorities, consider long-term career goals, and explore opportunities that align with both financial needs and the desire to make a meaningful impact.

Pathways and Perspectives: Cat Kozlowski on Navigating Law with Innovation and Integrity

Counsel, Polsinelli

Cat Kozlowski, with a foundation in mathematics and computer science, has carved a distinctive path in the legal profession. Their educational journey began at a relatively small school, where they pursued legal studies on a near full scholarship, a testament to their academic prowess and determination. This choice was not merely a matter of financial necessity but a strategic decision that set the stage for a career marked by innovation and a deep understanding of the intersection between law and business.

After completing their education, Cat ventured into the legal world, where they quickly distinguished themselves through their work. With over a decade of experience spanning roles at law firms and as an in-house legal consultant, Cat has developed a broad and nuanced understanding of the healthcare industry, from small retail companies to billion-dollar health systems. Their expertise lies in operational and transactional matters, the Health Insurance Portability and Accountability Act of 1996 (HIPAA) and state privacy laws, and the practical aspects of medical staff integration with hospital operations. This diverse experience has equipped Cat with a unique ability to anticipate challenges and devise innovative solutions, making them a valued advisor in the field.

Beyond their professional achievements, Cat has actively contributed to fostering inclusivity within the legal community as the Cochair of their firm's LGBTQ+Resource Group.

Path to Business Law

Cat Kozlowski's path into business law was not a straightforward journey but one marked by curiosity and a drive to find where their skills could make the most significant impact. Initially drawn to the legal field by the potential to solve complex problems, Cat's background in mathematics and computer science provided a unique lens through which they viewed legal challenges. "I'm a natural project manager," Cat explained, reflecting on their early involvement in various organizations where they frequently found themselves in leadership roles. This knack for creating order out of chaos and making systems work efficiently was a precursor to their eventual gravitation toward business law.

The turning point came when Cat, recognizing the limitations of their knowledge in traditional legal roles, sought to expand their horizons. They recounted an early experience that significantly influenced their career direction: "I tracked down the attorney for Burt Rutan and Virgin Galactic in the U.S. and took them out to lunch." It was this initiative and willingness to step into the unknown that led them to the advice that would shape their career: either become a lobbyist in Washington or learn business law. This advice resonated with Cat, sparking an interest in transactional work and setting them on the path to becoming a business law specialist.

Challenges and Triumphs

Throughout their career, Cat has navigated a series of challenges that have tested their resolve and honed their skills as a business lawyer. One such challenge emerged early in their career, rooted in the adversarial nature of litigation and a law firm that did not align with their values. Cat recalls a significant moment of dissonance: "I really struggled with discovery . . . being told, wait, no, don't send anything. You're going to send objections first, and then they're going to threaten to pull you in court . . . Why are we wasting this time? Oh, because it's profitable to us." This experience highlighted a fundamental conflict between Cat's values and the profit-driven aspects of some legal practices, prompting them to reflect deeply on the type of lawyer they aspired to be.

Cat's dedication to finding a resolution that benefits all parties involved often sets them apart from their peers. They shared an innovative approach to settling cases, a method not universally welcomed in their professional environment. "I usually would just drag both sides in a room and be like, hey, opposing counsel, can we talk in the hallway for a minute? And leave the two in the room . . . nine times out of ten, they would start talking." This strategy, while effective, was frowned upon, underscoring the tension between traditional legal practices and Cat's forward-thinking methods.

Cat's personal journey and identity played a significant role in the challenges they faced. Working in an environment that was not always accepting or understanding of diverse identities added another layer of difficulty. "I'm genderqueer, I'm pansexual, and the people I was working under were incredibly homophobic and sexist." Despite these adversities, Cat's resilience and commitment to authenticity never wavered.

Through these experiences, Cat learned the importance of aligning personal values with professional practice. Their journey underscores the necessity of creating spaces in the legal field that respect and celebrate diversity, encourage innovative problem solving, and prioritize the well-being of all parties involved. Cat's story offers a powerful message to aspiring business lawyers: success is not just about navigating legal complexities but also about fostering an environment of respect, understanding, and ethical practice.

Advice for Business Lawyers

Cat's journey in the field of law is filled with invaluable lessons for anyone looking to make their mark. Reflecting on their experiences, Cat offers advice for aspiring business lawyers. "First and foremost, understand that this field is constantly evolving. You need to be adaptable, willing to learn, and proactive in seeking out new knowledge," they emphasize. This attitude of continuous learning was pivotal in Cat's transition from a background in mathematics and computer science to a successful career in law. They stress the importance of being open to change and the unexpected directions your career might take.

Cat's proactive approach to reaching out to established professionals for guidance underscores the value of building relationships in the field. "Don't be afraid to reach out to people whose work you admire. More often than not, they're willing to share their insights and experiences," Cat advises.

Finally, Cat encourages aspiring lawyers to prioritize their values and personal happiness in their career choices. "It's easy to get caught up in the prestige or the money, but at the end of the day, it's about finding work that fulfills you," they reflect. Cat's own career decisions, from tackling the challenges in the healthcare industry to advocating for inclusivity within the legal community, were driven by a desire to make a meaningful impact. They urge future business lawyers to seek roles that align with their passions and to remember that success is not solely defined by traditional metrics of achievement but by the satisfaction and joy derived from the work itself. ”

Skills Development and Law School Experience

Developing Key Legal Skills

In the journey of becoming a successful lawyer, particularly in the field of business law, the development of certain key legal skills is indispensable. Alongside these technical skills, soft skills play a crucial role in shaping a lawyer's career, especially in the early stages where mentorship and formative opportunities often stem from personal connections.

Cultivating Critical Thinking

- **Exercises for Enhancing Analytical Skills:** Engage in activities that challenge your reasoning and analytical abilities. Participating in moot court competitions, case study groups, or legal debate forums can be highly beneficial.
- **Application in Real-World Scenarios:** Seek opportunities to apply your critical thinking skills in practical settings, such as internships or legal clinics, where you can work on actual cases under supervision.

Mastering Negotiation Techniques

- **Negotiation Workshops and Simulations:** Attend workshops that focus on negotiation skills. Participating in simulated negotiations can provide hands-on experience and feedback from experts.
- **Understanding Different Negotiation Styles:** Learn about various negotiation styles and strategies. There are many books on the topic. Understand when to apply different tactics, such as collaborative versus competitive approaches, depending on the situation.

Enhancing Legal Writing

- **Writing Workshops and Courses:** Enroll in legal writing workshops or courses. These can provide structured guidance and improve your ability to articulate complex legal arguments effectively.
- **Practice Through Briefs and Memos:** Regularly practice writing case briefs, memos, and other legal documents. Seek feedback from professors or mentors to refine your writing skills.

Developing Soft Skills

- **Communication Skills:** Engage in activities that require public speaking, such as mock trials or legal presentations. Effective communication is key to clearly conveying legal concepts to clients and colleagues.
- **Empathy and Client Management:** Participate in client counseling competitions or volunteer at legal aid clinics to develop empathy and client management skills. Understanding client perspectives is crucial for effective legal representation and building trust.
- **Building Personal Connections for Mentorship:** Attend networking events, join legal associations, and actively seek mentorship opportunities. Building relationships with experienced professionals can provide invaluable guidance and open doors to career-enhancing opportunities.

Leveraging Technology

- **Familiarity with Legal Tech Tools:** Stay abreast of the latest legal technologies. Familiarity with case management software, legal research tools, and emerging tech such as AI in law can give you an edge in a tech-driven legal environment.
- **Incorporating Tech in Legal Learning:** Use technology to enhance your legal education. This can include using online resources for research, participating in virtual internships, or attending webinars on legal tech trends.

The development of both technical and soft skills is a continuous process that extends beyond law school. By focusing on critical thinking, negotiation, legal writing, and soft skills, aspiring lawyers can lay a strong foundation for a successful career in business law. Remember, these skills are not just about excelling in legal tasks; they are about becoming a well-rounded professional who can effectively connect with clients, colleagues, and mentors. Actively seeking opportunities for skill development and being open to learning and adapting will position you for success in the dynamic and competitive world of business law.

In the world of law, the journey through law school is filled with unique opportunities designed to prepare students for their future careers. Beyond the essential academic curriculum, engaging in internships, participating in legal clinics, and competing in moot court competitions stand out as cornerstone experiences. These elements not only complement theoretical knowledge with practical application but also foster skill development and offer valuable networking opportunities. This comprehensive guide explores how to fully leverage these opportunities, setting a strong foundation for a successful legal career.

Leveraging Internships

Finding Internships

- **Researching Opportunities:** Begin by identifying your interest areas within the legal field. Use resources such as online job boards, law firm websites, and professional associations to discover internships that align with your interests, be it in civil rights, corporate law, or environmental law.
- **Networking:** Leverage networking as a key strategy to find internship opportunities. Engage with law school alumni, attend networking events, and connect with professionals on platforms such as LinkedIn. Law school alumni can be particularly insightful, offering advice and potentially knowing of opportunities within their networks.
- **Law School Resources:** Use your law school's career services office, which often maintains lists of internship opportunities and has established relationships with firms and organizations that routinely offer positions to students. Career advisors can also assist in tailoring your resume and cover letter for a stronger application.

Securing Internships

- **Application Preparation:** When you have identified potential internships, meticulously prepare each application. Tailor your resume and cover letter to highlight relevant experiences, coursework, and any legal skills pertinent to the internship. Express your enthusiasm for the specific area of law and articulate your objectives for the internship experience.

- **Follow-Up:** Demonstrating initiative, follow up on your applications with a polite inquiry about the status, showing your keen interest in the position.
- **Interview Readiness:** Prepare for interviews by researching the organization thoroughly. Be ready to discuss your alignment with their mission, recent cases or projects, and how your interests and experiences contribute to their needs. Practice common interview questions and engage in mock interviews offered by career services to bolster your confidence.

Maximizing the Internship Experience

- **Setting Learning Objectives:** Initiate your internship by setting clear learning objectives with your supervisor, aligning your goals with the organization's needs. This proactive approach ensures the internship is tailored to your educational and career aspirations.
- **Engaging in a Variety of Tasks:** Seek exposure to a wide range of tasks and express your eagerness to participate in different aspects of legal work. This varied exposure offers a comprehensive view of legal practice and allows you to identify areas of interest and strength.
- **Building Professional Relationships:** Use your internship as an avenue to expand your professional network. Participate in events, connect with colleagues, and engage with other interns to forge relationships that could support and guide your career trajectory.
- **Seeking Mentorship:** Identify potential mentors among the attorneys you work with. A mentor can offer invaluable advice, feedback, and insights into the legal profession, facilitating your professional development and opening doors to future opportunities.

Engaging in Legal Clinics

Legal clinics represent a pivotal component of the law school experience, offering students the chance to work on real cases under the guidance of experienced attorneys and faculty members. These clinics serve diverse clients, providing critical legal services while allowing students to develop practical legal skills.

- **Choosing the Right Clinic:** Reflect on your career goals and interests to select a clinic that aligns with your aspirations. Research available clinics, considering the types of cases handled and the expertise of supervising attorneys. Choose clinics that offer the opportunity to develop skills relevant to your career path.

- **Skills Development:** Clinics are invaluable for gaining hands-on experience, from client interviews and legal research to court appearances. They foster client communication skills, collaborative work, and a deeper understanding of legal ethics and professional responsibility.

Participating in Moot Court

Moot court competitions are integral to law school education, simulating appellate court proceedings and honing students' legal argumentation and presentation skills.

- **Preparing for Competitions:** Success in moot court demands thorough legal research, effective brief writing, and the development of compelling oral arguments. Participants improve their ability to think on their feet and respond to judges' questions with poise and confidence.
- **Benefits of Participation:** Moot court enhances public speaking, legal reasoning, and presentation skills. It also provides opportunities to network with the legal community, including peers, faculty, and practicing attorneys, which can be invaluable for future career opportunities.

The journey through law school is enhanced by actively engaging in internships, legal clinics, and moot court competitions. These experiences are crucial for bridging the gap between theoretical knowledge and practical application, developing essential legal skills, and building a professional network. By strategically leveraging these opportunities, law students can lay a solid foundation for their legal careers, ensuring they are well prepared for the challenges and opportunities ahead.

Mastering Litigation and Leadership: Insights from James Williams

Seattle Office Managing Partner, Perkins Coie

James Williams stands as a distinguished figure in the realm of trial and complex business litigation, bringing over three decades of experience to his role as the Seattle Office Managing Partner at Perkins Coie. His journey into law began with a solid foundation laid at The Citadel, followed by further legal studies at the University of Virginia School of Law. Williams's career is marked by a series of courtroom victories, arbitrations, mediations, and effective litigation management, showcasing his prowess in navigating the intricacies of legal disputes across a wide spectrum of issues. These include breach of contract, fraud, product liability, and more, where he has consistently delivered results for both plaintiffs and defendants.

Beyond his legal practice, Williams has demonstrated a commitment to legal leadership and community service. His professional roles extend into national, regional, and local levels, including significant positions within Perkins Coie and active participation in the wider legal community. Notably, his election to the American Law Institute and his involvement with the American Bar Association highlight his influence and respect within the field. Williams's dedication to mentorship and pro bono work, particularly in the realm of civil rights, underscores his belief in the power of law as a force for positive change.

Williams's unique background, from his early years on a South Carolina farm to his military service in the U.S. Air Force, has informed his approach to law and leadership. This diverse experience has equipped him with a distinctive perspective on the challenges and opportunities within the legal profession. As readers delve into his insights and advice, they will find a wealth of knowledge and inspiration for their own careers in business law.

Building and Maintaining Professional Networks

Williams stresses the significance of staying in touch with peers from undergraduate and law school years, recognizing them as potential referral sources. Williams points out, "The lesson I should have learned early, and I didn't, was to stay in contact with the people who you liked when you were in undergrad or in law school, because all of them could be potential referral sources." This insight highlights the long-term value of nurturing connections made during one's educational journey, emphasizing that these relationships can evolve into professional opportunities.

He further elaborates on the nature of law as a relationship business, where personal connections often lead to work referrals. Williams suggests keeping these relationships "warm" without an immediate goal of gaining work from them. He explains, "It's just staying in contact. And firms will often underwrite the cost of doing that, whether it's going to lunch or having some activity or event where you reconnect with that person." This approach fosters a genuine connection that, over time, may naturally develop into a professional relationship. Williams advises against overtly selling oneself as a young lawyer, instead recommending a focus on maintaining a genuine connection that can later serve as a foundation for business development when one has developed a specific expertise.

Williams's advice culminates in the concept of becoming a subject matter expert as a pivotal moment in a lawyer's career. He notes, "And when you have something to sell, you'll know it because you start developing an expertise in an area or doing a certain thing that people say you're known for." This expertise, combined with preexisting warm relationships, creates a sweet spot for developing business where trust and professional respect are already established.

Mentorship and Professional Growth

Williams firmly believes in the transformative power of mentorship in shaping a lawyer's career. He asserts, "Mentors are fundamental. No one in this profession gets ahead alone." Williams's own journey in the legal field underscores the importance of having mentors who can guide, advise, and champion a young lawyer's growth. He recommends seeking mentors both within and outside one's organization, as they can offer varied perspectives and support. Inside an organization, mentors can provide invaluable insider knowledge and help navigate the often complex dynamics of a law firm. Williams suggests looking for mentors who can explain the unspoken cultural nuances and expectations, assist in understanding work assignments, and act as champions for career advancement.

Outside the organization, mentors serve as sounding boards for issues that might be too sensitive to discuss internally and can offer candid feedback on career progress. Williams highlights the importance of having a diverse group of mentors to cover different aspects of professional development. He shares, "I would have a variety of mentors filling a variety of functions within my professional life." This diversity in mentorship ensures that young lawyers can receive comprehensive guidance tailored to their unique career paths.

Engaging with mentors requires tact and respect for their time and expertise. Williams advises young lawyers to approach potential mentors with an understanding of the value of the mentor's time and not to be a burden. He suggests finding ways to add value to the mentor's work or life as a means of fostering a mutually beneficial relationship. "What is it that you can do for them that would be of benefit?" he asks, emphasizing the importance of making the relationship reciprocal whenever possible. This approach helps not only in building strong mentor–mentee relationships but also in laying the groundwork for a successful career in law.

Engaging in Professional Development Activities in Law School

Professional development activities enable law students to enhance their skills, expand their networks, and lay a robust foundation for their future careers. From participating in law school organizations, contributing to law journals, and attending networking events, to seeking mentorship, these activities enrich classroom learning with practical experience and professional growth. This chapter explores various professional development avenues available to law students, offering insights on maximizing these opportunities for a comprehensive legal education and successful career outset.

Introduction to Professional Development in Law School

Professional development serves as a crucial link between academic study and the practical realities of a legal career. While rigorous coursework provides the theoretical foundation necessary for legal expertise, engagement in professional development activities bolsters this knowledge with crucial practical skills and real-world insights. Participation in law school organizations, law journals, networking events, and mentorship presents students with invaluable opportunities to apply classroom learning in practical settings, develop professional competencies, and establish a robust professional network. These experiences significantly enhance a student's legal education and competitiveness in the job market, offering a deeper understanding of the legal profession, potential career paths, and the development of essential interpersonal and professional skills crucial for long-term success.

Participating in Law School Organizations

Participation in law school organizations provides students with a unique opportunity to enrich their legal education, develop essential professional skills, and build a supportive network of peers and mentors. These groups act as a practical bridge to law and a community for personal and professional development.

> **Types of Organizations and Their Roles:** Law schools host various organizations, each with specific goals. These include academic-focused groups such as law reviews, advocacy and interest groups dedicated to particular legal areas, and professional development organizations offering networking events and workshops.
>
> **Benefits of Active Participation:** Active involvement is an investment in future careers and personal development. Leadership roles enhance managerial skills, while membership allows for the practical application of legal skills. In addition, these organizations serve as platforms for community service and advocacy.

Building a Support Group: Participation also facilitates the creation of a support group, providing friendship, a sense of belonging, and a network of peers sharing similar interests and career goals. These organizations are invaluable for meeting mentors and professionals offering guidance and opportunities.

Choosing the Right Organizations: Considerations include aligning with career interests, enhancing desired skills, experiencing diversity, and finding community and support. It is also vital to manage involvement to complement, not compromise, the law school experience.

Contributing to Law Journals

Contributing to law journals is both prestigious and enriching, offering significant benefits in legal scholarship, professional development, and the enhancement of crucial legal skills. These student-run publications, guided by faculty, play a pivotal role in the legal landscape by disseminating research and contributing to academic debate.

Role of Law Journals in Legal Scholarship and Development: They allow for the dissemination of research, exploration of legal theories, and commentary on current issues, enriching the legal community and elevating a student's profile in the competitive legal field.

The Contribution Process: Involves submitting an article or note for peer review, engaging in extensive legal research, drafting, revising articles, and navigating complex legal databases. This process hones research, writing, critical thinking, collaboration, and detail-oriented skills, preparing students for nuanced legal practice.

Maximizing Networking Events in Law School

Networking is an essential component of building a successful legal career. Law school events, bar association meetings, and professional conferences offer invaluable opportunities for students to connect with practitioners, alumni, and peers. These connections can provide mentorship, advice, and potential job opportunities. Effectively navigating these events is crucial for establishing a robust professional network.

Understanding the Value of Networking in the Legal Profession

Networking in law goes beyond merely exchanging business cards; it is about forging relationships that foster career development. Through networking, students can gain insights into various legal fields, discover job openings, and find mentors to guide their early careers. A strong network also serves as a platform for idea exchange, collaboration on projects, and obtaining referrals.

Strategies for Effective Networking at Law School Events

- **Preparation:** Research attendees, especially guest speakers or panelists, to prepare meaningful questions and conversation starters.
- **Engagement:** Actively participate by asking questions and showing genuine interest in others' experiences. Networking is about mutual learning and sharing of goals and interests.
- **Follow-Up:** Send thank-you messages post-event to express gratitude and reinforce connections. Suggest further meetings or discussions when appropriate.
- **Using Social Media:** Use platforms such as LinkedIn to maintain contact with professional connections, share achievements, and engage in legal discussions. Ensure your profile is professional, current, and reflective of your career aspirations.

Building and Maintaining Professional Relationships

- **Finding Like-Minded Individuals:** Seek out organizations and events where you feel a sense of belonging and connection. Affinity groups and places where people share common interests or backgrounds can be particularly valuable.
- **Consistency:** Regular attendance at legal networking events and active participation in legal communities or organizations help maintain strong connections.
- **Mutual Support:** Approach networking with a mindset of how you can help others. Offering assistance without expecting anything in return can encourage reciprocal support.
- **Personalization:** Customize your interactions based on others' interests and expertise. Authentic connections are formed from genuine interactions and shared experiences.
- **Professionalism:** Always maintain professionalism in your interactions. This includes being respectful, punctual, and prepared.

Networking should be viewed as a long-term investment in your legal career. By approaching it with intention, preparation, and an authentic, service-minded attitude, you can maximize the opportunities presented by law school events and professional conferences. The relationships you build during law school can offer guidance, opportunities, and a sense of community throughout your legal career.

Using Faculty Guidance

Tapping into Faculty Knowledge and Experience

- **Office Hours and Consultations:** Leverage office hours for deep dives into subjects that interest you, gaining personalized advice related to your courses, areas of interest, or career aspirations.
- **Classroom Engagement:** Participate actively in class to enhance learning and stand out to professors, who can be pivotal in recommending you for opportunities.

Seeking Academic and Career Advice

- **Career Path Discussions:** Consult with professors about career paths in the legal field, especially areas matching their expertise for unique insights.
- **Guidance on Specializations:** For those considering a legal specialization, discussions with relevant faculty can offer invaluable insights into practical aspects, ongoing research, and trends.

Involvement in Faculty-Led Research Projects and Initiatives

- **Research Assistance:** Volunteering in research projects offers in-depth knowledge in specific legal areas and enhances research, writing, and analytical skills.
- **Participation in Faculty Projects:** Engaging in projects such as legal clinics or advocacy campaigns broadens practical legal skills under experienced mentorship.

Building Professional Relationships with Faculty

- **Networking and Recommendations:** Strong relationships with professors can lead to valuable recommendations and networking opportunities.
- **Mentorship Opportunities:** Some faculty may offer mentorship, providing guidance and support through your legal career journey.

Leveraging Legal Professionals' Insights

Engaging with Legal Professionals

- **Guest Lectures and Workshops:** Attend these events to gain realistic views of legal careers and learn about new legal areas and issues.
- **Active Participation:** Be proactive during these events. Asking questions and showing interest can facilitate future networking opportunities.

Learning from Real-World Experiences

- **Informational Interviews:** Arrange interviews with legal professionals to gain firsthand insights into daily work and challenges within specific legal fields.
- **Networking Events:** Use these events to build connections and gather advice, remembering that a broad network can lead to opportunities.

Applying Insights to Your Career Path

- **Real-World Application:** Reflect on insights from professional interactions to clarify career goals and guide your decisions.
- **Mentorship Opportunities:** Displaying interest and initiative can lead to mentorship relationships, offering further guidance and support.
- **Sharing with Peers:** Discuss insights with classmates to deepen understanding and foster a collaborative environment.

Balancing Academic Rigor with Practical Experience

For aspiring attorneys, law school is about more than mastering legal theories; it is about integrating practical experiences, developing professional relationships, and honing business development skills. This comprehensive approach is crucial for both law school success and long-term career advancement.

- **Effective Time Management and Strategic Prioritization** are essential for balancing academic responsibilities with practical experiences and networking opportunities.
- **Selective Engagement** in internships and extracurriculars ensures each activity aligns with career goals and enhances understanding of the law.
- **Acknowledging the Continuous Challenge** of balancing professional development emphasizes the need for ongoing growth and skill development beyond law school.

Effective Time Management and Strategic Prioritization

- **Strategic Planning:** Use digital calendars and planning tools to effectively balance academic obligations with practical legal experiences and networking activities.
- **Long-Term Goal Setting:** Prioritize activities aligned with career aspirations, acknowledging necessary trade-offs for future benefits.

Seamless Integration of Practical Experiences

- **Selective Engagement:** Choose internships, clinics, and extracurriculars that enrich legal understanding and contribute to professional networking.
- **Maximizing Nonacademic Periods:** Leverage summers and breaks for internships or pro bono work to apply learned theories in real-world contexts.

Acknowledging the Continuous Challenge of Balancing Professional Development

- **Ongoing Professional Growth:** Recognize that the challenge of integrating academic work with practical experience extends into professional life.
- **Developing Key Professional Skills:** Law school offers opportunities to develop essential soft skills like effective communication and client management alongside legal expertise.

Leveraging Support Systems

- **Faculty and Mentor Guidance:** Seek insights from faculty and mentors to navigate law school complexities and early career stages effectively.
- **Building and Maintaining Relationships:** Engage with a diverse network from the start to foster a culture of mutual support and open career opportunities.

Reflective Practice

- **Commitment to Self-Reflection:** Engage in regular reflection to foster personal growth and adapt strategies for balancing various aspects of professional development.

Engaging in professional development activities during law school is crucial for laying a solid foundation for a successful legal career. Students are encouraged to proactively participate in law school organizations, contribute to law journals, network extensively, and seek mentorship. These experiences not only enrich legal education but also enhance resumes, making students more competitive in the job market and better prepared for the challenges and opportunities of their future careers in law.

Navigating the Legal Job Market: Strategies from Application to Acceptance

Navigating the legal job market is a nuanced process that begins with crafting standout applications and extends to making strategic decisions upon receiving job offers. It involves not only showcasing your legal expertise but also highlighting your unique skills and experiences. Effective networking and personal branding play crucial roles in uncovering opportunities and making lasting impressions. The interview stage is your opportunity to demonstrate your fit within an organization, requiring preparation and insight into the firm's culture and values. Finally, evaluating job offers and negotiating terms are critical steps in aligning your career aspirations with the right opportunity. This journey is about more than finding a job; it is about strategically positioning yourself for a fulfilling career in law.

Tailoring Your Application for Legal Job Opportunities

When applying for positions in the legal field, it's essential to present an application that stands out and effectively communicates your suitability for the role. Here's how to tailor your application materials effectively:

Customized Resumes and Cover Letters

Understand the Organization:

- Research the law firm or organization extensively. Understand their culture, areas of expertise, and recent accomplishments.
- Use this information to align your application with their values, style, and needs.

Use AI Tools:

- Leverage AI-powered tools to craft resumes and cover letters that are spot-on in terms of relevance and precision.
- Ensure that these tools accentuate the aspects of your experience and skills that are most pertinent to the job.

Personalize Each Application:

- Avoid generic applications. Customize each resume and cover letter to the specific job and firm.
- Mention specific reasons why you are interested in the firm and how your skills and interests align with their work.

Connect through Your Network:

- If possible, make connections within the organization before applying. Networking can provide insider insights and potentially an internal referral.

- Mention these connections in your cover letter to add a personal touch and demonstrate your genuine interest.

Highlighting Relevant Experience

Showcase Legal Internships and Clinics:

- Highlight any legal internships, clinics, or practical experiences that are directly relevant to the position.
- Detail the skills acquired and how they translate to the responsibilities of the job you're applying for.

Project Experience in Law School:

- If you've worked on significant projects or papers in law school, especially those relevant to the firm's specialty, make sure to include them.
- Explain how these experiences have prepared you for the legal challenges you might face in the role.

Quantify Achievements:

- Use numbers and data to quantify your achievements where possible. For example, mention the number of cases handled, the amount of funds raised in a legal fundraiser, or the scale of a research project.

Skills and Competencies:

- Identify key skills that are highly valued in the legal profession, such as analytical thinking, attention to detail, and effective communication.
- Emphasize soft skills like teamwork, time management, and client relations, particularly if you have tangible examples or stories that showcase these abilities.

Include Nonlegal Experience if Relevant:

- If you have work experience outside the legal field, include it if it demonstrates transferable skills or unique perspectives beneficial to a legal career.

Customize Your Skills Section:

- Tailor the skills section of your resume to match the job description. Highlight the skills that are most relevant to the job you are applying for.

A well-tailored application is crucial in the competitive legal job market. By customizing your resumes and cover letters and highlighting relevant experience effectively, you demonstrate your commitment and suitability for the role.

Remember, a tailored application shows effort and keen interest, and it can significantly enhance your chances of being noticed and ultimately, hired.

Preparing for Legal Job Interviews

Interview preparation is crucial for aspiring lawyers. It's about showcasing not only your legal acumen but also your understanding of the firm and your ability to fit into its culture. Here's how to prepare effectively:

In-Depth Research

Firm or Organization History:

- Investigate the firm's history, key practice areas, and any notable cases or achievements.
- Understand its position in the legal market, recent developments, and future goals.

Lawyer Profiles and Current Work:

- Study the bios of the firm's attorneys, especially those you'll be meeting. Look for shared experiences, alma maters, or interests.
- Familiarize yourself with their current cases, publications, or speaking engagements.

Use Various Sources:

- Read through the firm's website, news sections, LinkedIn updates, and recent press releases.
- Check legal news websites for any mentions of the firm or its lawyers.

Prepare Questions:

- Prepare insightful questions based on your research. This shows engagement and a deep interest in the firm's activities.

Mock Interviews

Practice with Peers and Mentors:

- Conduct mock interviews with peers, mentors, or law school career advisors.
- Seek feedback on your answers, body language, and overall demeanor.

Use AI Tools:

- Leverage AI-powered interview training tools for additional practice.

- These tools can provide a safe space to practice and often offer constructive feedback.

Professionalism and Video Interviews

Professional Attire:

- Dress professionally, even if the interview is virtual. Choose attire that reflects the firm's culture but always errs on the side of formality.
- Ensure your outfit is neat, well-fitted, and appropriate for a legal setting.

Mastering Video Interview Techniques:

- For video interviews, test your technology beforehand. Ensure your camera and microphone work well.
- Pay attention to lighting and background. Choose a quiet, well-lit space with a neutral background.

Presenting Yourself:

- Work on your interpersonal skills. Be friendly, enthusiastic, and professional in your demeanor.
- Practice maintaining eye contact, a confident posture, and clear, articulate speech.

Body Language:

- Be mindful of your body language. Sit upright, use hand gestures moderately, and maintain a positive, engaged facial expression.
- Avoid fidgeting, which can be distracting and convey nervousness.

Conveying Enthusiasm and Competence:

- Express enthusiasm for the role and the firm. Show that you are not only capable of the job but also excited about the opportunity to contribute.
- Share specific reasons why you are attracted to this particular firm or role.

A well-prepared candidate is more likely to succeed in legal job interviews. By conducting thorough research, practicing with mock interviews, and presenting yourself professionally—especially in video interviews—you demonstrate your commitment and fit for the role. Remember, professionalism, preparedness, and a genuine enthusiasm for the legal profession are key to making a positive impression.

Strategies to Understand and Evaluate Culture

Direct Networking and Conversations:

- Use LinkedIn to connect with current and former employees of law firms, corporations, or government agencies. Personalized messages can lead to informative discussions about their experiences and the workplace culture.

Online Research:

- Websites like Vault, Glassdoor, and Indeed provide employee reviews and ratings, offering insights into the work environment, management style, and job satisfaction.
- Follow firms or organizations on LinkedIn for updates and news. This can reveal their values, employee achievements, and community involvement.

Interview Strategies:

- In interviews, inquire about mentorship, work–life balance, and team collaboration.
- For law firms, ask about their approach to handling high-pressure situations, client relationships, and career advancement opportunities.

Culture-Specific Questions to Ask:

- How does the firm/organization handle feedback and performance reviews?
- What are their policies on work–life balance, remote work, and employee well-being?
- For law firms, ask about their approach to associate development, client engagement, and pro bono work.

Using LinkedIn for Deeper Insights:

- Employee profiles on LinkedIn can give you a sense of the professional growth and development opportunities within the firm or organization.
- Company pages and employee-shared content can offer a glimpse into the day-to-day work life and firm culture.

Thoroughly researching and understanding the culture of potential legal workplaces is crucial for your career satisfaction and growth. Use online platforms, direct networking, and specific inquiries to gain a comprehensive understanding of the work environment in law firms, in-house departments, and government agencies. This informed approach will help you find a workplace where you can thrive both professionally and personally, aligning with your values and career aspirations.

Evaluating Career Growth Opportunities for First-Time Job Seekers in Law

When starting out in your legal career, it's essential to consider not just your immediate job role but also the long-term growth and development opportunities that potential employers offer. Here's a detailed guide on evaluating these prospects:

- **Understanding Advancement Pathways:**
  - Research the firm or organization's career progression structure. Is there a clear path to becoming a partner, senior counsel, or a leader in a specific legal domain?
  - Inquire about the typical timeline for promotions and the criteria used for advancement. Do they prioritize seniority, merit, or a combination of both?
  - Understand the turnover rate at the organization. A high rate might indicate issues with job satisfaction or advancement opportunities.
- **Transparent Career Pathways:**
  - During interviews or networking opportunities, ask about examples of individuals who have successfully climbed the ladder within the organization. This can provide a realistic picture of career progression.
  - Be wary of vague answers about growth opportunities. Look for organizations that can provide concrete examples of career development paths.
- **Training Programs:**
  - Find out if the firm or organization offers formal training programs. This includes induction training for new hires, ongoing legal education, and skill-specific training such as negotiation, litigation techniques, or contract drafting.
  - Ask about opportunities to work in different legal areas or departments. This kind of exposure can be crucial for broadening your legal expertise.
- **Leadership and Management Training:**
  - Inquire about training in soft skills like leadership, management, and client development. These skills are vital for lawyers aspiring to take on senior roles or to build and lead their own teams.
  - Look for firms that invest in their employees' leadership skills, as this indicates a commitment to nurturing well-rounded legal professionals.

- **Continuing Legal Education (CLE) and Resources:**
    - Check if the organization supports and funds continuing legal education. CLE is crucial for staying updated with legal trends and maintaining your license.
    - Assess the availability of resources such as legal research tools, access to legal databases, and support staff. These resources are essential for efficient and effective legal practice.

- **Mentorship and Networking Opportunities:**
    - Seek firms that have formal mentorship programs. Having a mentor in the early stages of your career can significantly impact your professional development.
    - Organizations that encourage networking and participation in legal associations and conferences can also be beneficial for your career growth.

Evaluating career growth opportunities is a critical step in choosing your first legal employer. Firms and organizations that provide clear advancement paths, comprehensive training programs, and support for professional development are more likely to foster your growth as a lawyer. Remember, your first job is not just about the work you do today but also about the opportunities it opens up for your future in the legal profession. Be thorough in your research and don't hesitate to ask direct questions about career development during your job search process.

Exploring Alternative Legal Roles for Law Graduates

Law graduates have a wealth of opportunities beyond traditional law firm or in-house roles. Skills acquired in law school are highly valued across various sectors, offering unique career paths.

Nontraditional Paths Overview

- **Legal Technology:** Engage in roles contributing to the development of legal research, e-discovery, and client management software. Opportunities include product development, legal analysis, and customer success roles.
- **Legal Consulting:** Consulting firms value law graduates for their analytical skills and regulatory knowledge. Positions range from compliance and risk management to legal operations consulting.
- **Nonprofit Organizations:** Work in advocacy, research, and policy development for organizations focusing on legal issues, human rights, or policy. These roles offer a chance to make significant social impacts.
- **Educational and Research Institutions:** Consider roles in academic research, teaching, or administration within law schools and research institutions, allowing for deeper specialization and contribution to legal scholarship.

Flexibility and Openness

- Be flexible and open to diverse roles that leverage your legal training.
- Network and explore industries and sectors where legal expertise is valued, even if they fall outside traditional legal job descriptions.

The Value of a Legal Education

- Legal education develops skills such as critical thinking and understanding of regulatory frameworks, applicable in various contexts.
- A legal background provides a unique perspective beneficial in numerous alternative roles.

Career Development Strategies

- **Diverse Experiences:** Early career flexibility can lead to unexpected and enriching paths, broadening your legal and industry knowledge.
- **Networking and Continuous Learning:** Build connections across industries and stay informed about trends, particularly in sectors where legal skills are increasingly vital, such as fintech, healthtech, or policy advisory.

Embrace the Journey

Embarking on nontraditional paths can lead to a dynamic and fulfilling career. Your legal foundation opens doors to myriad opportunities. Be proactive in exploring these avenues to find a career that aligns with your passions and goals.

Making Informed Decisions in Your Legal Career

Embarking on a legal career involves making critical decisions that align with your personal and professional aspirations. Below are detailed strategies to help guide these decisions.

Reflect on Personal Goals and Values

- **Career Ambitions:**
  - Take time to introspect on where you see yourself in the next five, ten, or twenty years. Are you aiming for a partnership in a law firm, a senior in-house counsel role, or a position of influence in the public sector?
  - Think about the type of work you want to be doing. Do you see yourself thriving in the fast-paced environment of corporate law, the nuanced world of IP law, or the socially impactful area of public interest law?

- **Personal Values:**
  - Identify what drives you ethically and morally. If social justice is a priority, consider paths such as nonprofit organizations or government roles. If innovation excites you, look toward firms specializing in technology or intellectual property.
  - Consider the type of clients you want to serve and the impact you wish to have. Do you want to assist large corporations in navigating legal challenges, or do you prefer helping individuals and communities?

Seeking Guidance and Support

- **Career Counseling:**
  - Most law schools offer career services that provide personalized guidance. Schedule meetings with career counselors who can help you explore various legal career paths and understand market trends.
  - Use these sessions to discuss your strengths, weaknesses, and areas of interest. Career counselors can help align your skills with suitable legal paths.
- **Alumni and Peer Insights:**
  - Reach out to alumni who are now working in areas you're interested in. Their recent experience in the job market can provide valuable insights.
  - Conduct informational interviews. These are informal conversations where you can ask about their career path, experiences, and advice for someone entering the field. To conduct an effective informational interview:
    - Use LinkedIn to identify potential interviewees. Look for alumni from your law school or individuals working in your area of interest.
    - Send a polite, concise message explaining that you're a law student interested in learning about their career path. Be clear that you're seeking advice and insights, not a job.
    - Prepare specific questions. Ask about their day-to-day responsibilities, what they enjoy about their work, challenges they face, and any advice they have for someone starting out.
    - Express gratitude after the interview and keep the connection alive. These contacts can become valuable parts of your professional network.

Making informed decisions at the start of your legal career is crucial for long-term satisfaction and success. Reflect deeply on your personal goals and values, and actively seek guidance and insights from available resources and connections.

Your law school's career services, along with alumni and peer networks, are invaluable in this journey. By aligning your career path with your aspirations and values, and by leveraging the support around you, you set the foundation for a fulfilling and impactful legal career.

Understanding Market Trends: Strategies for First-Time Job Seekers in Law

Researching Current Legal Market Trends

- **Using Online Resources:**
  - Leverage legal industry publications, online forums, and news platforms to stay updated on market trends. Websites such as the American Bar Association, Law.com, and legal blogs offer insights into evolving legal fields and market demands.
  - Follow industry thought leaders on social media and professional platforms like LinkedIn to gain insights into emerging legal trends and discussions.
- **Attending Industry Events and Webinars:**
  - Participate in legal industry conferences, webinars, and workshops. These events are not only excellent for networking but also provide a pulse on current and future legal market trends.
  - Use these opportunities to engage with speakers and attendees, asking questions about market shifts and areas of growing legal demand.
- **Engaging with Legal Recruiters and Career Advisors:**
  - Schedule meetings with legal recruiters and your law school's career advisors. They can provide valuable information on which legal sectors are hiring and what skills are in demand.
  - Recruiters and career advisors can also offer insights into salary trends, firm cultures, and job market forecasts, helping you align your career plans with market realities.

Specialization vs. General Legal Practice

- **Assessing the Benefits of Specialization:**
  - Evaluate the advantages of specializing in a niche area. Specialization can make you more attractive to firms and clients seeking specific expertise, such as environmental law, intellectual property, or cybersecurity law.
  - Research the demand for various specializations, considering long-term career prospects and your own interests.

- **Considering a General Legal Practice:**
  - A broad general legal practice can offer flexibility and a wide range of experiences. It's especially beneficial if you're unsure about your long-term career path or if you enjoy a diverse legal workload.
  - Understand that a generalist approach may be more suited to certain work environments, such as small to midsized firms, in-house legal departments, or public sector roles.

Making Informed Career Decisions

- **Aligning Career Choices with Market and Personal Interests:**
  - Balance your personal interests with market demand. While it's important to consider market trends, aligning your career with your interests and strengths will lead to greater job satisfaction and success.
  - Regularly reassess your career path in light of market changes and personal growth to ensure you're on track with your professional goals.
- **Continuous Market Awareness:**
  - Stay informed about the legal market throughout your career. The legal industry is dynamic, and areas of high demand can shift. Ongoing education and adaptability are key to staying relevant and successful.

For first-time job seekers in law, understanding and adapting to market trends is crucial. Whether you choose to specialize or maintain a general legal practice, aligning your career with both market demands and personal interests is essential. Stay informed, flexible, and proactive in your career planning to navigate the ever-evolving landscape of the legal profession successfully.

Thoughtful Consideration of Job Offers in Legal Careers

As the final step in the early career decision-making process, evaluating job offers requires a careful and comprehensive approach. Young lawyers must consider a range of factors beyond the immediate allure of salary to ensure that their first professional role sets the stage for a fulfilling and successful legal career.

Evaluating Beyond Salary

- **Quality of Work and Learning Opportunities:**
  - Assess the type of work you will be doing. Does it align with your areas of interest or specialization? Will it challenge you and help you grow as a lawyer?

  - Consider the learning opportunities available. Does the firm or organization invest in ongoing training and professional development? Will you have access to mentors and senior lawyers who can guide you?

- **Potential for Work–Life Balance:**
  - Investigate the firm's or organization's approach to work–life balance. Understand expectations regarding working hours, flexibility, and time off.
  - Remember, a well-rounded life contributes to your effectiveness and satisfaction as a lawyer. A role that respects your personal time and health is crucial for long-term success.

Fit and Comfort with the Role

- **Alignment with Career Aspirations:**
  - Reflect on how the offer aligns with your long-term career goals. Does it provide a stepping stone toward your desired career path?
  - Consider the trajectory of growth within the organization. Does it offer clear advancement opportunities that align with your professional objectives?
- **Compatibility with Personal Working Style:**
  - Evaluate the working environment and culture. Is it collaborative or competitive? Does it match your working style and personality?
  - Consider how comfortable you feel with the team and the organizational ethos. A supportive and compatible work environment is key to thriving in your new role.
- **Balancing Personal and Professional Life:**
  - Factor in how the role will affect your personal life. Consider the location, commute, and the impact on your family or personal commitments.
  - Ensure that the role allows you to maintain a healthy balance between your professional responsibilities and personal life.

When evaluating job offers, it is essential to look at the complete picture. A thoughtful approach that weighs salary alongside quality of work, learning opportunities, work–life balance, and alignment with personal and professional goals will lead to a more informed and satisfactory decision. Remember, the right job is not just about financial rewards; it is also about growth, fulfillment, and a harmonious integration into your overall life journey. Your first role in the legal profession sets the foundation for your future, so choose wisely, considering all aspects that contribute to a rewarding and sustainable career in law.

Insider Strategies for Legal Job Seekers: Insights from Kate Reder Sheikh

Partner—Associate Practice Group, Major, Lindsey & Africa

Kate Reder Sheikh's career in the legal profession is marked by a blend of specialized legal expertise and a deep commitment to fostering diversity and mentorship within the field. She began her educational journey at Wesleyan University, where she earned a Bachelor of Arts in English, laying a solid foundation in critical thinking and communication. Her pursuit of law led her to the University of North Carolina School of Law, where she obtained her Juris Doctor degree. This academic background equipped her with the legal acumen and ethical framework necessary for a successful career in law.

Upon entering the legal profession, Kate initially focused on family law, dedicating a significant part of her early career to serving the LGBTQ community. This work, especially before the landmark Obergefell decision, showcased her ability to navigate complex legal landscapes with empathy and precision. However, the evolution of her practice area and a desire to impact the legal profession more broadly prompted a shift in her career trajectory. She transitioned into legal recruitment, where she has made a notable impact by placing talented associates and partners in law firms, with a particular emphasis on mental health support and diversity.

Currently, as a partner at Major, Lindsey & Africa, Kate leverages her extensive experience and deep roots in the San Francisco Bay Area's legal market to match candidates with firms that align with their career aspirations and values. Her approach is characterized by a commitment to understanding the unique needs of both law firms and candidates, ensuring a fit that benefits all parties involved. Through her work, Kate continues to be a driving force in promoting diversity and inclusion in the legal profession, guiding the next generation of legal professionals toward fulfilling and impactful careers in business law.

Steering the Start of a Legal Career in Business Law

Starting a career in business law can be challenging, yet rewarding, with the right strategies and mindset. Kate emphasizes the importance of networking, particularly with alumni from one's law school. This approach not only fosters a sense of community but also opens doors to opportunities within and across law firms. For those considering a switch in practice areas, Kate suggests leveraging these connections to gain insights into the day-to-day realities of different specializations. This internal network can be instrumental in making informed decisions about one's career path.

Another critical aspect of navigating the early stages of a legal career is building a strong reputation from the outset. Kate points out that coming into a new role with enthusiasm and a willingness to tackle any task can set a positive tone that benefits one's career long term. She advises against immediately diving into pro bono work in big law firms, suggesting instead that new attorneys focus on proving their capabilities in billable work before pursuing their passion for making a positive change. This strategic patience ensures that when the time comes to engage in pro bono projects, they do so from a position of strength and established competence.

Kate also highlights the importance of understanding the operational aspects of a law firm, especially for first-generation professionals. Knowing whom to approach with a client's email or how to handle specific situations can be as crucial as legal expertise itself. She recommends building relationships with paralegals and asking plenty of questions to navigate the firm's processes effectively. For first-generation law students and attorneys, finding a mentor who has navigated similar challenges can provide invaluable guidance and support.

Key Milestones and Turning Points

Throughout her career, Kate has encountered several pivotal moments that not only tested her resolve but also significantly shaped her professional journey. One such moment came early in her career when she decided to transition from practicing family law to legal recruitment. This shift was not just a change in job function but a leap into a completely different aspect of the legal profession. It required Kate to leverage her legal skills in new ways, assessing not just the legal acumen of candidates but also their fit within various law firm cultures. This move was a gamble that paid off, allowing her to make a broader impact on the legal profession by ensuring that law firms were not just staffed, but staffed with individuals who could contribute to a more diverse and inclusive workplace.

Whether it was shifting career paths or tackling challenging placements, Kate's experiences underscore that success often requires stepping out of one's comfort zone and embracing the unknown. Her journey serves as a testament to the fact that while the path to success in law may be fraught with challenges, it is those very challenges that provide the opportunity for growth and development.

Navigating the Job Market with Emerging Technology and Global Trends

The legal profession, particularly within the realm of business law, is poised on the cusp of transformation, driven by rapid technological advancements and shifting societal expectations. Kate observes that the integration of technology into legal practice is not just changing how tasks are accomplished but also what clients expect from their legal advisors. As digital platforms become more prevalent, the ability to understand and leverage technology for legal research, case management, and client communication will become indispensable. Moreover, the rise of legal tech start-ups signifies an era where legal services are increasingly productized and delivered in more efficient, user-friendly formats.

In addition to technical skills, Kate emphasizes the growing importance of soft skills, particularly adaptability, emotional intelligence, and cross-cultural communication. The global nature of business today requires lawyers to navigate diverse legal systems and cultural norms seamlessly. As business law becomes more intertwined with international markets, the ability to understand and respect different perspectives will be crucial for successful negotiation and dispute resolution.

For law students and early career attorneys looking to thrive in this evolving landscape, Kate recommends a proactive approach to learning. This includes staying abreast of technological trends impacting the legal industry, seeking opportunities for cross-disciplinary education, and cultivating a global mindset through internships or studies abroad. Equally important is the development of a robust professional network that spans beyond the legal field, to include tech professionals, entrepreneurs, and international counterparts. By preparing for these shifts, aspiring legal professionals can position themselves at the forefront of the future of business law, ready to tackle the challenges and opportunities that lie ahead. ”

Transitioning to Legal Practice

From Classroom to Courtroom: Bridging the Gap

The transition from law school to legal practice is a critical phase in a lawyer's career, marking the shift from academic learning to the practical application of legal skills in real-world scenarios. This chapter, "From Classroom to Courtroom: Bridging the Gap," guides new attorneys through understanding what lies ahead after law school and how to best position themselves for success in the legal profession.

Preparing for the Professional Shift

The move from an academic setting to professional practice involves more than a change of environment; it necessitates a fundamental shift in mindset and approach. New attorneys must adapt to the demands and dynamics of legal practice, where theoretical knowledge meets practical application. Key areas of focus include the following:

- **Understanding Professional Expectations:** The legal profession demands a high level of professionalism, including adherence to ethical standards, client confidentiality, and a commitment to learning and improvement.
- **Developing Practical Legal Skills:** Although law school provides a theoretical foundation, practical skills such as legal writing, client counseling, negotiation, and courtroom advocacy are honed through experience. Seeking opportunities for hands-on learning, such as internships or clinics, can facilitate this skill development.

Navigating Early Career Challenges

The initial years of legal practice come with their own set of challenges, from managing workloads to building a professional identity. Addressing these challenges head-on is crucial for early career development:

- **Effective Workload Management:** Learning to efficiently manage time and responsibilities is essential for handling the often demanding workload of legal practice. Developing strong organizational skills and learning to prioritize tasks can help new attorneys manage their caseloads effectively.
- **Building Professional Networks:** Establishing connections within the legal community is vital for career advancement. Networking, mentorship, and involvement in professional organizations can provide support, guidance, and opportunities for growth.
- **Ethical and Professional Conduct:** Upholding the highest standards of ethical and professional conduct is paramount in legal practice. New attorneys must familiarize themselves with the ethical rules and standards governing the profession and incorporate them into their practice.

Strategies for Successful Transition

To successfully navigate the transition from law school to legal practice, new attorneys should employ several strategies:

- **Embrace Lifelong Learning:** The legal field is constantly evolving, making ongoing education and adaptation a necessity. Engaging in CLE and staying abreast of legal developments are key to maintaining competence.
- **Seek Mentorship and Feedback:** Building relationships with more experienced attorneys can provide invaluable insights and guidance. Actively seeking feedback on your work can also accelerate your professional development.
- **Prioritize Professional Development:** Beyond mastering legal skills, focusing on professional development areas such as client relationship management, business development, and understanding the business aspects of legal practice can enhance a lawyer's career trajectory.

Understanding what's next after law school and strategically preparing for the transition to legal practice are critical steps in building a successful legal career. By focusing on professional development, embracing the practical application of legal skills, and navigating early career challenges with resilience and adaptability, new attorneys can position themselves for success in the dynamic and rewarding field of law.

Navigating Different Legal Environments

Navigating Different Legal Environments: Big Law, Boutique Firms, and In-House Legal Departments

Transitioning into the dynamic legal profession, early career lawyers are presented with a spectrum of environments where law is practiced. Each environment, ranging from the expansive corridors of Big Law firms to the specialized focus of boutique practices, and the strategic realm of in-house legal departments, presents its unique set of challenges, cultures, and growth opportunities. Understanding the distinctive features of each setting is crucial for new attorneys aiming to navigate their professional journeys effectively.

Big Law Firms: Navigating the Halls of Power and Prestige

Large law firms, commonly known as "Big Law," stand out for their formidable presence across global or national stages, offering a comprehensive suite of legal services to high-profile clients. These institutions are hallmarks of prestige and power in the legal world, where associates are immersed in:

- **High Expectations and Demanding Workloads:** The allure of Big Law comes with the reality of long hours and high-pressure projects. Associates are expected to deliver exceptional work under tight deadlines, catering to the sophisticated needs of corporate clients.

- **Structured Growth and Specialization:** Career progression in Big Law is often well-defined, with a clear hierarchy guiding advancement. Associates are encouraged to specialize, honing their expertise in areas critical to the firm's client services.
- **Professional Development Opportunities:** Despite the competitive environment, Big Law firms invest in their associates' growth through extensive training programs, mentorship, and access to cutting-edge legal resources and technologies.

Boutique Law Firms: Mastering Niche Expertise in a Collaborative Setting

In contrast, boutique law firms offer a more intimate setting where specialization and personal client relationships take center stage. These firms are characterized by the following:

- **Focused Expertise and Client Interaction:** Boutique practices allow lawyers to become deeply versed in specific legal niches. Early and direct involvement in cases facilitates a richer client interaction experience, often missing in larger firms.
- **Work–Life Balance:** Although the work remains demanding, boutique firms may offer a more manageable balance between professional responsibilities and personal life, appreciating the value of well-rounded lawyers.
- **Collaborative Cultures:** The smaller scale of boutique firms nurtures a supportive atmosphere. Teamwork and mentorship are pillars of the culture, fostering a conducive environment for professional and personal development.

In-House Legal Departments: The Intersection of Law and Business

Transitioning to an in-house legal role means stepping into the world of corporate decision making. Lawyers in these departments work directly for corporations or organizations, offering the following:

- **Diverse Legal Work:** In-house attorneys address a broad spectrum of legal issues, from navigating contracts and compliance to managing intellectual property and litigation, all within the context of the company's industry.
- **Integration with Business Strategy:** This role requires a seamless blend of legal expertise and business acumen. Lawyers provide advice that not only addresses legal compliance but also influences strategic business decisions.

- **Work–Life Balance and Corporate Benefits:** In-house positions often come with more predictable schedules and a suite of corporate benefits, reflecting the broader company culture and offering a different quality of life compared with private practice.

Adapting to Different Legal Settings

Successfully adapting to these varied legal environments demands an agile mindset, a commitment to education, and an introspective understanding of one's career ambitions and personal values. For those embarking on their legal careers, considerations such as preferred work style, the level of direct client interaction desired, and long-term aspirations are key in selecting an environment that aligns with their professional journey and personal fulfillment.

By thoughtfully evaluating the contrasts and opportunities presented by Big Law, boutique practices, and in-house departments, new attorneys can make informed decisions that resonate with their individual goals, setting the stage for a rewarding and impactful career in law.

Intersecting Paths: Matt McFarlane's Transition from Science to Legal Innovation

Cofounder of Boutique Law Firm, Grout

Matt McFarlane's professional journey is a testament to the power of interdisciplinary skills and the pursuit of diverse interests. With a solid foundation in science, holding an ScB in Biochemistry from Brown University and a PhD in Molecular & Cellular Physiology from Stanford University School of Medicine, Matt's initial career path seemed firmly rooted in the world of academic research and biotechnology. However, his trajectory took a unique turn when he decided to pursue a career in law, enrolling at Fordham University School of Law to obtain his JD. This decision marked the beginning of a distinctive blend of analytical rigor and creative problem solving in the legal profession.

The motivation behind Matt's transition from science to law was not a sudden epiphany but a gradual realization of his desire for a different kind of impact. Despite his deep engagement with scientific research, he found himself drawn to the challenges and opportunities presented by the legal field. The skills he developed during his time in the sciences—critical thinking, complex problem solving, and a meticulous attention to detail—proved to be invaluable assets in his legal studies and subsequent practice.

Matt's unique background has allowed him to bring a fresh perspective to the practice of law, particularly in the realms of intellectual property and business law. His ability to understand and communicate complex technical concepts has been a significant advantage, enabling him to bridge the gap between scientific innovation and legal protection. This blend of skills has not only set him apart in his field but also underscored the importance of diverse educational backgrounds in enriching the legal profession. Through his career journey, Matt exemplifies how embracing one's varied interests and skills can lead to a fulfilling and impactful career in law.

Navigating Diversity and Inclusion in Legal Spaces

Matt McFarlane's insights into diversity and inclusion within the legal profession stem from a rich tapestry of experiences, particularly highlighted by his transition from a large firm in a bustling market to a more isolated practice. This shift exposed him to the stark contrasts in professional environments and the implications for diversity and inclusion. In larger markets, the conversation around diversity seemed to be advancing, albeit slowly, with firms taking deliberate steps toward creating more inclusive spaces. These efforts, as Matt observed, often felt like navigating through new territory with a mix of enthusiasm and uncertainty. Despite the challenges, there was a sense of movement toward embracing a broader definition of diversity that went beyond mere demographics to include diversity of thought and experience.

Matt's reflections on diversity and inclusion extend beyond the conventional discussions. He emphasizes that diversity of thought and the willingness to challenge traditional ways of doing things are crucial for the legal profession to evolve and better serve society. This perspective is particularly relevant in the context of professional disparities between major markets and more isolated areas. It highlights the need for a more inclusive approach that values different viewpoints and experiences, fostering an environment where innovation can thrive. Through his experiences, Matt underscores the importance of embracing diversity and inclusion not as mere goals or checkboxes but as fundamental values that enrich the legal profession and enhance its ability to serve a diverse clientele.

Building a Fulfilling Legal Career

In his journey through the legal profession, Matt emphasizes the importance of intentionality in building a fulfilling career. He believes that understanding what you truly want from your career and taking deliberate steps toward it is crucial. "The fastest way to create the most impact is to do it with some intention," Matt shares. This approach involves not only setting clear career goals but also actively seeking opportunities that align with those goals. For Matt, this meant transitioning from patent litigation to a more generalist approach, allowing him to engage with work that resonated with his interests and values.

Another significant challenge Matt discusses is the aspect of self-marketing for lawyers, a concept many find uncomfortable. He points out that while lawyers may not see themselves as salespeople, effectively communicating one's expertise and value is essential. "If the right people know who you are, you can provide the most benefit," he asserts. This does not necessarily require traditional sales tactics but rather positioning oneself in a way that makes your skills and interests clear to potential clients and employers. By doing so, lawyers can attract work that is not only professionally rewarding but also personally fulfilling.

Finally, Matt highlights the power of positioning oneself to attract the right clients and work. He advises lawyers to focus on building connections with people who can refer or directly offer the kind of work they are most passionate about. This approach has been instrumental in his own career, enabling him to engage with projects and clients that align with his interests and values. Through his experiences, Matt illustrates that with thoughtful positioning and a clear understanding of one's professional goals, it is possible to craft a legal career that is both impactful and fulfilling.

Building a Professional Identity in the Legal Field

Transitioning from law school into the professional legal world involves much more than acquiring a robust set of legal skills; it demands the cultivation of a professional identity that resonates within the legal community. This process is essential for early career lawyers, setting the stage for their roles, relationships, and reputation in the field.

Creating a Reputation and Professional Identity

Showcase Your Expertise: Establish your areas of interest and actively engage in activities that highlight your knowledge and skills. Contributing to legal discussions, writing insightful articles, or participating in legal panels not only enhances your visibility but also establishes you as an expert in your chosen areas. This visibility, coupled with your expertise, forms the foundation of your professional reputation.

Engage with the Legal Community: Building a strong professional network is essential. Active involvement in bar associations, legal forums, and networking events provides opportunities to connect with mentors, peers, and influencers who can significantly impact your career trajectory. These interactions not only foster professional relationships but also enhance your reputation within the legal community.

Consistent Professionalism: Professionalism extends beyond the courtroom or office—it encompasses all aspects of your presence, including how you conduct yourself online and in social settings. Adhering to the highest standards of integrity, responsibility, and diligence in all your professional undertakings reinforces your reputation and solidifies your professional identity.

Balancing Personal Values and Professional Ethics

Aligning Values with Practice: It is imperative to choose roles and environments that resonate with your personal values. Whether your passion lies in social justice, corporate law, or public service, finding alignment between your work and your principles is crucial for genuine satisfaction and authenticity in your professional life.

Ethical Practice: The bedrock of the legal profession is its commitment to ethics. An unwavering adherence to ethical standards not only fosters trust among clients and colleagues but also enhances your professional identity as a lawyer committed to upholding the law and its values.

Reflect and Adapt: Continuous self-reflection and adaptability are key to developing a professional identity that truly represents you. Regularly evaluate how your choices align with your professional aspirations and be open to adapting your path to reflect the evolving landscape of the legal field.

Professional Presence in the Digital Age

The digital realm has become an integral part of professional life. How you present yourself online—in virtual meetings, through your professional profiles, and in digital communications—plays a significant role in shaping your professional identity. A thoughtful approach to your digital presence, emphasizing consistency, professionalism, and engagement, can significantly enhance your reputation and professional relationships.

Digital and Physical Consistency: Ensure that your online persona reflects the same level of professionalism as your in-person presence. This includes your email communication, your online profiles and commentary, and how you appear and conduct yourself on the phone and on video calls. This coherence between your digital and physical appearances reinforces your professional identity and builds trust with your audience.

Professional Image and Attire: Aligning your attire with your career goals and personal brand is crucial. Your choice of clothing should communicate your effort toward professionalism and confidence, supporting your professional aspirations to meet expectations of key stakeholders in your success and contributing to a positive first impression.

Elevating Visibility and Reputation: Actively seek opportunities to increase your visibility and establish your reputation as a knowledgeable and reliable legal professional. Whether through publishing articles, participating in legal discussions, or leading initiatives within professional organizations, each action you take should align with your professional goals and contribute to the development of your professional identity.

Crafting a professional identity in the legal field is an ongoing process that requires strategic effort and attention to detail. By showcasing your expertise, engaging with the legal community, adhering to professional ethics, and managing your digital presence, you create a strong foundation for a successful and fulfilling legal career. Your professional identity, shaped by your actions, decisions, and the way you present yourself, becomes a cornerstone of your career, influencing opportunities, relationships, and how you are perceived within the legal community.

Mentorship and Professional Relationships

The Importance of Mentorship in Law

Mentorship is a cornerstone of professional development in the legal field, serving as a conduit for knowledge, guidance, and opportunities. It plays a crucial role in shaping the career paths of new attorneys, offering a framework for learning that extends beyond the confines of traditional legal education. This section delves into how mentorship influences legal careers and provides strategies for cultivating productive mentor–mentee dynamics.

Shaping Career Paths and Opening Opportunities

Guidance and Insight: Mentors provide invaluable guidance on navigating the complexities of legal practice, from managing client relationships to understanding the intricacies of courtroom etiquette. Their insight can help mentees avoid common pitfalls and make informed decisions about their career trajectories.

Access to Opportunities: A mentor can open doors to opportunities that might otherwise be inaccessible. Through their networks, mentors can introduce mentees to potential employers, recommend them for positions, or involve them in high-profile cases, significantly accelerating their professional growth.

Professional and Personal Growth: Beyond career advancement, mentorship fosters professional and personal growth. Mentors can challenge mentees to set higher goals, encourage them to step out of their comfort zones, and provide support during challenging times, contributing to their overall development as legal professionals.

Initiating the Search for a Mentor

Identifying Potential Mentors: Begin by scanning your immediate environment and broader network for mentor candidates. This could include the following:

- **Law School Connections:** Professors whose classes sparked your interest or alumni who have taken a path you aspire to follow. These individuals often offer a wealth of knowledge and insights into navigating the legal profession.
- **Professional Associations:** Active participation in bar associations or special interest legal groups can introduce you to potential mentors who are established in your area of interest.
- **Legal Events and Seminars:** Attend industry conferences, workshops, and seminars. Speakers or attendees at these events can be valuable mentor resources, offering perspectives from within your desired field.

Leveraging Online Platforms: Use professional social networks such as LinkedIn to identify and connect with potential mentors. A polite, well-crafted message that expresses a genuine interest in their career and seeks guidance can open doors to fruitful conversations.

Cultivating a Meaningful Relationship

Initial Outreach: When reaching out, be specific about why you're seeking their mentorship. Mention any commonalities or specific aspects of their career that resonate with you. This personalized approach shows sincerity and preparation.

Establishing Mutual Goals: Early in the relationship, discuss your goals and what you hope to gain from the mentorship. Similarly, inquire about how you can assist or bring value to your mentor. Setting mutual expectations can help ensure the relationship is beneficial for both parties.

Consistent Engagement: Regularly update your mentor on your progress and setbacks. These updates not only keep the relationship active but also demonstrate your growth and responsiveness to their advice.

Respectful of Their Time: Understand that mentors are often busy professionals. Schedule meetings or check-ins at their convenience, and always come prepared with specific topics or questions to make the most of your time together.

Being a Proactive and Engaged Mentee

Goal-Oriented Learning: Set clear, achievable objectives for what you aim to learn or accomplish through the mentorship. Share these goals with your mentor to guide the direction of your interactions.

Embrace Feedback: Be open to constructive criticism. Demonstrating a willingness to learn and adapt based on feedback is crucial for personal and professional development.

Apply Lessons Learned: Show your mentor that their advice does not fall on deaf ears. Apply their guidance to your actions and decisions, and share your successes and lessons learned from failures.

Contributing to the Mentorship Ecosystem

Giving Back: Find ways to reciprocate the mentor's generosity. This could involve offering assistance with research, sharing articles of mutual interest, or supporting their professional events and endeavors.

Expanding Your Network: Introduce your mentor to other professionals in your network when relevant. This reciprocal networking can add value to their professional life.

Becoming a Mentor: In the spirit of paying it forward, consider mentoring junior peers or law students. Sharing your journey and insights can enrich your understanding and appreciation of the legal field, while also honing your leadership and advisory skills.

Fostering meaningful mentor–mentee relationships is a dynamic process that requires initiative, commitment, and a genuine desire to grow. By actively seeking out mentors, cultivating these relationships with care, and eventually contributing back to the mentoring cycle, you set the stage for a rewarding journey in the legal profession.

Advancing Beyond Initial Mentorship Connections

Building Upon Demonstrated Potential

To advance beyond the initial stages of securing a mentorship, it is imperative to continue demonstrating your potential and dedication. This commitment shows not only your appreciation for the mentorship received but also your ongoing desire to grow within the legal field. Engaging deeply in your work and seeking opportunities to showcase your abilities further cement your reputation as a diligent and aspiring legal professional.

Broadening the Spectrum of Mentorship

Diversifying your mentorship circle is crucial for a well-rounded professional development. While one mentor can provide valuable insights, embracing advice and guidance from multiple mentors offers a kaleidoscope of perspectives, enriching your understanding and approach to legal challenges. This diversity in mentorship can introduce you to new areas of law, different working styles, and innovative problem-solving techniques, thereby enhancing your adaptability and resourcefulness.

Actionable Strategies for Deepening Mentor Relationships

Learning and Growth: Show your mentors that their investment in you is yielding positive results. Share your successes and learning moments, demonstrating how their guidance has directly impacted your professional journey.

Contributing Value: As your relationship with your mentor evolves, look for ways to add value back to your mentor's professional life. This could be through collaboration on projects, offering assistance with research, or even providing insights into areas of your expertise.

Respectful Persistence: Maintaining a mentorship relationship requires a delicate balance of persistence and respect for the mentor's time and commitments. Regular, meaningful interactions that respect this balance can strengthen the mentor–mentee bond.

Empowerment Through Mentorship

Nurturing Confidence and Belonging: For first-generation and diverse lawyers, mentorship can play a pivotal role in navigating the legal profession with confidence. A mentor who understands and acknowledges the unique challenges faced can offer targeted advice and support, making the legal landscape less daunting.

Creating Pathways for Success: Effective mentorship provides more than just career guidance; it opens doors to opportunities that might otherwise remain inaccessible. Mentors can introduce you to networks, recommend you for positions, and advocate on your behalf, helping to accelerate your career progression.

The Cycle of Mentorship: The ultimate testament to a successful mentor–mentee relationship is the transition from being mentored to becoming a mentor yourself. Sharing the knowledge and insights you've gained with the next generation of lawyers not only contributes to the profession's growth but also enriches your own understanding and appreciation of the law.

By embracing these strategies and understanding the dynamic nature of mentorship, you position yourself for a rewarding and impactful career in law. Mentorship, when approached with intention and dedication, becomes a cornerstone of professional development, laying the groundwork for a legacy of excellence and mentorship within the legal community.

Jeannine Del Monte: Navigating Legal Practice Through Mentorship

Vice President, Assistant General Counsel, Wells Fargo

Jeannine Del Monte serves as the Vice President, Assistant General Counsel at Wells Fargo, where she plays a pivotal role in navigating the complex interplay between legal requirements and business strategies. Her responsibilities include identifying and leveraging digital and technological opportunities to enhance return on investment (ROI) and ensure regulatory compliance. With a keen understanding of the legal landscape, Jeannine's expertise extends across privacy, cybersecurity, vendor management, and compliance, making her an invaluable asset to Wells Fargo's legal team.

Prior to joining Wells Fargo, Jeannine held the position of Chief Legal Officer at Athas Capital Group. In this role, she was instrumental in identifying legal and compliance risks, as well as uncovering business opportunities. Her efforts significantly contributed to the company's strategic decision-making, particularly in areas related to mergers and acquisitions, lending, risk and compliance, information technology and cybersecurity, and vendor management. Jeannine's ability to manage all regulatory interactions and serve as the primary liaison for regulators further underscores her comprehensive skill set.

Jeannine's career also includes a significant tenure at Pacific Western Bank, where she served as Senior Vice President, Associate General Counsel. Here, she led operations counsel, supported over seventy California branches, and was the bank's leading voice on privacy and cybersecurity matters.

Through her roles at Wells Fargo, Athas Capital Group, and Pacific Western Bank, Jeannine has demonstrated an exceptional ability to bridge the gap between legal advisement and business operations. Her forward-thinking approach to legal challenges, combined with her deep understanding of the banking and financial sectors, positions her as a thought leader in the field.

Career Transitions and Decision Making

Jeannine's career trajectory is marked by thoughtful transitions that reflect both a strategic approach to her career and a deep understanding of the legal landscape within the banking and financial sectors. Initially embarking on her legal journey in a law firm setting, Jeannine quickly recognized her interest in banking and finance due to its unique blend of litigation and transactional work. However, her desire for more transactional experience led her to pivot toward roles that offered a closer alignment with her interests and skills. This shift was not without its challenges, as it required her to adapt to new environments and expectations, particularly the need to balance legal advisement with business objectives. Jeannine's move to in-house roles was propelled by an understanding of the value she could bring to a business by directly influencing its operations and strategy.

In-house legal roles demand a wide array of skills beyond legal expertise, something Jeannine was keenly aware of as she navigated her career transitions. Collaboration, the ability to receive and provide feedback, and a willingness to participate in group projects emerged as crucial for success. Perhaps most importantly, she emphasized the need for in-house counsel to support business needs while effectively communicating the legal implications of business decisions. This balancing act requires a nuanced understanding of both the legal and business landscapes, a skill Jeannine honed through her experiences across various roles.

Jeannine's project management experience further illustrates the impact of legal work on business operations. She recounts the gratification derived from seeing a cybersecurity foundation project come to fruition, highlighting the critical role legal professionals play in facilitating technological advancements and ensuring regulatory compliance. This project not only allowed the company to achieve its objectives but also underscored the importance of legal expertise in navigating complex technological and regulatory environments.

Through her career transitions, Jeannine has demonstrated the importance of adaptability, strategic decision making, and a deep commitment to aligning legal advice with business needs. Her journey offers valuable insights for legal professionals aspiring to make a similar transition, emphasizing the need for a broad skill set, the ability to navigate complex business environments, and the satisfaction that comes from directly contributing to a company's success.

Mentorship, Networking, and Building Expertise

Reflecting on her experiences, Jeannine highlights the importance of engaging with mentors and leveraging professional networks, especially for those navigating the complexities of business law. Despite not having a traditional mentorship experience early in her career, Jeannine emphasizes the value found in collegial relationships and informal mentorship. These connections, she notes, have been instrumental in her development, allowing her to exchange ideas, seek advice, and gain insights from more experienced colleagues. For Jeannine, the essence of mentorship lies in the support and guidance that can be found within one's professional circle, underscoring the importance of building and nurturing these relationships over time.

Jeannine also speaks to the significance of specialization, particularly in areas such as cybersecurity and privacy, which are increasingly relevant in today's digital landscape. She advises aspiring legal professionals to identify areas of interest early on and to pursue specialized knowledge through both formal education and self-directed learning. Jeannine's own expertise in privacy and cybersecurity was cultivated through a combination of certifications, participation in relevant work groups, and a proactive approach to staying abreast of emerging trends and regulations. This dedication to building expertise not only positioned her as a valuable asset within her organizations but also highlights the importance of continuous learning in maintaining relevance in a rapidly evolving field.

Networking, according to Jeannine, is another cornerstone of professional growth. She encourages early career attorneys to engage with industry groups, attend conferences, and participate in professional organizations, such as the Association of Corporate Counsel. These platforms offer invaluable opportunities for connecting with peers, discovering mentorship opportunities, and gaining exposure to different facets of the legal and banking industries. Jeannine's own experiences underscore the reciprocal nature of networking, where offering support and sharing knowledge contribute to the development of a robust professional network that can provide guidance, opportunities, and support throughout one's career. ”

Effective Networking

Networking is foundational to building a thriving legal career. It transcends the traditional view of networking as merely exchanging business cards or connecting on LinkedIn. Effective networking is about cultivating meaningful, long-term professional relationships, enabling ongoing learning, and supporting career advancement. At its core, successful networking is driven by authenticity, engaging in activities that genuinely interest you, and forming connections with individuals with whom you resonate on a personal and professional level. This authentic approach not only deepens relationships but also transforms networking from a chore into a rewarding and enriching part of your professional journey.

Key Takeaways

- **Strategic Networking:** Treat networking as a deliberate strategy within your career development plan. It's an investment in your future, paving the way for opportunities, mentorships, and collaborations that can significantly influence your career trajectory.
- **Purposeful Relationship Building:** Concentrate on nurturing a network that actively supports and contributes to your career goals. This involves more than just expanding your contact list; it's about fostering relationships that provide mutual growth and learning opportunities.
- **The Power of Authenticity:** Authenticity is the cornerstone of effective networking. Genuine interactions not only lead to stronger connections but also ensure that your network is built on a foundation of trust and mutual respect. Authentic networking encourages open exchanges of ideas, experiences, and support, creating a robust professional network that thrives on sincerity and shared interests.

Understanding Networking's Role in Career Development

Networking plays a crucial role in career development, acting as a bridge to opportunities that are often hidden from the traditional job market. It's the key to unlocking mentorships, strategic partnerships, and invaluable insights into the complexities of the legal profession. For new attorneys and law students, networking provides a platform to showcase their enthusiasm, knowledge, and potential, making them visible to the key influencers who can help shape their careers.

Networking is not just about finding the next job opportunity; it's about building a foundation for a dynamic and fulfilling legal career. It allows for the exploration of diverse legal paths, understanding industry trends, and discovering areas of law that might align with personal passions and career aspirations.

How to Leverage Networking for Career Development

- **Identify Opportunities for Engagement:** Seek out networking events, professional associations, and online forums that align with your career interests. Being in spaces that resonate with your career goals increases the likelihood of meeting like-minded professionals who can provide guidance and support.
- **Showcase Your Expertise and Willingness to Learn:** Use networking opportunities to demonstrate your knowledge and your openness to new experiences. Sharing your insights and showing genuine curiosity about others' experiences can make you a memorable and valued connection.
- **Follow Up and Stay Connected:** After making new connections, take the initiative to follow up and nurture those relationships. A simple message reflecting on your conversation, sharing an article of mutual interest, or suggesting a follow-up meeting can keep the dialogue going and solidify your new connections.
- **Offer Value:** Remember that effective networking is reciprocal. Be ready to offer your skills, knowledge, or support to others in your network. This could mean providing feedback, offering to help with a project, or introducing them to another contact. By offering value, you strengthen your relationships and establish yourself as a proactive and contributing member of your professional community.

By embracing networking as a strategic and authentic part of your career development, you open doors to a world of opportunities that can enrich your legal career in ways that go beyond the conventional job search. Networking, when done effectively, lays the groundwork for a robust, supportive, and dynamic professional network that propels your career forward.

Strategies for Effective Networking

To navigate the complex landscape of the legal profession successfully, adopting strategic networking practices is essential. Here's how to refine your approach for more impactful connections:

- **Focus on Depth:** Prioritize depth and quality in your networking interactions. Meaningful conversations are more likely to lead to lasting professional relationships than superficial exchanges. Aim to leave every networking opportunity with a few significant connections rather than a stack of business cards with no real connection.
- **Reciprocity Is Key:** Networking is a two-way street. Always look for ways to provide value back to those in your network. This could be in the form of sharing an article relevant to their work, offering your expertise on a subject, or even making an introduction to another professional who could help them. Similarly, do not hesitate to reach out for advice or insights when needed, but do so respectfully and with appreciation for the other person's time.
- **Diverse Connections:** Broaden your network by engaging with professionals from various sectors within the legal community and related fields. This diversity can provide a broader perspective on the industry, open up unexpected opportunities, and enrich your professional experience.

Building a Professional Network

A robust professional network is a critical asset in the legal profession. It provides support, advice, opportunities, and a sense of community. Here's a guide to strategically building your professional network:

Attending Industry Events with Purpose:

- **Research and Selectivity:** Research upcoming events and select those most aligned with your interests and career goals. This targeted approach ensures you're in the right room with professionals and potential mentors who can influence your career positively.
- **Preparation:** Before the event, set clear objectives. Identify speakers or attendees you want to connect with and prepare thoughtful questions or conversation starters relevant to their expertise.
- **Follow-Up:** After the event, reach out to the connections you made with a personalized message. Reference specific discussions you had to strengthen the connection and suggest a follow-up meeting if appropriate.

Joining Legal Associations for Active Engagement:

- **Selection:** Choose legal associations that not only align with your professional interests but also offer active engagement opportunities, such as committees, panels, or volunteer roles.
- **Contribution:** Actively contribute to the association's initiatives. This could involve writing for their newsletter, participating in events planning, or volunteering for pro bono activities. Active involvement raises your profile and demonstrates your commitment to the profession.

Leveraging Social Media Effectively:

- **Professional Presence:** Build a strong professional presence on platforms like LinkedIn. Ensure your profile is complete, professional, and highlights your skills, experiences, and areas of interest.
- **Content Sharing and Engagement:** Share insightful content related to your field, engage with posts by commenting thoughtfully, and contribute to discussions. This visibility can attract connections who share your interests.
- **Networking Intentionally:** Use social media to reach out to professionals you admire. When making a new connection, include a personalized message explaining why you're reaching out and what you hope to learn or discuss with them.

Using Networking to Gain Insights

Networking serves as a key to unlocking the vast knowledge pool within the legal community, providing insights that are crucial for both personal growth and professional advancement.

- **Informational Interviews:** Identify and reach out to attorneys whose career paths or specialties align with your interests. These discussions are invaluable for gaining insights into different legal fields, understanding the day-to-day realities of specific roles, and receiving tailored advice on navigating your career.
- **Industry Trends:** Use your network to stay ahead of industry trends and legal innovations. Attend webinars, join legal think tanks or special interest groups, and follow influential legal professionals on social media. Engage in discussions and share your viewpoints to deepen your understanding and visibility in these areas.
- **Knowledge Exchange:** Establish a give-and-take relationship within your network. Share your unique insights, case studies, or latest findings with peers. This reciprocal exchange fosters a learning community and strengthens your professional bonds.

Job Opportunities through Networking

The hidden job market in the legal profession is vast, with many positions filled through networking and personal referrals. Here's how to strategically uncover these opportunities:

- **Alumni Networks:** Leverage your law school's alumni network for insights into various legal sectors and potential job openings. Alumni events and dedicated online platforms can be rich sources of connections and advice.
- **Legal Associations and Conferences:** Active participation in legal associations and attendance at industry conferences put you in direct contact with potential employers and inform you about unadvertised job openings. Volunteer for committees or speaking opportunities to increase your visibility.
- **Social Media Presence:** A robust online presence can attract opportunities directly to you. Regularly update your LinkedIn profile with your latest accomplishments and engage with content relevant to your career interests. Use hashtags and follow industry-related discussions to connect with hiring managers and recruiters.

Advanced Networking Strategies

As legal professionals progress, their networking needs and strategies evolve. Here are ways to enhance your networking practices:

- **Strategic Relationship Building:** Focus on nurturing a few key relationships with individuals who can act as mentors, sponsors, or gateways to new opportunities. Quality trumps quantity in advanced networking.
- **Thought Leadership:** Establish yourself as a thought leader in your area of expertise by publishing articles, speaking at industry events, and contributing to legal discussions. This visibility can attract advanced career opportunities and collaborations.
- **Long-Term Connection Maintenance:** Use a personal Customer Relationship Management (CRM) software tool or a simple spreadsheet to keep track of your contacts, last interaction, and notes about personal interests or professional goals. Regular, personalized check-ins can keep relationships warm and productive.
- **Cross-Industry Networking:** Expand your network beyond the legal field to include professionals in industries related to your practice area. This broadens your perspective, opens up interdisciplinary opportunities, and can provide a competitive edge in your legal practice.

- **Mentoring Others:** As you advance in your career, offering mentorship to junior colleagues can not only help them grow but also expand your own network as they progress in their careers. This reciprocal growth strengthens the legal community and your position within it.

Elevating Your Networking Efforts

Elevating your networking efforts is essential for growing your legal career. It involves not just expanding your network but also enhancing the quality of your interactions within it.

- **Active Contribution:** Make it a habit to regularly share legal updates, insights, or helpful resources with your network. This could be through social media posts, email newsletters, or direct communication. Your contributions should add value, provoke thought, or offer solutions to common challenges faced by your peers.
- **Participation in Legal Webinars and Roundtables:** Actively participating in or even organizing webinars and roundtable discussions on pertinent legal issues can significantly boost your standing as a thought leader in your field. These platforms offer you a stage to share your expertise, debate on hot-button issues, and showcase your depth of knowledge to a broader audience.
- **Skill-Sharing Sessions:** Organizing or participating in skill-sharing sessions can be a great way to both learn and teach. These sessions provide a platform for exchanging valuable skills and knowledge that can enhance your professional capabilities and those of your peers.
- **Consistent Engagement and Personalized Interactions:** Regular and meaningful engagement with your network is key to deepening professional relationships. Personalize your interactions by referencing past conversations, congratulating them on their achievements, and offering your support. This approach shows that you value the relationship beyond just professional gain.

Overcoming Networking Challenges

Networking comes with its set of challenges, especially for those who may not naturally lean toward social interactions.

- **Small Group Engagements:** If large networking events feel overwhelming, focus on smaller, more intimate gatherings where you can have meaningful conversations. These settings often lead to deeper connections and can be less intimidating.

- **Initiating Meaningful Discussions:** Start discussions on topics you are passionate about or that are currently trending in the legal field. This can make interactions more engaging and less forced, providing a solid foundation for building relationships.
- **Integrating Networking into Your Routine:** View networking as an integral part of your professional development. Schedule regular intervals for networking activities, making it a habit rather than an occasional endeavor.

Recognizing the value that networking brings to your career can transform it from a daunting task to a rewarding part of your professional journey.

Measuring Networking Success

- **Setting Specific Goals:** Define what success looks like for your networking efforts. This could range from gaining a certain number of new contacts in your preferred legal area to securing mentorship or finding new job opportunities.
- **Reflecting on Career Impact:** Regularly assess how networking has influenced your career development. Have you gained new insights, learned about unanticipated job openings, or developed new skills through your network?
- **Assessing Relationship Depth:** The quality of the connections you make can often be more important than the quantity. Strong, mutually beneficial relationships are a significant indicator of successful networking.

The Future of Networking in Law: A Comprehensive Approach

As the legal profession navigates through an era of rapid technological advancements and shifting work paradigms, the essence of networking is also evolving. The future of networking in law is set to embrace a hybrid model, integrating the efficiency of digital platforms with the irreplaceable value of in-person connections. Here's an in-depth look at how to adapt and thrive in this new networking landscape.

Embracing Technology for Initial Connections

- **Digital Platforms as Networking Tools:** Leverage platforms such as LinkedIn, Twitter, and specialized legal forums to make initial connections. These platforms offer the convenience of reaching out to legal professionals globally, enabling you to expand your network beyond geographical boundaries.

- **Virtual Conferences and Webinars:** Participate actively in virtual conferences and webinars. These events not only offer valuable learning opportunities but also provide platforms for you to contribute to discussions, showcase your knowledge, and connect with other attendees.
- **Online Branding:** Develop a strong online presence that reflects your professional interests, achievements, and expertise. Regularly publish articles, share insightful commentary on recent legal developments, and engage with content posted by your connections and industry leaders.

In-Person Events for Deeper Connections

- **Strategic Attendance at Conferences and Seminars:** Selectively attend in-person events that are most relevant to your areas of interest or where you can meet influencers and potential mentors in your field. Prioritize events that offer opportunities for meaningful engagement over those with only superficial networking potential.
- **Hosting Meetups and Roundtables:** Consider organizing small, in-person meetups or roundtable discussions on niche topics. These gatherings can foster deeper conversations and build stronger connections among participants who share specific interests within the legal domain.

Staying Top of Mind through Digital Presence

- **Consistent Online Engagement:** Maintain a consistent digital presence by sharing your professional achievements, insights into legal trends, and participation in both virtual and physical networking events. This not only keeps you visible to your network but also demonstrates your active engagement in the legal profession.
- **Interactive Content:** Create and share interactive content, such as polls, Q&A sessions, or live discussions, to encourage engagement from your network. This interactive approach can help in keeping your digital presence dynamic and engaging.

Leveraging Groups for Visibility and Alignment

- **Targeted Group Participation:** Actively participate in online groups and forums that are closely aligned with your professional goals. Contributing valuable insights and resources in these groups can elevate your status as a knowledgeable and engaged legal professional.
- **Creating Special Interest Groups:** If existing groups do not meet your needs, consider creating a special interest group. This can attract like-minded

professionals and establish you as a leader within a particular niche or area of legal expertise.

Adapting Networking Strategies for a Hybrid World

- **Flexible Networking Approach:** Develop a flexible approach to networking that allows you to seamlessly transition between digital and in-person engagements. Recognize the unique benefits each mode offers and tailor your strategy accordingly.
- **Blended Networking Events:** Embrace and participate in blended networking events that offer both virtual and physical participation options. This hybrid format can broaden the reach and inclusivity of networking activities, allowing for a more diverse and expansive professional network.

The future of networking in law demands adaptability, a willingness to embrace new technologies, and an understanding of the enduring value of personal connections. By integrating digital and in-person networking strategies, legal professionals can build resilient, dynamic networks that support their career growth and adapt to the evolving landscape of the legal profession.

Long-Term Professional Relationship Building

The fabric of a thriving legal career is often woven not merely through individual prowess or relentless effort but significantly through the robustness and depth of one's professional networks. Echoing the findings of the landmark Harvard Study of Adult Development—one of the most extensive examinations of adult life—relationships stand as a pivotal determinant of happiness and success. Within the legal sector, the value of these relationships extends beyond personal satisfaction, encompassing professional progression, mentorship possibilities, and client relations.

- **Sustained Success Foundations:** Enduring professional relationships within the legal arena are pillars of continuous support, counsel, and business exchange. They cultivate an atmosphere of trust, respect, and reciprocal advantage—qualities indispensable for maneuvering the intricacies of legal practices. Such relationships often burgeon into repeated collaborations, referrals, and joint ventures, pivotal for career longevity and development.
- **Mentorship and Career Direction:** The mentor–mentee dynamic exemplifies the enduring influence of professional bonds. A mentor, familiar with your professional journey, can offer bespoke guidance, detailed critiques, and access to tailored opportunities that resonate with your career

evolution. This enduring interaction deepens the mentorship experience, rendering it significantly enriching for both individuals involved.

- **Client Development and Loyalty:** In client relations, patience and persistence are rewarded. Clients entrenched in a profound, trusting rapport with their legal advisors are more inclined to continue their partnership and advocate for your services. Commitment to understanding a client's industry, preempting their requirements, and consistently delivering superior legal counsel nurtures a collaboration that may extend over years, if not decades.

Strategies for Cultivating Lasting Relationships

Cultivating enduring professional relationships is a cornerstone of a successful and satisfying legal career. These bonds, founded on mutual trust and respect, can accompany you throughout your career, offering support, advice, and openings. Here's a guide to ensuring your professional connections not only persist but also flourish alongside your career trajectory.

Deepening Mentor and Peer Connections

- **Learning and Sharing:** As you and your colleagues progress, continuously seek new avenues for mutual learning. Sharing insights and challenges can fortify your relationship, turning it into a wellspring of mutual growth.
- **Support Beyond Professionalism:** Extend and seek support beyond immediate career objectives, embracing life's broader milestones. Celebrating each other's personal triumphs and offering a shoulder during tough times can cement these relationships beyond mere professional contexts.
- **Evolving Dynamics:** Be open to the natural evolution of your relationships. A mentor might transition into a collaborator, or a peer might emerge as a business partner. Embrace these changes, recognizing the dynamic nature of professional relationships.

Sustaining Client Relationships Over Decades

- **Transcending Transactions:** Approach each client interaction as an opportunity to forge a lasting bond, not just complete a business transaction. Being attuned to and anticipating their legal needs over time can position you as an irreplaceable counsel.
- **Delivering Consistent Value:** Maintain relevance by staying informed about your clients' industries and offering proactive legal counsel. This

strategy not only secures client retention but also makes you a likely candidate for referrals.

- **Adding a Personal Touch:** Incorporating personal details into your interactions and reaching out during pivotal moments can elevate a purely professional relationship to a personal connection, fostering loyalty and profound trust.

Building a Community

- **Creating Shared Spaces:** Engage in or establish forums that nurture long-term professional connections. From legal discussion groups to charitable initiatives, shared experiences can act as a binding agent for these relationships.
- **Redefining Mentorship:** As you advance, take on the mentor role for the next generation of legal professionals. This not only allows you to contribute back to the community but also keeps your network fresh and diverse.
- **Celebrating Milestones Together:** Make it a point to recognize and celebrate the key moments within your professional relationships. Whether marking the anniversary of a collaboration or a significant personal achievement, such acknowledgments reinforce the importance of these enduring connections.

Embracing Strategic Reciprocity

- **Foster a Cycle of Giving:** Actively seek opportunities to contribute to the successes of your network—be it through referrals, sharing expertise, or being an innovative sounding board. Such strategic reciprocity enriches the relationship, creating a robust network of support and collaboration.

Balancing Relationships with Professional Responsibilities

Achieving a harmonious balance between fostering professional relationships and meeting work obligations is essential for a successful and satisfying legal career. Here are actionable strategies to integrate relationship building into your professional routine without compromising your duties.

Integrating Relationship Building with Professional Activities

- **Leverage Dual-Benefit Opportunities:** Identify and engage in activities that serve both your professional growth and networking goals. Speaking at

CLE seminars, for instance, not only sharpens your expertise but also puts you in front of potential mentors and collaborators. Similarly, participating in legal committees or volunteer projects can enrich your professional network while contributing positively to the community.

Scheduling Time for Relationships

- **Dedicate Time for Networking:** Allocate specific slots in your schedule for cultivating professional relationships, treating these moments with the same level of importance as your work tasks. Regular meetups with mentors, catch-up calls with peers, or networking events should be marked in your calendar as nonnegotiable commitments.

Prioritizing Key Connections

- **Focus on Impactful Relationships:** Although the legal field offers numerous networking opportunities, not all connections will significantly benefit your career. Invest your energy in deepening bonds with individuals who have been pivotal to your journey or with whom you share common professional aspirations.

Setting Boundaries Between Work and Networking

- **Manage Time Effectively:** Establish clear boundaries to maintain a healthy balance between work and networking. This might mean respectfully declining certain invitations during busy periods to ensure neither your work quality nor your key relationships suffer due to overcommitment.

Being Strategic in Participation

- **Select Events Wisely:** Choose to attend networking events, conferences, and seminars that resonate with your career objectives. This focused approach ensures that your networking efforts are both productive and enjoyable, connecting you with like-minded professionals and potential mentors.

Reflecting and Adapting

- **Evaluate and Adjust:** Periodically review the effectiveness of your balancing act between work and networking. Consider whether your relationship-building activities are leading to meaningful connections and whether your work is benefiting from these efforts. Be ready to adjust your strategies to find a more optimal balance.

Leveraging Technology to Sustain Connections

The digital era has significantly transformed the way we maintain professional relationships. With the advent of social media platforms, legal technology tools, and virtual networking opportunities, sustaining connections with colleagues, mentors, and peers worldwide has become more accessible and efficient.

Social Media as a Networking Catalyst

- **LinkedIn and Beyond:** Platforms such as LinkedIn serve as powerful tools for lawyers aiming to keep their professional networks vibrant. Regularly updating your profile, sharing legal developments, and interacting with others' posts not only keeps your presence active but also signals your continuous engagement with the legal field.

Embracing Legal Technology Platforms

- **Enhanced Collaboration:** Legal technology platforms offer more than just case management or research capabilities; they provide forums for discussion, networking features, and collaborative workspaces. Engaging with these platforms keeps you at the forefront of legal innovation while fostering meaningful professional relationships.

Advantages of Digital Communication

- **Ease of Connection:** The convenience of digital communication tools—whether it's a quick email, a social media message, or a video call—means that staying in touch has never been easier. These interactions ensure that your professional relationships remain strong, regardless of geographical distances.

Incorporating these technological advancements into your networking efforts ensures that your professional connections are not just maintained but actively nurtured, supporting your career's growth and evolution.

Networking Beyond Immediate Circles

Expanding your professional network beyond familiar legal territories can open doors to unexpected opportunities, innovative ideas, and enriching collaborations. Diversifying your connections by reaching out to professionals in different fields and from various backgrounds can significantly enhance your legal practice and perspective.

Exploring Cross-Disciplinary Connections

- **Engaging with Adjacent Sectors:** Connecting with professionals in related areas such as finance, technology, or health care can provide a richer understanding of the multifaceted nature of legal issues and solutions. These relationships are particularly valuable in today's interconnected legal environment, where cross-disciplinary knowledge is increasingly crucial.

Embracing Diversity in Networking

- **Cultivating a Varied Network:** A diverse professional network—one that spans different industries, cultural backgrounds, career stages, and life experiences—enriches your legal practice. It encourages innovative problem solving, offers insights into a broader client base, and contributes to creating a more inclusive legal community.

Embracing a proactive and heartfelt approach to nurturing professional relationships is more than a strategic career move; it's a commitment to cultivating a community that sustains and enriches you personally and professionally. Each connection you make is an opportunity not just for career advancement but for genuine human interaction and growth. As you journey through your legal career, cherish these relationships, recognizing their profound impact on your happiness, fulfillment, and success. By fostering these connections with sincerity and care, you're not just building a network; you're creating a supportive professional family that will accompany you at every milestone. Let this approach guide you, and you'll find that the rewards extend far beyond the courtroom or office, touching every aspect of your life with joy and meaning.

It's Your Career: Insights with Kari Jensen Thomas

Business Development Training & Alumni Engagement, Faegre Drinker

Kari Jensen Thomas spearheads the firm's business development training programs and alumni engagement initiatives. With a rich background in the legal profession, Kari's journey is marked by a series of strategic moves that saw her transition from practicing law to focusing on the crucial aspects of professional development and networking within the legal community. Her educational foundation, coupled with her hands-on experience in various facets of the legal world, has equipped her with a unique perspective on the dynamics of law practice and the importance of continuous professional growth.

Personal Insights and Advice

Kari offers advice for those embarking on a career in business law, emphasizing the importance of understanding the broader business context of clients. "You're not just getting to know the issue at hand . . . you need to get to know that client, that business entity," she advises. This holistic understanding of a client's business, including their industry, priorities, customers, and competitors, is crucial. Kari stresses that such knowledge enables lawyers to provide added value, making them indispensable to their clients. She encourages lawyers to be vigilant and proactive in acquiring this knowledge, suggesting that this effort, although not billable, is a strategic investment in one's career.

For those just starting out or considering a shift to business law, Kari underscores the importance of networking and relationship building, not just externally with clients but also within one's own firm and the broader legal community. "The relationships you build, the people you meet, and the connections you make are all part of your professional toolkit," she says. She advises law students and early career lawyers to engage genuinely with others, be open to learning, and take initiative in their professional development. "It's your career," Kari reminds us, "and the more you invest in it, the more rewarding it will be."

Navigating Career Evolution and Challenges

In a legal career, especially in business law, being able to adapt and learn continuously is key. Every lawyer's journey involves navigating through changes, tackling various roles, and always seeking new knowledge. This process builds resilience and helps maintain authenticity in a demanding profession.

However, challenges such as shifting market trends, navigating office politics, and overcoming personal obstacles are part of the territory. Addressing diversity, equity, and inclusion (DEI) is also crucial, pushing for a profession that is as diverse as the society it serves.

Beyond professional life, finding a balance with personal life and focusing on personal development are important for a fulfilling career. This means looking after your well-being, building a supportive network, and managing career changes thoughtfully.

Through these experiences, we see that a legal career is more than just a job—it is a journey of continuous growth and learning, facing challenges head-on, and striving for both professional success and personal fulfillment.

Career Adaptability and Growth: Stories of Career Transitions, Embracing Diverse Roles, and Continuous Learning

Embracing Career Transitions in Business Law

Embracing career transitions within business law not only marks a significant step in a lawyer's professional journey but also requires a strategic, well-thought-out approach to navigate successfully. Whether you're moving from traditional corporate law roles to emerging business law specializations or shifting focus within the vast expanse of business law itself, understanding the intricacies of career change and adopting effective transition strategies are paramount.

Understanding the Dynamics of Career Change

Career transitions in business law are often spurred by a combination of factors, including personal interest in a burgeoning area of law, market demand for specialized legal services, or shifts in regulatory landscapes that open up new legal frontiers. Transitioning effectively demands a keen awareness of the motivations driving the change, a clear vision of the desired endpoint, and a comprehensive understanding of the new specialization's scope. This understanding forms the basis for identifying the skill sets and knowledge areas that will be pivotal in the new role.

Actionable Insights

- Conduct in-depth research on the target specialization, focusing on current trends, key players, emerging legal challenges, and opportunities within the niche.
- Analyze case studies or profiles of professionals who have successfully made similar transitions. Note the pathways they took, the obstacles they encountered, and how they overcame them.

Strategies for Smooth Transitions

Leveraging existing expertise while acquiring new competencies is crucial in transitioning smoothly between different areas of business law. This involves a multifaceted approach, encompassing education, networking, practical experience, and personal branding.

Pursue Targeted Education and Training: Identify and fill knowledge gaps by enrolling in specialized legal courses offered by accredited institutions, attending webinars and workshops focused on the latest developments in your target area, and obtaining relevant certifications to bolster your credentials.

Seek Mentorship and Guidance: Find mentors who are well-established in your area of interest. Look for mentorship opportunities through professional associations, alumni networks, or legal conferences. A mentor can offer not just insights and advice but also critical feedback and encouragement.

Engage in Strategic Networking: Actively participate in industry events, join specific legal associations or groups, and engage in online forums dedicated to your new specialty. Networking should be intentional; focus on building relationships that provide mutual value, rather than merely expanding your contact list.

Gain Practical Experience: Seek opportunities to apply new skills in real-world settings. This could involve taking on pro bono cases related to your new field, participating in legal clinics, or undertaking project work that allows you to demonstrate your emerging expertise. Practical experience not only reinforces your learning but also enhances your resume.

Communicate Your Transition Effectively: Craft a compelling narrative around your career shift, highlighting how your background and newly acquired skills make you uniquely qualified for roles in the new specialization. Update your LinkedIn profile, resume, and personal website to reflect this narrative, ensuring consistency across all professional touchpoints.

Leverage Digital Platforms: Use platforms such as LinkedIn to showcase your transition journey. Share articles, case studies, and personal insights related to your new field. Engaging with content not only boosts your visibility but also positions you as an emerging thought leader in the area.

Volunteer for Leadership Roles: Taking on leadership roles in relevant legal associations or committees can significantly enhance your profile in the new specialization. Leadership roles offer a platform to demonstrate your commitment, engage deeply with current issues, and influence the direction of the specialization.

- Stories of Successful Shifts: Profiles of business lawyers who have transitioned into or within business law, highlighting the strategies that contributed to their success.

From Law to Leadership: Edythe Repoff's Path to Influencing Business Strategy

President/Chief Operating Officer at New Omni Bank

With an early inclination toward making a global impact, Edythe Repoff's career trajectory was shaped by her foundational years at Rutgers Law School. Chosen for its strong reputation in public interest work and its affordability, Rutgers laid the groundwork for her to explore the intersections of law, business, and international affairs. This choice was not just practical but strategic, aligning with her aspirations to engage in work that reached across borders.

Following her graduation, the reality of the economic landscape in 2009 steered Edythe toward a position at a law firm. Here, she was part of the USA China Law Group, a role that allowed her to maintain her commitment to international business despite the shift from her initial public interest focus. This period offered her a practical understanding of the complexities of international business law and set the stage for her subsequent career evolution.

Edythe's career took a significant turn when she transitioned from practicing law to taking on the role of the first general counsel at a company. This position was not just a job change but a pivot point that demanded a broadening of her skill set beyond the legal domain. It required her to navigate the intricacies of corporate operations and to foster trust and understanding among her colleagues about the value of legal insight in business decisions.

The culmination of Edythe's career journey saw her stepping into the role of President/Chief Operating Officer at New Omni Bank. Her story is particularly relevant for those at the crossroads of law and business, illustrating that the path to leadership can be as unconventional as it is rewarding.

Transitioning from Law to Leadership

Edythe's transition from practicing law to becoming the chief operating officer of New Omni Bank marked a significant shift in her career trajectory. As the first general counsel for a company, she found herself in a unique position to shape the legal framework within the organization. Edythe recounted the initial challenges of educating her colleagues on the value of legal insight in business decisions. Her role required not just legal expertise but also the ability to build trust across departments. She emphasized the importance of small wins in establishing credibility, such as revising loan document terms to reduce legal risk, which in turn, helped her colleagues appreciate the protective role of legal counsel in their operations.

The move from legal counsel to chief operating officer was not a straightforward path. It necessitated a broad expansion of her skill set beyond the confines of law. Leadership, finance, and accounting were areas where her legal background offered less direct preparation. Edythe highlighted how mentorship played a pivotal role in her development during this transition. The guidance from experienced professionals helped her navigate the complexities of her new role. In addition, her participation in the Pacific Coast Banking School, a program akin to an executive MBA with a focus on banking, was instrumental in deepening her understanding of the banking industry. This formal education, combined with mentorship, equipped her with the knowledge and confidence to tackle the multifaceted challenges of her leadership position.

In her role as chief operating officer, Edythe applied her legal acumen in new ways, focusing on strategic planning and operational efficiency. Her legal background provided a strong foundation for understanding regulatory and compliance issues critical in the banking sector. However, she quickly learned that success in her new role also depended on her ability to lead teams, make financial decisions, and foster a culture of trust and collaboration. These experiences underscored the transferable nature of legal skills, demonstrating that with the right opportunities and support, lawyers can effectively transition into leadership roles within the business world. Edythe's journey from the legal department to the executive suite illustrates the potential for career growth when one is open to learning and taking on new challenges.

The Role of Lawyers in Business

Edythe's insights into the role of lawyers in business illuminate the nuanced shift from private practice to in-house counsel, and eventually, to a leadership position that goes beyond traditional legal functions. In her early career, the focus was on detailed legal research, memo writing, and contract drafting—skills that are honed in law school and essential in law firms. However, as she transitioned to an in-house role, the emphasis moved from comprehensive legal analyses to the ability to succinctly quantify legal risks and offer direct, actionable advice. This change reflects a broader understanding of business needs, where decisions must be made swiftly and based on clear, concise information.

In her capacity as general counsel and later as a leader within the business, Edythe had to recalibrate her approach to legal advice. She found that business executives, particularly CEOs, require distilled information that directly impacts decision-making processes. The ability to quantify legal risks in a manner that is both comprehensible and practical for business leaders became paramount. This skill—a departure from the exhaustive legal explanations typical in law firms—underscores the adaptability required of in-house counsel. Edythe's experience highlights the critical need for lawyers in business settings to not only grasp the legal dimensions of issues but also communicate their implications efficiently and effectively.

Edythe's reflections on the role of legal risk in business decisions shed light on the broader context in which corporate lawyers operate. She observed that legal risk is but one factor among many that business leaders consider when making decisions. This realization was, in her words, a "shock to the ego," challenging the preconception that legal considerations are paramount. Instead, she learned that understanding the business's overarching goals and the myriad factors influencing its direction is crucial. This broader perspective is essential for lawyers who wish to contribute meaningfully to business strategies and outcomes.

Understanding Employee Motivations and Career Planning

Edythe believes that recognizing the diverse aspirations within a team is crucial for fostering a productive and harmonious work environment. For Edythe, this means actively engaging with team members to discern their professional goals and the kind of support they require to achieve them. This approach is not only about facilitating individual growth but also about aligning personal ambitions with the organization's objectives, thereby ensuring mutual advancement.

In her experience, Edythe found that creating opportunities for open dialogue about career aspirations can significantly impact employee satisfaction and retention. She emphasizes the importance of leaders being approachable and willing to invest time in their team members. This investment includes offering guidance, sharing insights from one's own career journey, and facilitating connections that can help employees navigate their professional paths. For early career attorneys and law students, this insight highlights the value of seeking mentors who demonstrate a genuine interest in their mentees' development and are committed to helping them succeed.

Edythe's approach to leadership and career planning illustrates the benefits of being adaptable and open to learning from various sources, including one's own team. She advocates for a leadership style that is inclusive, one that recognizes the contributions of every team member, regardless of their role. By understanding the motivations of employees, leaders can tailor their management strategies to support each individual effectively, thereby enhancing team cohesion and driving the organization forward. For those at the beginning of their careers in law and business, Edythe's story serves as a reminder that success often lies in the willingness to explore unconventional paths and the readiness to adapt to new challenges and opportunities. ”

Diverse Roles in Business Law

Exploring the realm of business law reveals a spectrum of career paths that extend far beyond the traditional law firm setting. As the legal industry evolves, opportunities in in-house counsel roles, legal consulting, entrepreneurship, and beyond are increasingly becoming pivotal to the tapestry of legal careers. Understanding these nontraditional paths can not only broaden one's career prospects but also align professional pursuits with personal interests and lifestyle preferences.

Exploring Nontraditional Careers

Legal Consulting: Legal consultants offer expert advice to law firms, businesses, and nonprofits on specific legal issues, compliance strategies, and operational efficiencies. This career path is ideal for those who enjoy variety, strategic problem solving, and the flexibility of project-based work.

Actionable Steps:

- Build a strong foundation in a specialized area of business law to offer as your consulting niche.
- Foster relationships with law firms and businesses through networking and by showcasing your expertise at industry events and in legal publications.
- Consider joining a consulting firm or starting your own consultancy to gain credibility and access to a broader client base.

Entrepreneurship in the Legal Sector: For those with an entrepreneurial spirit, launching a legal tech start-up or founding a boutique law firm specializing in a niche area of business law can be highly rewarding. This path requires a combination of legal expertise, business savvy, and a deep understanding of market needs.

Actionable Steps:

- Identify gaps in the legal market where technology or innovative legal services could offer solutions.
- Participate in legal innovation hubs, tech incubators, or entrepreneurship workshops to refine your business idea and acquire start-up skills.
- Network with potential investors, partners, and mentors who can provide guidance and support as you develop your business plan and launch your venture.

Cross-Disciplinary Roles: Many business lawyers find fulfilling careers at the intersection of law and other fields, such as finance, technology, or environmental advocacy. These roles may involve regulatory compliance, intellectual property management, or sustainable business practices.

Actionable Steps:

- Pursue dual degrees or continuing education in law and the complementary field of interest.
- Engage with professionals from both industries to understand the synergies and opportunities for cross-disciplinary work.
- Look for roles in organizations or projects that value interdisciplinary approaches and offer the chance to apply your dual expertise.

Exploring nontraditional careers in business law not only expands your professional horizons but also allows for greater personalization of your career path. Whether you're drawn to the strategic depth of in-house counsel roles, the dynamic challenges of legal consulting, the innovative potential of entrepreneurship, or the integrative approach of cross-disciplinary work, the business law landscape is rich with opportunities. Embracing these diverse roles requires curiosity, adaptability, and a proactive approach to career planning, ensuring that you can navigate the evolving legal market with confidence and purpose.

The Value of Diverse Experiences

Diverse career experiences within the realm of business law provide not just a breadth of legal knowledge but also a more nuanced, holistic understanding of how law intersects with the broader business ecosystem. Embracing a variety of roles and challenges throughout one's career enriches a lawyer's perspective, making them more adaptable, empathetic, and effective in their practice. Here's how varied career experiences contribute significantly to a lawyer's growth and understanding of business law:

Enhanced Problem-Solving Skills: Exposure to different facets of business law, from contract negotiations in a corporate setting to intellectual property disputes in a tech start-up, cultivates a versatile problem-solving toolkit. Lawyers who have navigated diverse legal landscapes can approach complex legal issues with a more creative and informed perspective, drawing on a wide array of past experiences.

Actionable Steps:

- Seek opportunities to work in different legal environments, such as rotating through departments within a firm or taking on secondments in industry.
- Volunteer for pro bono work that challenges you to apply your skills in new contexts, further broadening your experience base.

Broader Industry Insight: Varied experiences enable lawyers to understand the intricacies of multiple industries, from finance and technology to health care and entertainment. This insight is invaluable in business law, where legal strategies must often be tailored to fit the specific operational, regulatory, and competitive landscapes of the client's industry.

Actionable Steps:

- Attend industry-specific seminars and workshops to gain insights into the challenges and trends affecting different sectors.
- Network with professionals outside of law to learn about their industry's needs and how legal services can be best positioned to meet those needs.

Improved Client Relations: Lawyers with diverse experiences are better equipped to empathize with clients from various backgrounds and industries. They can communicate more effectively, having a deeper understanding of the client's perspective and the pressures they face, which fosters stronger, more trusting client relationships.

Actionable Steps:

- Develop strong listening skills to better understand the unique context and needs of each client.
- Tailor your communication style to match the client's level of legal understanding and industry-specific concerns.

Adaptability to Change: The legal field and the world of business are both rapidly evolving. Lawyers with a wide range of experiences are more adaptable to change, whether it's navigating new legal regulations, embracing technological advancements, or advising clients entering emerging markets.

Actionable Steps:

- Stay informed about developments in law and business by subscribing to relevant publications and attending industry conferences.
- Pursue continuous education and training in areas of law that are emerging or undergoing significant change.

Personal Growth and Fulfillment: Diverse career experiences not only enhance professional capabilities but also contribute to personal growth. They offer a sense of accomplishment and fulfillment that comes from overcoming varied challenges and continuously learning.

Actionable Steps:

- Reflect regularly on your career path, acknowledging the skills and insights gained from each experience.
- Set personal and professional goals that encourage you to step out of your comfort zone and tackle new challenges.

The value of diverse experiences in business law cannot be overstated. They prepare lawyers for the complexities of advising businesses in an interconnected, rapidly changing world. By actively seeking out varied roles and challenges, lawyers can ensure they remain relevant, resilient, and ready to provide the highest level of service to their clients.

Crafting Your Path: Insights from Amy Lerner-Hill on Legal Careers

General Counsel, RBC Bank (U.S.) and Head, U.S. Privacy & AML, Royal Bank of Canada

Amy Lerner-Hill's career has been characterized by a blend of ambition, adaptability, and a keen sense of the evolving landscape of business law. As General Counsel for RBC Bank (U.S.) and Head of U.S. Privacy & AML for the Royal Bank of Canada, Amy oversees the delivery of legal services, managing legal risks related to privacy and AML matters for the bank's U.S. entities. This role places her at the forefront of strategic business initiatives and product development, where she works directly with senior management to navigate the intricate regulatory and legal challenges that come with operating in the financial sector. Prior to her current position, Amy served as Deputy General Counsel at City National Bank for over a decade, where she was responsible for a broad array of legal functions, including litigation, investigations, regulatory enforcement, and more.

The Art of Adaptation: From Law Firm to In-House Counsel

Amy's decision to transition from a regional law firm to an in-house counsel role was driven by a blend of personal reflection and professional ambition. She recognized a growing sense of stagnation in her law firm role, noting that she wasn't as stimulated by the work as she once was. This realization came during a period when the legal industry was undergoing significant changes, particularly with the onset of the Great Recession, which reshaped the landscape of legal work. Amy observed shifts in the type of work coming into firms, including a surge in banking-related cases due to the economic downturn. Despite having the opportunity to stay within the law firm environment, possibly in a different firm, she felt a compelling urge to seek out new challenges and shake things up in her career.

The move to an in-house position at a bank marked a significant pivot in Amy's career trajectory, introducing her to a distinctly different work environment and set of responsibilities. One of the most notable changes was the shift from acting primarily as an advisor to becoming a business partner. In her in-house role, Amy found herself deeply involved in strategic business initiatives, working closely with senior management and other stakeholders. This required not only a solid understanding of legal principles but also a keen sense of business acumen and the ability to navigate complex regulatory landscapes.

Building and maintaining relationships became a cornerstone of her in-house role. Unlike the more transactional nature of client interactions in a law firm, working in-house meant collaborating with colleagues across various departments on a daily basis. Amy emphasized the importance of being able to build connections with people internally, as these were the individuals she would work with closely to advance the bank's objectives. This emphasis on relationships extended to her approach to legal challenges; rather than simply advising on what could not be done, Amy focused on finding solutions that would enable the business to move forward, aligning legal advice with business goals. This mindset underscored the transition from a purely advisory role to that of a true business partner, marking a significant adaptation in her approach to legal practice.

Mentorship and Growth: Building a Career on Solid Foundations

Amy's journey in the legal profession underscores the pivotal role mentorship played in her career, both as a mentee and later as a mentor herself. She quickly identified individuals who could serve as mentors, making it a point to absorb the wealth of knowledge they had to offer. "I've always had female mentors," Amy recalls, highlighting the ease and comfort she found in these relationships. These mentors, experienced bank lawyers, provided her with invaluable insights, significantly shaping her understanding and approach to legal practice. From them, Amy learned not just about the technical aspects of law but also about navigating the professional landscape, emphasizing the importance of presence and engagement within the firm and broader legal community.

As a mentee, Amy demonstrated a proactive stance, seeking feedback and embracing both positive and negative critiques with an open mind. She recalls how her mentors would offer practical advice, from the importance of attending department meetings to refining her approach to drafting legal documents. This openness to feedback and willingness to go above and beyond in her responsibilities were key to her development. Amy's experience illustrates the essence of a productive mentor–mentee relationship: a mutual commitment to growth, with mentors providing guidance and mentees actively engaging in the process.

Transitioning into the role of a mentor herself, Amy reflects on the qualities that make a good mentor and how to foster a nurturing mentor–mentee relationship. She emphasizes the importance of protection and support, recalling how her mentor would shield her from less desirable assignments and provide a safe space for discussing professional challenges. This protective aspect, coupled with the provision of constructive feedback and opportunities for growth, constitutes the foundation of effective mentorship. Amy's journey from mentee to mentor highlights the cyclical nature of mentorship in professional development, underscoring its significance in building a successful career in law.

Hiring Philosophy: Beyond the Prestige of Law Schools

Amy's approach to hiring diverges from the traditional emphasis on the prestige of a candidate's law school. Instead, she places a significant value on practical skills, such as effective communication and proficient writing. This perspective stems from her understanding that the essence of legal work often lies in one's ability to articulate complex ideas clearly and interact effectively with clients, colleagues, and courts. "I look less at the school or what they even did before, unless it's relevant," Amy explains, underscoring the importance of practical skills over academic pedigree.

Her hiring philosophy is rooted in the belief that a strong legal professional is not solely defined by their educational background but by their diverse experiences and willingness to embrace various challenges. Amy highlights the significance of candidates who have demonstrated an ability to present in front of people, whether through classes, mock trials, or other public speaking opportunities. These experiences, she believes, are crucial in developing the communication skills necessary for a successful legal career.

Amy values candidates who exhibit a pleasant demeanor and the social etiquette essential for dealing with clients and colleagues daily. This focus on interpersonal skills and adaptability reflects a broader understanding that the legal profession is as much about building relationships as it is about legal expertise. Through her hiring practices, Amy seeks to identify individuals who not only have a solid legal foundation but also possess the practical, personal skills needed to navigate the complexities of the legal field effectively.

The Imperative of Continuous Learning

Lifelong learning stands as a foundational pillar for any legal professional aiming to excel and stay relevant amid the rapidly evolving legal and business landscapes. Here's why continuous learning is crucial and how legal professionals can embed this principle into their careers:

Staying Ahead of Legal Developments: The legal framework governing business practices is constantly subject to amendments, revisions, and overhauls. To effectively advise and represent clients, lawyers must be abreast of the latest legal developments, from regulatory changes to landmark case law. This ensures that their counsel is not only accurate but also strategically forward-looking.

Actionable Steps:

- Regularly attend CLE courses and seminars focused on business law.
- Subscribe to and actively read legal journals and newsletters that spotlight current legal trends and case law.
- Engage with legal thought leaders and experts on social media platforms to gain insights into emerging legal challenges and solutions.

Understanding Emerging Technologies: The integration of technology in business operations introduces new legal challenges and areas, such as cybersecurity, data privacy, and intellectual property in the digital age. Lawyers with a grasp of these technologies and the related legal issues are better positioned to offer comprehensive advice to tech-savvy clients and businesses.

Actionable Steps:

- Attend workshops or online courses that explore the intersection of technology and law, focusing on areas like cybersecurity and digital IP rights.
- Join interdisciplinary forums or tech-focused legal groups to discuss and learn about the legal implications of new technologies.
- Partner with technology professionals for joint learning sessions, enhancing your understanding of tech-driven legal issues.

Enhancing Client Services: The continuous acquisition of knowledge allows lawyers to provide more innovative and effective solutions to their clients. It enables them to approach legal problems from various angles, consider novel strategies, and offer advice that aligns with the latest industry practices and legal standards.

Actionable Steps:

- Seek feedback from clients on areas where they need more support and tailor your learning to meet these needs.

- Develop a practice of reading widely, not just legal texts, to gain broader insights into business strategies, economic trends, and global issues that could impact your clients.
- Implement a strategy for staying informed about industry-specific news and technological advancements that could impact your clients, utilizing this knowledge to proactively address potential legal issues before they arise.

Personal and Professional Growth: Beyond staying competitive, lifelong learning contributes to personal satisfaction and professional growth. It fosters a mindset of curiosity, openness to new ideas, and the humility to recognize that there is always more to learn. This attitude not only enriches a lawyer's own life but also inspires colleagues and clients alike.

Actionable Steps:

- Set personal learning goals each year, focusing on both legal and nonlegal areas of interest.
- Share your learning journey with peers and mentor others, creating a culture of continuous improvement within your network or organization.
- Engage in professional networking and join study groups focusing on both legal and nonlegal interests to diversify your knowledge base and bring fresh perspectives to your practice.

Adapting to Career Transitions: As lawyers navigate through different phases of their careers, continuous learning facilitates smoother transitions, whether it's moving into a new legal specialty, taking on leadership roles, or venturing into entrepreneurship within the legal domain.

Actionable Steps:

- Engage in cross-disciplinary learning to broaden your skill set and prepare for diverse roles within the legal field.
- Utilize online platforms and university programs to pursue formal education or certifications that align with your career aspirations.
- Attend career development seminars and personal growth workshops that focus on skills such as leadership, negotiation, and emotional intelligence, which are vital for navigating career changes and embracing new opportunities within the legal field. Consider working with a specialized coach.

Advancing Specialization through Education and Certification

Legal professionals can distinguish themselves and stay ahead by pursuing advanced education and specialized certifications. These avenues not only deepen your expertise but also showcase your dedication to maintaining a cutting-edge understanding of your field to clients, colleagues, and the broader legal community.

Postgraduate Studies in Business Law

Purpose and Benefits

- Embarking on postgraduate studies, such as obtaining an LLM (Master of Laws) in areas such as international business law or corporate governance, equips you with comprehensive knowledge and a nuanced understanding of complex legal subjects.
- These programs offer unique opportunities to engage with thought leaders, access the latest legal research, and network with peers from diverse legal backgrounds.

Actionable Steps

- Carefully select programs that match your career ambitions and interests, evaluating the program's faculty, curriculum, and networking opportunities.
- Investigate financial aid options, such as scholarships and grants, and consider flexible learning schedules to accommodate professional commitments.

Certifications in Specialized Areas

Purpose and Benefits

- Obtaining certifications in areas like compliance or intellectual property law demonstrates specialized competency and commitment, enhancing your professional standing and marketability.
- These certifications can set you apart in your practice area, making you more attractive to prospective clients and employers.

Actionable Steps

- Research certifications recognized within the business law community for their rigor and relevance.
- Dedicate time to prepare for certification exams, using preparatory courses and studying comprehensive legal materials.

Workshops and Short Courses

Purpose and Benefits

- Participating in targeted workshops and short courses offers timely updates on legal trends, practical skill enhancement, and familiarity with new technologies affecting business law.
- These educational formats are tailored to fit the busy schedules of professionals, enabling immediate application of learned skills to legal practice.

Actionable Steps

- Keep an eye on offerings from reputable legal education providers and professional associations.
- Choose workshops that promise practical, actionable skills, such as advanced contract drafting techniques or updates on digital currency regulations.

Leveraging Online Learning Platforms

Purpose and Benefits

- Online learning platforms such as Coursera and LinkedIn Learning make learning accessible and flexible, covering a broad spectrum of topics relevant to law and business, from foundational principles to cutting-edge legal tech.
- Courses often include interactive components, such as peer discussions and practical case studies, enriching the learning experience.

Actionable Steps

- Explore and enroll in courses that align with your specialization goals, prioritizing those developed by prestigious institutions and featuring industry experts.
- Opt for courses offering certificates upon completion to enhance your professional profile and resume.

Pursuing further education and certification is a proactive strategy for legal professionals aiming to specialize in business law. By embracing continuous learning and seeking out opportunities for specialization, you not only enrich your own professional journey but also elevate the legal services you provide, ensuring they are both comprehensive and cutting edge.

Leveraging Learning for Career Advancement in Business Law

In the dynamic world of business law, embracing continuous education is a strategic approach to career advancement. It positions you as an adept professional capable of adeptly handling the complexities of the field. Below, we explore strategies for integrating ongoing learning into your career development plan.

Elevating Expertise through Continuous Education

Purpose and Benefits

Continuous learning keeps you informed about the latest legal trends, technologies, and regulatory changes, showcasing your dedication to excellence. Specializing in niche areas within business law sets you apart, making you a sought-after expert.

Actionable Steps

- Carve out weekly time slots for engaging with legal journals or attending webinars on emerging business law topics. For example, subscribing to "The Business Law Section" of the American Bar Association can keep you updated with specialized content.
- Follow industry thought leaders on platforms like LinkedIn or Twitter and subscribe to legal innovation newsletters to stay ahead of the curve.

Using Education for Networking and Visibility

Purpose and Benefits

Educational forums offer rich networking opportunities with legal peers and thought leaders, opening doors to mentorships or collaborations. Active engagement in these settings boosts your visibility and cements your reputation as a knowledgeable professional.

Actionable Steps

- Participate in legal conferences or seminars and initiate conversations with speakers and attendees. For instance, attending the annual ABA Techshow can expand your network with tech-savvy legal professionals.
- Volunteer as a speaker at educational events or contribute insightful articles to legal publications. This not only enriches the legal discourse but also underscores your expertise in your specialty.

Translating Education into Practical Applications

Purpose and Benefits

Applying what you've learned in real-world scenarios enhances client service and case outcomes, reinforcing your role as a proactive, innovative legal advisor.

Actionable Steps

- Analyze your current cases to identify how recent learnings can be applied for strategic advantage. Implementing a new legal technology you learned about in a recent seminar, for example, could streamline your case management process.
- Keep your clients in the loop about your continuous education efforts and explain how these endeavors directly benefit their legal standing. This transparency not only builds trust but also demonstrates your commitment to leveraging the latest legal insights for their advantage.

Educating Yourself through Leadership and Thought Leadership

In the realm of business law, continuous learning isn't confined to traditional educational settings; it extends into active participation in the field through leadership roles and thought leadership. Here's how embracing these opportunities can serve as a dynamic educational tool, furthering your expertise while elevating your professional stature.

Purpose and Benefits

- **Leadership Roles:** Taking on leadership positions within legal associations, committees, or your firm does more than just adorn your resume. These roles challenge you to apply your knowledge in real-world settings, pushing you to stay informed about the latest developments in business law. Leadership allows you to influence the profession's trajectory and actively contribute to its evolution, offering profound learning opportunities in the process.
- **Thought Leadership:** Engaging in thought leadership activities—such as writing articles, contributing to legal podcasts, or speaking at industry conferences—positions you as an authority in your field. This not only enhances your professional brand but also compels you to deepen your understanding of complex legal topics. The research and preparation involved in these endeavors serve as an invaluable learning process, enabling you to explore and clarify your insights on nuanced legal issues.

Actionable Steps

Identify Opportunities for Leadership: Look for positions within your professional circle that align with your areas of expertise and interest. Whether it's heading a committee at a legal association or leading a project team within your firm, choose roles that challenge you and offer room for growth.

Volunteer Strategically: Seek out volunteer opportunities that require skills you aim to hone. For example, if you wish to improve your public speaking, volunteer to present at legal seminars. This approach allows you to develop specific competencies while contributing meaningfully to your field.

Develop a Thought Leadership Plan: Craft a strategy for sharing your knowledge and insights with a broader audience. This might involve starting a legal blog, pitching articles to legal journals, or offering to speak at industry events. Consider topics that you're passionate about or areas where you want to deepen your expertise. The process of researching, writing, and presenting not only solidifies your understanding but also exposes you to feedback and perspectives from peers, further enriching your learning experience.

By integrating leadership and thought leadership into your professional development strategy, you transform your career advancement journey into an educational adventure. Not only do you position yourself as a knowledgeable authority, but you also ensure ongoing personal and professional growth. This proactive approach to learning—leveraging every opportunity to educate yourself through active participation and contribution—sets the foundation for a dynamic and influential career in the legal profession.

Fostering Resilience in Business Law Careers

Developing Professional Resilience

In the dynamic realm of business law, resilience transcends being a mere attribute to become an essential quality for enduring success. Cultivating professional resilience entails adopting a mindset that perceives challenges as avenues for growth rather than as barriers. For attorneys immersed in the intricacies of business law, this signifies the importance of adaptability, initiative, and the readiness to recalibrate strategies in alignment with shifts in market dynamics or legal frameworks. Here's how resilience can be developed and nurtured:

Continuous Skill Development

In a field as fluid as business law, staying at the forefront of knowledge is imperative. Continuous skill enhancement ensures preparedness for forthcoming challenges, equipping lawyers with the ability to navigate through complexities with ease. This might involve the following:

- **Specialization:** Delving deeper into specific domains of business law to build expertise that stands out, whether it's in mergers and acquisitions, financial regulation, or intellectual property rights.
- **Diversification:** Broadening the scope of your expertise to encompass emerging areas, including legal technology applications, privacy laws, or cross-border transaction regulations. This not only prepares you for a broader range of scenarios but also positions you as a versatile professional in the field.

Embracing Change

The willingness to adapt is paramount in the rapidly evolving landscape of business law. Embracing change is about more than just survival; it's about thriving in a profession characterized by continuous evolution. This includes the following:

- **Technological Adoption:** Integrating new technologies into your practice to enhance efficiency, client communication, and data management. From blockchain to AI-driven contract analysis, staying abreast of technological advancements can significantly bolster your legal practice.
- **Adaptation of Legal Specialization:** The legal needs of businesses are constantly changing. Being open to shifting your focus or expanding your specialization in response to these needs not only helps your clients but also ensures your relevancy in the market.
- **Business Model Innovation:** The way legal services are delivered is undergoing a transformation. Exploring alternative business models, such as virtual law firms or subscription-based legal services, can open new avenues for growth and client engagement.

Developing resilience in the field of business law is an ongoing process that requires a proactive approach to learning, a willingness to embrace change, and a commitment to excellence. By focusing on continuous skill development and being open to adapt, lawyers can ensure they are well-equipped to navigate the challenges and opportunities that lie ahead in their careers.

Learning from Challenges

In the rigorous and often unpredictable field of business law, resilience is more than just a buzzword; it's a fundamental characteristic of successful practitioners. Learning from challenges and transforming setbacks into stepping stones for professional growth are pivotal. This resilience is not innate but cultivated through experiences, mindset shifts, and deliberate practice. Key insights include the following:

Analyzing and Reflecting on Setbacks: Every setback, be it a lost case, a client's departure, or a regulatory overhaul that upends a familiar legal landscape, offers a wealth of learning opportunities. The key is to approach these situations with a mindset geared toward growth rather than defeat. This involves the following:

- **Conducting thorough analyses** of what went awry and why, without resorting to self-criticism or assigning blame.
- **Extracting lessons** from these experiences to enhance future legal strategies and client interactions.

Embracing Failure as a Growth Mechanism: The concept of failure in the legal profession, particularly in business law, is often stigmatized. However, redefining failure as an essential component of learning and growth can transform the way legal challenges are perceived and tackled. This mindset shift encourages the following:

- **Risk-taking and innovation** in legal practices, knowing that not every venture will succeed but each will provide valuable insights.
- **Resilience in the face of adversity**, fostering a culture where setbacks are viewed as integral steps in the journey toward mastery and success.

The Crucial Role of Mentorship and Networking in Fostering Resilience in Business Law

The journey through the legal landscape is marked by successes, failures, and constant change, making resilience not just beneficial but also necessary for long-term success and well-being. Mentorship and networking emerge as foundational pillars in building this resilience, offering a scaffold of support, wisdom, and resources that empower legal professionals to navigate challenges with grace and adaptability.

Mentorship: A Beacon for Navigating Storms

Personal and Professional Growth: A mentor, with their wealth of experience and understanding of the legal profession's intricacies, acts as a lighthouse, guiding mentees through turbulent times. They provide the following:

- Insight into the ebb and flow of a legal career, emphasizing that challenges are not only common but also surmountable.

- Personalized advice and strategies tailored to the mentee's unique circumstances, fostering a growth mindset and resilience.

Example: Consider a scenario where a young attorney faces their first major case setback. A mentor who has experienced similar trials can share their own story of overcoming such obstacles, offering practical advice and emotional support that reframe the challenge as a growth opportunity rather than a career-defining failure.

Networking: Creating a Supportive Professional Community

Knowledge Sharing and Community Support: A vibrant network of peers and colleagues provides a rich tapestry of support, encompassing emotional solidarity and practical advice. This community can:

- Serve as a forum for exchanging coping strategies and resources, reinforcing the idea that setbacks are part of the learning and growth process in law.
- Cultivate a sense of belonging, significantly impacting one's resilience by providing a reminder that challenges are a collective experience rather than individual battles.

Example: After facing a challenging period of professional stagnation or loss, an attorney can turn to their network for support. Through conversations, they might discover new opportunities for professional development or be reminded of the commonality of their experience, offering both solace and actionable paths forward.

Fostering a Culture of Resilience

The integration of mentorship and networking into the fabric of a legal professional's career is not just about building individual resilience; it's about nurturing a resilient legal community. By openly sharing experiences of overcoming adversity, legal professionals can contribute to a culture where resilience is valued and fostered. This culture not only aids in personal recovery and growth but also strengthens the collective ability of the legal profession to adapt and thrive in the face of challenges.

Actionable Steps

- Seek out mentors and build a diverse professional network before challenges arise, laying the groundwork for support when needed.
- Actively participate in legal forums, associations, and events that emphasize personal growth, resilience, and community support.
- Share your own experiences of overcoming challenges within your professional circles, contributing to a culture of openness and resilience.

Human Connections in Legal Practice: The Bridget Mayer Briggs Approach

Partner, Blank Rome

Bridget Mayer Briggs is a Partner in Business Litigation at Blank Rome, where she leverages her expertise in white-collar investigations, regulatory litigation, and class action defense matters. With an academic foundation in business from her undergraduate studies, Bridget took a leap into the legal field driven by her fascination with the justice system and a desire to continue learning.

Following her clerkship for Judge Margaret B. Seymour, Bridget's career path led her to Blank Rome, where she has made substantial contributions, particularly in areas that straddle the lines between criminal and civil litigation. Her work often involves navigating complex legal landscapes, including civil RICO (the Racketeer Influenced and Corrupt Organizations Act), the False Claims Act, and the FCPA, among others. Bridget's ability to dissect and understand intricate legal and business issues has been pivotal in her role, especially in conducting internal investigations and advising clients on compliance matters to mitigate risks and prevent potential litigation.

Navigating the Intersection of Criminal and Civil Law

Bridget finds herself at the forefront of an evolving legal landscape where the lines between criminal and civil law frequently blur. Her work primarily revolves around white-collar investigations, regulatory litigation, and class action defense matters. Bridget's journey into this niche was somewhat serendipitous, driven by her innate curiosity and a desire to be where she could be most useful. Starting with a focus on white-collar work, which often entailed business litigation elements due to regulatory violations and compliance issues, she noticed how intertwined criminal law aspects were with business litigation. This realization steered her toward specializing in areas that require a nuanced understanding of both criminal and civil law.

A key aspect of Bridget's approach to legal practice is her emphasis on strategic thinking and understanding the bigger picture. She believes that to effectively navigate the complex scenarios her clients face, it's crucial to think beyond the immediate task at hand. This involves considering the ripple effects of legal actions, the next steps for the company, and the overall litigation strategy. Bridget's ability to anticipate future challenges and opportunities allows her to offer comprehensive counsel to her clients, helping them make informed decisions amid uncertainty.

Bridget's success in blending criminal and civil law is also a testament to her belief in the importance of seeing complexity in every situation and acknowledging that nuance matters. Her practice is not just about defending clients in court but understanding their unique challenges and perspectives. This approach enables her to devise strategies that not only address the legal issues at hand but also consider the broader implications for the client's business and reputation. By adopting this holistic perspective, Bridget ensures that her clients are well-equipped to navigate the intricacies of their legal battles and the potential consequences they face.

Advice for Aspiring Business Lawyers

Bridget emphasizes the importance of gaining business experience for those aspiring to enter the field of business law. She believes that understanding the business context in which legal decisions are made can significantly enhance a lawyer's ability to serve their clients effectively. Bridget advises law students and early career attorneys to seek opportunities that expose them to the business world, whether through internships, part-time jobs, or even coursework that focuses on business principles. This exposure, she argues, not only broadens one's perspective but also aids in understanding the incentives and motivations behind the decision-making processes of law firms and their clients.

Understanding the incentives behind decisions is crucial, Bridget notes. It's not just about the legal outcome but also about how these outcomes align with the client's business objectives and risk tolerance. She encourages aspiring lawyers to ask questions that go beyond the surface, aiming to grasp the full picture of a client's situation. This level of understanding, Bridget believes, is what can set a lawyer apart in the competitive landscape of business law.

Bridget points out that being true to oneself and focusing on sincerely connecting with clients can significantly impact a lawyer's career. Bridget stresses that clients value lawyers who are not only competent in their legal expertise but are also approachable and empathetic. These qualities, she believes, are essential in establishing trust and fostering long-term client relationships. Bridget's own approach to law emphasizes empathy and understanding, which has not only differentiated her in her field but also deepened her connections with her clients, allowing her to provide more tailored and impactful legal advice.

The Human Element in Legal Practice

Bridget understands that behind every legal case, there are individuals trying their best to navigate complex and often daunting scenarios. She emphasizes that situations are rarely black and white, and it's the nuances that truly matter. This perspective shapes her approach to legal practice, where she sees her role not just as an attorney but as a guide helping clients through their challenges. By acknowledging that everyone makes mistakes, and that these mistakes don't define a person's character or worth, Bridget fosters an environment where clients feel understood and supported.

Her empathetic approach is particularly evident in how she deals with clients facing potential litigation or criminal consequences stemming from poor decision making. Bridget stresses the importance of not casting blame too quickly or harshly, as doing so overlooks the complex web of factors that lead to most legal issues. Instead, she focuses on helping her clients understand their situations better, guiding them toward making informed decisions about their next steps. This often involves discussing the broader impacts of their choices, not only on their legal standing but also on their personal lives and businesses.

Bridget's dedication to understanding her clients' perspectives enables her to offer more personalized and effective legal counsel. She believes in the power of empathy and understanding, qualities that allow her to connect with her clients on a deeper level. By viewing her clients as whole people rather than just cases to be won or lost, Bridget is able to navigate the legal system more effectively. This human-centered approach not only aids in achieving better outcomes for her clients but also contributes to a more compassionate and equitable practice of law. ”

Authenticity and Values in Law

Aligning Careers with Personal Ethics

In the competitive and demanding world of law, the pursuit of success often brings lawyers face to face with ethical dilemmas and challenges to their personal values. Navigating these waters while maintaining one's integrity requires a strong sense of self and a commitment to authenticity. This alignment between personal ethics and professional practice is not only crucial for personal satisfaction but also enhances trust and credibility with clients and colleagues. Here's how legal professionals can ensure their career paths in business law are in harmony with their core values:

Self-Reflection and Value Assessment: The first step in aligning your career with your personal ethics is to conduct a thorough self-assessment of your values, beliefs, and what you stand for. This introspective process involves the following:

- Identifying your core values and understanding how they translate into your professional life. For instance, if transparency and fairness are values you hold dear, consider how these can be manifested in your approach to client dealings and case management.
- Regularly revisiting and reassessing your values, as personal growth and experiences may lead to shifts in what you prioritize and stand for.

Career Choices and Ethical Practice: Making career decisions that reflect your personal ethics involves being selective about the roles you take on, the clients you represent, and the cases you pursue. This conscious choice-making ensures that your work in business law is not just a means to an end but a reflection of your identity and values. This can be achieved by the following:

- Researching potential employers, partners, and clients to ensure their business practices and ethical standards align with your own.
- Being willing to say no to opportunities that conflict with your ethical standards, even if they promise financial gain or career advancement.

Advocacy for Ethical Standards: Beyond personal practice, aligning your career with your values involves advocating for high ethical standards within your workplace and the broader legal community. This advocacy can take various forms, including the following:

- Leading by example through your conduct and decision-making processes.
- Actively participating in discussions and initiatives aimed at promoting ethical practices in business law.
- Mentoring younger lawyers and sharing insights on navigating ethical dilemmas while maintaining personal integrity.

Balancing Professional Ambitions with Ethical Considerations: The drive for success in business law often requires balancing ambition with ethical considerations. This balance is critical for long-term fulfillment and maintaining a positive reputation in the legal community. Strategies include the following:

- Developing a clear understanding of your personal and professional boundaries.

- Engaging in continuous learning and professional development focused on ethics in business law.
- Seeking out role models and mentors who exemplify a harmonious blend of professional success and ethical practice.

Authenticity as a Foundation for Trust: Ultimately, the alignment of your career in business law with your personal ethics enhances your authenticity, which is a cornerstone of trust and respect in professional relationships. Authenticity fosters genuine connections with clients, colleagues, and the community, laying the foundation for a rewarding and impactful career. Maintaining this alignment requires the following:

- Regular self-reflection and honest assessment of your career path and decisions.
- Open communication about your values and ethical standards with your professional network.
- A commitment to continuous growth and adaptation, ensuring that your practice of business law remains a true reflection of your authentic self.

By prioritizing authenticity and aligning your career with your personal values and ethics, you ensure that your professional journey in business law is not only successful but also deeply fulfilling and reflective of who you are as an individual. This alignment serves as a beacon, guiding your decisions and actions toward positive outcomes for yourself, your clients, and the broader community.

From Torts to Trust: Miko Ando Brown's Legal Evolution at Airbnb

Associate General Counsel, Community Trust, Airbnb

Miko Brown serves as the Associate General Counsel at Airbnb, Inc., where she leads the Community Trust team. Her journey into the legal profession is marked by a significant evolution of interests and expertise. Initially, Miko's encounter with torts during her law school years was less than favorable. The complexity and nuances of tort law did not immediately resonate with her, leading to an early aversion. However, this initial disinterest did not define her career trajectory. Instead, it set the stage for a remarkable transformation as she delved deeper into the world of law.

After completing her education, Miko embarked on a path that would see her defending high-profile companies in catastrophic personal injury lawsuits across the nation. This role not only demanded a deep understanding of the very torts she once disliked but also required a keen insight into product liability law—a field where Miko found her passion. Her expertise and dedication in this area propelled her through the ranks of the legal profession, eventually leading her to become a partner at prominent law firms before taking on her current role at Airbnb.

Miko's transition from a skeptic of torts to a champion of personal injury defense and product liability law underscores a fundamental truth about careers in law: interests can evolve, and early challenges can pave the way to unexpected and fulfilling paths. Her story is a testament to the importance of remaining open to change and the value of persistence in the face of initial disinterest or difficulty. Now, at Airbnb, Miko leverages her extensive legal experience to lead initiatives that protect and foster trust within the global community that the platform serves.

Advice for Early Career Attorneys

Miko stresses the significance of choosing a law firm that provides meaningful experience right from the start. For law students and early career attorneys, the decision is not just about joining a prestigious name but finding a place where you can actively contribute and grow. "It's crucial to be in an environment where you're not just observing but actually doing the work," she says. This hands-on experience is invaluable, as it not only hones your legal skills but also builds your confidence in handling complex cases.

Being proactive in seeking out responsibilities is another piece of advice Miko shares. She believes in the importance of demonstrating initiative and a willingness to take on challenges. "If you show that you're capable of driving projects forward and leading, opportunities will open up for you," Miko explains. It's about making your capabilities known and seizing the opportunities to lead and manage, which are critical skills in any legal career.

Miko advises job seekers to ask potential employers for examples of the type of work they will be doing. This not only helps in setting the right expectations but also shows the employer that you are serious about contributing to their team. "You need to demonstrate that you're not just there to fill a seat but to make a difference," she adds. This approach has been instrumental in Miko's career, allowing her to take on more responsibilities and eventually lead a team of eight lawyers at Airbnb. Her journey underscores the importance of being a go-getter in the legal field, a quality that can significantly impact your career trajectory.

Miko's Role at Airbnb

In her role at Airbnb, Miko manages a diverse legal team tasked with a dual focus: proactive risk mitigation and reactive incident response. This balance requires a nuanced understanding of the platform's operations and the potential legal challenges it faces. The proactive side involves developing and implementing strategies to prevent safety incidents and discrimination, both on and off the platform. On the reactive side, Miko's team is responsible for handling any incidents that do occur, ensuring that responses are swift, effective, and legally sound. This dynamic aspect of her work keeps her engaged and constantly on her toes, as the landscape of online community trust is ever-evolving.

Leading a team of eight lawyers, Miko's management style is informed by her experiences both as a partner in law firms and now in her current role. She notes significant differences in her responsibilities, particularly in the broader scope of her current work which extends beyond legal defenses to include the formulation of policies and practices that safeguard the Airbnb community. Her role requires not just legal expertise but also strategic thinking and leadership skills. Miko finds this blend of responsibilities enriching, offering her a unique opportunity to impact the platform and its users directly.

Miko's transition from a law firm partner to an in-house counsel at a major tech company like Airbnb has been marked by a shift in focus toward more collaborative and preventive legal work. At the law firm, her work was primarily reactive, centered on defending clients after incidents had occurred. Now, her role encompasses a broader spectrum of legal and ethical considerations, aiming to prevent issues before they arise. This shift has not only broadened her professional skills but also deepened her commitment to creating a safe and inclusive environment for Airbnb's global community.

Passion for Diversity and Inclusion

Central to Miko's philosophy and Airbnb's ethos is a deep-seated commitment to diversity and inclusion. For Miko, these are not just buzzwords but pivotal principles that guide hiring practices, team dynamics, and decision-making processes. She underscores the importance of embedding diversity and inclusion into the core values of any organization, advocating for these principles to be considered in promotion criteria as well. This approach not only enriches the workplace culture but also enhances the creative and problem-solving capabilities of the team, as diverse perspectives are key to navigating the complex challenges of today's legal landscape.

Miko's work and advocacy serve as a compelling call to action for law firms and corporations alike to prioritize diversity and inclusion not only as moral imperatives but also as strategic assets. By sharing her story, she hopes to inspire other legal professionals to champion these values within their organizations, recognizing that a genuine commitment to creating an inclusive environment is essential for long-term success and sustainability. Through proactive initiatives and a steadfast commitment to diversity, Miko exemplifies how legal professionals can drive meaningful change, both within their companies and in the broader community they serve. ”

Global Perspectives on Business Law Careers

The Global Legal Market: Opportunities and Challenges

The interconnected global legal market presents both expansive opportunities and unique challenges for business lawyers. As companies operate on an increasingly international scale, the demand for legal professionals who can adeptly navigate cross-border transactions, understand diverse regulatory environments, and manage international legal complexities continues to grow. This section delves into how embracing the global legal market can significantly enhance your career in business law, outlining actionable strategies for seizing international opportunities and overcoming the hurdles inherent in global legal practice.

Embracing International Opportunities for Business Lawyers

Diverse Clientele and Cross-Border Expertise

- **Opportunity:** Lawyers with a global outlook have the unique advantage of advising on intricate international mergers, acquisitions, and partnerships, serving a diverse international clientele. This exposure not only enriches your professional experience but also elevates your profile within the legal community.
- **Actionable Steps:** Build your expertise in international business law through advanced studies or certifications. Engage actively in global legal networks

by participating in international forums, workshops, and conferences where you can connect with potential international clients and partners.

Navigating Multinational Compliance

- **Opportunity:** Mastery in coordinating multinational regulatory compliance positions you as an indispensable asset to global enterprises. The ability to guide businesses through the labyrinth of international regulations and standards is a highly marketable skill.
- **Actionable Steps:** Keep abreast of global regulatory trends through continuous education and professional development opportunities. Forge connections with international legal experts to facilitate a collaborative approach to complex compliance issues.

Specialization in Dispute Resolution

- **Opportunity:** The growing preference for resolving international disputes through arbitration and mediation offers a lucrative niche for lawyers. Specializing in these areas can lead to engagement in high-stakes, high-profile international cases.
- **Actionable Steps:** Pursue specialized training or certifications in international arbitration and mediation. Participate actively in international moot court competitions or intern with firms known for their dispute resolution prowess.

Overcoming Challenges in Global Legal Practice

Cultural and Linguistic Fluency

- **Challenge:** Successful international legal practice demands more than just legal expertise; it requires cultural understanding and language proficiency to communicate effectively across borders.
- **Actionable Steps:** Embark on language learning tailored to your areas of focus in international law. Engage with cultural competency programs to enhance your ability to navigate the subtleties of international legal negotiations and client interactions.

Adapting to Diverse Legal Systems

- **Challenge:** The variety of legal frameworks worldwide poses a significant challenge, requiring a versatile and informed approach to international legal practice.

- **Actionable Steps:** Subscribe to global legal databases and engage in partnerships with local counsel across jurisdictions to enrich your understanding of diverse legal systems. Attend comparative law seminars and workshops to refine your approach to multi-jurisdictional issues.

Ethical Navigation in International Contexts

- **Challenge:** Differing ethical standards and practices across jurisdictions necessitate a careful, informed approach to international legal work to maintain integrity and professionalism.
- **Actionable Steps:** Familiarize yourself with the International Bar Association's guidelines and other global ethical standards. Seek counsel from local legal authorities or ethics committees when facing ethical dilemmas in unfamiliar jurisdictions.

Thriving in the global legal marketplace requires a strategic blend of specialized knowledge, cultural fluency, and ethical vigilance. By proactively seeking opportunities for international engagement, continuously expanding your legal and cultural competencies, and navigating the complexities of global practice with integrity, you can forge a distinguished and rewarding career in the field of international business law. This proactive and informed approach not only advances your professional trajectory but also contributes to the evolving landscape of global business law.

Overcoming Professional Challenges: Addressing Challenges like Market Conditions, Institutional Dynamics, and Personal Setbacks

In the legal profession, practitioners are often confronted with a diverse array of challenges that span from external market pressures and internal organizational dynamics to personal setbacks and the ongoing struggle for diversity, equity, and inclusion. Navigating these obstacles requires a blend of resilience, adaptability, and strategic thinking. Understanding the intricacies of market conditions is crucial for staying relevant and competitive, while grasping the nuances of institutional dynamics can unlock opportunities for advocacy and career advancement. Personal setbacks, although daunting, offer unique opportunities for growth and learning, pushing professionals to redefine their paths and strategies. Moreover, addressing DEI challenges is not just a moral imperative but also a necessity for enriching the profession with diverse perspectives and fostering an inclusive environment. Together, these themes underscore the importance of a holistic approach to overcoming professional challenges, emphasizing the potential for personal development and systemic change within the legal landscape.

Navigating Market Conditions

Understanding and navigating market conditions are crucial for lawyers specializing in business law. Market fluctuations can significantly impact the demand for legal services, affecting everything from client budgets to the types of legal issues that become prevalent. Here's how you can effectively analyze and adapt to these conditions:

Analyzing Market Trends

Importance of Staying Informed

- Keeping abreast of market trends allows you to anticipate changes in the demand for various legal services. This foresight can help you adjust your practice areas or marketing strategies to align with emerging needs.
- Understanding economic indicators and their potential impact on your clients' industries enables you to provide more targeted and valuable legal advice, making you an indispensable resource.

Actionable Steps

- Regularly review industry reports, legal publications, and economic forecasts to stay informed about the current state of the market and potential future trends.
- Attend industry conferences and participate in legal forums where experts discuss the implications of market conditions on business law.

Adapting Legal Services to Market Needs

Tailoring Services

- As market conditions fluctuate, so too do the legal needs of businesses. By tailoring your services to meet these evolving needs, you can maintain or even grow your client base during challenging times.
- For example, during an economic downturn, there may be an increased demand for bankruptcy, restructuring, or compliance services. Conversely, periods of economic growth might see a rise in mergers and acquisitions or intellectual property protection.

Actionable Steps

- Analyze your client portfolio to identify which industries are most affected by current market conditions and adjust your service offerings accordingly.

- Develop flexible pricing models or alternative billing arrangements to accommodate clients' changing financial situations, ensuring that your services remain accessible and attractive.

Strengthening Client Relationships

Building Trust

- Strong client relationships are your best defense against the unpredictable nature of market conditions. Clients who trust and value your services are more likely to remain loyal, even when budget constraints arise.
- Transparent communication about market impacts on legal issues, and how you can assist, reinforces your role as a trusted advisor.

Actionable Steps

- Schedule regular check-ins with clients to discuss their concerns related to market conditions and explore how you can support their business through legal strategies.
- Offer proactive advice and insights on market trends that could affect their industry, highlighting your commitment to their success.

Leveraging Technology and Innovation

Embracing Legal Tech

- Technology can be a game-changer in responding to market conditions. Leveraging legal tech tools can improve efficiency, reduce costs, and enhance the quality of your services.
- Innovative solutions, such as AI for legal research or blockchain for contract management, can set your practice apart and attract clients looking for cutting-edge legal support.

Actionable Steps

- Invest in legal technology that streamlines your practice areas most affected by market changes. This could include tools for electronic discovery, document automation, or online client portals.
- Stay informed about the latest legal tech innovations and assess their potential impact on your practice. Consider attending tech-focused legal conferences or participating in webinars and online courses.

Navigating market conditions requires a proactive approach, where staying informed, adapting services, strengthening client relationships, leveraging technology, and continuous learning are key strategies. By employing these tactics, you can position yourself and your practice to thrive, regardless of the economic landscape.

Maram Salaheldin's Journey in Environmental Law and Corporate Advocacy

Senior Attorney, EHS&S, Clark Hill

Maram Salaheldin's journey into the legal profession is marked by a blend of passion, expertise, and a keen understanding of the evolving landscape of environmental, health, safety, and sustainability (EHS&S) challenges. With an educational background that spans continents, Maram's early aspirations to become a lawyer were fueled by her experiences growing up in the Middle East, where she was exposed to international human rights issues and conflict resolution from a young age. Her academic pursuits led her to the United States, where she completed her undergraduate studies in Houston, Texas, before earning her law degree in Maryland. Today, Maram serves as a Senior Attorney at Clark Hill, specializing in EHS&S matters.

In her role at Clark Hill, Maram leverages her extensive experience to counsel U.S. and multinational clients on EHS&S risks and liabilities associated with their operations and products. Her expertise is particularly critical in periods of change, such as expansion into new markets or navigating supply chain disruptions. Maram's work is at the intersection of environmental law and corporate strategy, where she helps clients manage the potential impacts of international laws and navigate the complexities of ESG issues. Her ability to fluently speak multiple languages, including Arabic and French, further enhances her capacity to address transnational operations and client needs effectively.

Before joining Clark Hill, Maram's career was shaped by her time as a consultant focused on EHS&S compliance and management systems. This experience provided her with a practical understanding of U.S. regulations, foreign laws, and international treaties, serving government and commercial clients across various sectors. It is this foundation that has enabled Maram to not only excel in her current role but also co-lead the firm's ESG & Sustainability advisory practice, demonstrating the critical role of environmental law in today's business environment.

Bridging Environmental Law and Corporate Strategy

Maram has observed a significant shift in the legal landscape, particularly in how environmental law increasingly intersects with corporate strategy. She notes, "Historically, you didn't really see environmental law and corporate law as overlapping because you were doing very specific subsets that funneled up into the corporate lawyer handling the transaction." However, the rise of ESG issues has changed this dynamic, bringing environmental considerations to the forefront of corporate decision making. Maram's work now often involves advising on ESG issues that have become material risks for businesses, demonstrating the evolving role of environmental law in guiding corporate strategy.

One example Maram shares involves her increased involvement with the SEC due to the regulatory focus on sustainability reporting. "I've been talking more about the SEC in the past two years than I ever thought I would," she says, highlighting the unexpected turn her career has taken. This shift is largely due to the regulatory crackdown on deceptive environmental claims, or "greenwashing," where companies make unsustainable sustainability claims. Maram's expertise in environmental law has become crucial for corporate clients navigating these new regulatory waters, underscoring the importance of environmental law expertise in today's business environment.

Maram's work illustrates how environmental lawyers are now integral to board-level and C-suite discussions on material risks related to climate change, human rights, and social impacts. "ESG by definition puts environmental issues at the forefront," she explains, pointing out how this has led to her involvement in high-level strategic decisions. Her role in bridging environmental law and corporate strategy not only showcases her expertise but also emphasizes the growing recognition of environmental considerations in shaping sustainable and compliant corporate practices.

The Path to Legal Expertise: From Consultancy to Law Firm Success

After completing her law degree, Maram faced the common challenge of finding a position that would sponsor her work visa, a hurdle that led her to explore opportunities beyond traditional law firms. Her fluency in Arabic became a crucial asset, opening the door to her first job at an international consulting firm. This role, while not initially what she envisioned for her legal career, provided her with a solid foundation in technical compliance and an understanding of environmental law's practical applications across different jurisdictions. Working with multinational companies, she helped bridge the gap between varying international and U.S. regulations, gaining a deep appreciation for the complexities of global compliance.

This early career experience in a consulting capacity was instrumental in shaping Maram's approach to environmental law. It exposed her to a wide range of challenges and solutions in the field, from managing medical waste in rural health clinics to navigating the intricacies of international environmental standards. Such experiences honed her ability to think pragmatically and work effectively with nonlegal professionals, skills that would prove invaluable in her later work at Clark Hill. Her consulting background, particularly her direct involvement with clients and on-site work, provided a practical understanding of business operations and the real-world implications of legal advice, setting her apart from peers who took more traditional legal paths.

By the time Maram joined Clark Hill, she brought with her not just expertise in environmental law but a comprehensive view of how legal advice impacts business operations and compliance strategies across borders. Her journey from consultancy to law firm success underscores the importance of adaptability, the value of practical experience, and the significant role language and cultural understanding play in the global practice of law. Maram's story is a testament to how nontraditional legal roles can equip attorneys with the diverse skills and perspectives necessary to address the complex environmental challenges facing today's multinational corporations.

Advocacy and Self-Advocacy in the Legal Profession

Maram points out the critical role of self-advocacy in the legal profession, a principle she has adhered to throughout her career. She notes, "It's definitely important to advocate for yourself. That's probably the number one thing that I would give as a piece of advice." This insight is not just theoretical for Maram; it is a practice she has lived by, especially in her efforts to launch and co-lead the ESG & Sustainability advisory practice at her firm. Her journey underscores the idea that lawyers, often so focused on advocating for their clients, sometimes neglect to advocate for themselves and their career aspirations.

Drawing from her own experiences, Maram shares that many lawyers, surprisingly, do not actively pursue their own interests or speak up about their career goals within their firms. This, she believes, is a missed opportunity for both personal growth and the advancement of the profession. "I'm always shocked at how many lawyers don't advocate for themselves," she remarks, pointing out that self-advocacy can lead to significant opportunities, such as her leadership role in ESG and sustainability. Maram's success in this area demonstrates what can be achieved when lawyers confidently present their ideas and seek support for initiatives they are passionate about.

Maram's advice to early career attorneys is clear: don't wait for opportunities to come to you. Instead, create them by being proactive about your interests and career goals. Her own story is proof of the power of self-advocacy in navigating the complexities of the legal profession and making a meaningful impact. By advocating for the establishment of the ESG & Sustainability advisory practice, Maram not only advanced her career but also contributed significantly to her firm's positioning in a rapidly evolving legal landscape.

Institutional Dynamics and Their Impact

Navigating Firm Politics in Business Law

Navigating the nuanced dynamics of law firm politics is essential for advancing in the field of business law. Success in this area involves more than just understanding legal principles; it requires strategic engagement with both the formal and informal structures that influence firm culture and decision-making processes. Below, we delve deeper into actionable strategies for navigating these dynamics effectively.

Understanding the Firm's Political Landscape

The political environment within a law firm can significantly impact your career trajectory. It encompasses power structures, key influencers, and the unwritten rules that govern interactions and decisions within the firm.

Actionable Steps

- **Conduct a Political Map Exercise:** Identify the power centers within your firm. This might include senior partners, influential practice groups, or administrative departments. Understanding these entities' interests and influence can guide your interactions and strategies.

- **Engage in Active Listening and Observation:** Spend time observing the dynamics during meetings and casual interactions. Note how decisions are made, who influences them, and the role of informal networks. This will help you understand the firm's culture and how to navigate it effectively.

Cultivating Strategic Relationships

Building and maintaining positive relationships within the firm is crucial for navigating its political landscape. These relationships can offer support, insights, and opportunities for advancement.

Actionable Steps

- **Identify Allies and Advocates:** Look for individuals within the firm who share your professional values and goals. These relationships can provide mutual support and advocacy in firm decisions.
- **Engage Across Hierarchies:** Build connections not just vertically within your practice area but also horizontally across different departments and levels of seniority. This broad network can offer diverse perspectives and opportunities.

Mastering the Art of Diplomacy

Diplomacy involves navigating firm politics with tact, respect, and the ability to find common ground among differing viewpoints.

Actionable Steps

- **Practice Empathetic Communication:** When discussing contentious issues, strive to understand others' perspectives fully before presenting your viewpoint. This approach can facilitate more productive conversations and solutions.
- **Develop Conflict Resolution Skills:** Engage in training or workshops that enhance your ability to manage and resolve conflicts effectively. This skill is invaluable in navigating firm politics and maintaining positive relationships.

Upholding Professional Integrity

In the complex world of firm politics, maintaining your ethical standards and professional integrity is paramount.

Actionable Steps

- **Adhere to Ethical Guidelines:** Familiarize yourself with both the legal industry's ethical standards and your firm's specific guidelines. Ensure your actions always align with these principles.
- **Seek Ethical Counsel:** When faced with ethical dilemmas, don't hesitate to consult with your firm's ethics committee or a trusted mentor. Their guidance can help you navigate difficult situations without compromising your principles.

Leveraging Mentorship and Networking

Mentors and a strong professional network can provide invaluable guidance and support as you navigate the firm's political landscape.

Actionable Steps

- **Seek Diverse Mentorship:** Cultivate mentorship relationships with individuals from various backgrounds and areas of expertise within the firm. These mentors can offer a wide range of perspectives and advice on navigating firm politics.
- **Invest in Networking:** Attend firm events, participate in industry associations, and engage in networking opportunities outside your immediate practice area. These activities can expand your professional network and initiate relationships with professionals who can offer helpful advice.

Navigating the politics of a law firm requires a nuanced approach that balances strategic engagement with the firm's dynamics, the cultivation of positive relationships, diplomatic communication, unwavering professional integrity, and active mentorship and networking. By implementing these comprehensive strategies, you can navigate firm politics effectively, paving the way for a successful and fulfilling career in business law.

Organizational Change: Adapting to mergers, acquisitions, or restructuring within legal institutions and its impact on business law practices

Organizational changes such as mergers, acquisitions, or restructuring within legal institutions significantly impact business law practices. These shifts require business law practitioners to exhibit adaptability and resilience to navigate the new landscape successfully. Here's a structured approach to managing organizational change effectively:

Anticipating the Impact

- **Understanding Organizational Objectives:** Recognize the reasons behind the organizational change—be it a merger, acquisition, or internal restructuring. Comprehending these motives can shed light on potential shifts in roles, responsibilities, and the overall direction of the law firm or department.
- **Preparatory Steps:**
  - Conduct research or attend briefings to grasp the strategic goals of the change.
  - Assess how these changes could affect your practice area and prepare for possible shifts in focus.

Maintaining Open Communication

- **Fostering Dialogue:** Open lines of communication are vital during transitions. Leadership should provide clear, timely information about the changes and how they impact various roles within the organization.
- **Actionable Steps:**
  - Seek out information and clarification on changes directly impacting your role.
  - Participate in discussions with peers and leadership to share concerns and suggestions, fostering a collaborative approach to navigating the change.

Adapting Your Practice

- **Aligning with New Directions:** As the firm's focus evolves, so too might the need for your legal expertise. This could involve expanding your knowledge base, exploring new client segments, or leading projects that align with the firm's new strategic direction.
- **Implementing Changes:**
  - Identify areas for growth or new services that align with the organizational change.
  - Propose initiatives or projects that contribute to the firm's goals, demonstrating your adaptability and initiative.

Networking Within the New Structure

- **Building New Relationships:** Changes often bring new team members or merge different organizational cultures. Actively building relationships within the new structure is essential for integration and finding new opportunities for collaboration.

- **Strategies for Integration:**
    - Reach out to new colleagues or teams to introduce yourself and learn about their expertise.
    - Organize or participate in cross-departmental meetings or team-building activities to foster a sense of unity and collaboration.

Embracing Flexibility and Resilience

- **Staying Agile:** The ability to remain flexible and positive in the face of change is crucial. This mindset can help mitigate the stress of transition and position you as a key player in the firm's future.
- **Cultivating Resilience:**
    - Adopt a proactive approach to change, seeking opportunities to contribute to the new organizational goals.
    - Stay open to learning and adapting your practices to fit the evolving needs of the firm and its clients.

Reflecting and Learning from the Experience

- **Gleaning Insights:** Every organizational change provides a unique learning opportunity. Reflecting on how the change was managed, the effectiveness of different strategies, and your personal adaptation process can offer valuable insights for future transitions.
- **Leveraging Lessons Learned:**
    - Document your observations and takeaways from the change process.
    - Share your experiences with colleagues, contributing to a collective knowledge base that can inform future organizational changes.

Organizational change in business law practices tests the adaptability and resilience of practitioners. By anticipating impacts, maintaining open communication, adapting practices, networking within the new structure, staying flexible, and reflecting on the experience, attorneys can navigate these changes successfully. This proactive and reflective approach not only aids personal growth but also contributes to the collective strength and agility of the legal institution.

Personal Setbacks and Professional Growth

Overcoming Career Obstacles: Addressing common career setbacks experienced by business law professionals, including job loss or demotion

Navigating personal setbacks is a pivotal aspect of any legal professional's career, particularly in the dynamic field of business law. Career obstacles such as job loss, demotion, or failed projects are not uncommon, yet they offer invaluable opportunities for reflection, learning, and ultimately, professional growth. Here's a narrative approach to overcoming these setbacks:

Understanding the Nature of Setbacks

The first step in overcoming career obstacles is recognizing that setbacks are a natural part of any professional journey. They are not reflections of failure but rather milestones for learning and development. In the competitive and ever-changing landscape of business law, external factors such as economic downturns, firm restructuring, or client loss can lead to situations such as job loss or demotion. Accepting the cyclical nature of these events helps in mentally preparing for and effectively managing them when they occur.

Reflecting and Learning

Once the initial emotional response to a setback has subsided, it is crucial to reflect on the experience. What led to the situation? Were there any warning signs? What could have been done differently? This introspection, while sometimes difficult, is essential for personal and professional growth. It allows for a clearer understanding of one's strengths and areas for improvement.

Seeking Support and Feedback

Reaching out to mentors, colleagues, or even a professional coach can provide perspective, advice, and support. These conversations can offer insights into how others have navigated similar challenges and can provide practical advice for moving forward. In addition, seeking feedback on your performance and approach can illuminate areas for development that you may not have recognized.

Developing a Plan for Moving Forward

Armed with a better understanding of the setback and how to address it, the next step is to develop a concrete plan for moving forward. This might involve additional training or education, rebranding oneself, networking to find new opportunities, or even exploring entirely new areas of business law. Setting specific, achievable goals as part of this plan provides direction and a sense of purpose.

Implementing and Adapting the Plan

As you implement your plan, remain open to new opportunities and be prepared to adapt your approach as necessary. The legal industry, particularly in areas such as business law, is continually evolving, and flexibility can open up paths you hadn't previously considered. Regularly assess your progress toward your goals and adjust your strategy to stay on track.

Maintaining Resilience and Positivity

Throughout this process, maintaining resilience and a positive outlook is key. Setbacks can be disheartening, but they do not define your career. With perseverance and a proactive approach, obstacles can transform into stepping stones for a more fulfilling and successful career path.

Sharing Your Experiences

Once you've navigated through a setback and found your footing again, consider sharing your experience with others. Contributing your story to discussions, mentorship conversations, or even writing about it can help those who might be facing similar challenges. Sharing not only aids others but also reinforces your own learning and growth.

Overcoming career obstacles in business law requires a balanced approach of introspection, planning, and action, supported by a network of colleagues and mentors. By viewing setbacks as opportunities for growth, embracing support, and maintaining resilience, legal professionals can navigate these challenges successfully, emerging stronger and more prepared for the future.

Merging Paths: Equity and Ambition in Nick Samedi's M&A Journey

Partner in M&A/Corporate Department at Lowenstein Sandler

Jean Nicolas "Nick" Samedi, a partner in the M&A/Corporate Department at Lowenstein Sandler, has a clear message for anyone standing at the crossroads of choosing a law school: think about where you want to end up, both geographically and in your career. Nick's own journey to law school was influenced by a mix of scholarship opportunities, proximity to family, and the strategic consideration of his future career path in M&A. He chose Georgetown University, situated in a location that, although not his ultimate destination, offered him a blend of academic rigor and access to the kind of legal markets he was interested in. This decision was not just about the prestige of the institution but was deeply intertwined with his long-term goal of practicing in New Jersey, away from the more traditional New York City law scene.

Nick points out the importance of being intentional about where you want to build your career and the role of a law school in that process.

He shares his own experience of conducting thorough research on the best law firms in New Jersey for M&A and using that information to guide his decisions during law school. This proactive approach not only helped him secure a position at a leading firm in his desired location but also underscores the value of foresight and planning in achieving career goals. Through his journey, Nick illustrates that choosing the right law school is about more than just academic excellence; it is about aligning one's education with their career vision and the geographical landscape of their future legal practice.

Cultivating Success: The Power of Relationships and Self-Advocacy

Reflecting on his time at Georgetown University during a period marked by intense competition, Nick recalls an environment where students felt compelled to outperform their peers at any cost. This hyper-competitive atmosphere, he notes, was not conducive to building the long-term professional networks that are crucial in the legal profession. Instead, Nick emphasizes the value of collaboration and mutual support among classmates. He points out that the very individuals one might view as competitors in law school can become invaluable contacts, clients, or collaborators in the future. The legal community is tightly knit, and the relationships formed during these formative years can significantly impact one's career trajectory.

Reflecting on his early years in the legal field, he acknowledges that his natural introversion and the merit-based values instilled in him as a first-generation American initially hindered his progress. He learned that success in law, particularly in client development, requires more than just hard work and competence; it demands visibility and vocal self-advocacy. Nick shares a pivotal moment in his career when a mentor highlighted the importance of making oneself known within the firm—not just as a diligent worker but as an integral part of the team with unique contributions. This realization prompted him to shift his approach, actively seeking opportunities to demonstrate his skills and value beyond the confines of his office.

Navigating Challenges: Resilience and Work–Life Balance in M&A Law

The field of M&A is renowned for its demanding pace and high stakes, a reality that Nick knows all too well. In his work with private equity and hedge fund clients, Nick has experienced firsthand the sacrifices required to succeed. The unpredictable hours and the need to be constantly available mean that personal plans often have to be set aside. "Every deal has its own cadence and flow," Nick explains, highlighting the necessity for lawyers in this field to be adaptable and ready to prioritize work at a moment's notice. This aspect of the job can be particularly challenging for one's family and significant other, requiring a level of understanding and resilience from both the lawyer and their loved ones.

Despite these challenges, Nick emphasizes the importance of perseverance and resilience, not just for the individual lawyer but also for their support network. The demanding nature of M&A law tests not only one's professional capabilities but also personal relationships. However, Nick believes that these challenges can be navigated successfully with the right mindset and support system. He candidly shares, "It's not just you. If you have a partner, it's you and your partner doing this." This collective perseverance is crucial, especially in a big law firm environment where the pressure to perform is constant.

Nick's journey in M&A law underscores the need for lawyers in this field to develop a sustainable approach to their work. Although the rewards of working on high-profile deals can be significant, the toll on personal life necessitates setting clear boundaries and fostering resilience. Nick's experience serves as a reminder that success in the demanding world of M&A requires not only legal acumen but also the ability to maintain a balance that supports both professional growth and personal well-being.

Fostering Diversity and Mentorship: Building a Supportive Legal Community

Understanding the challenges that underrepresented groups face in the legal profession, Nick played a pivotal role in creating a formal sponsorship program and diverse affinity groups within the firm. These initiatives aim to provide a supportive environment where all associates, regardless of their background, can receive the guidance and opportunities necessary for career advancement. By linking up-and-coming associates with experienced members of management, the sponsorship program facilitates meaningful career planning and development discussions, ensuring that diverse talent is not only recruited but also retained and nurtured.

Recognizing the detrimental impact of unequal work distribution on the morale and career progression of diverse attorneys, he advocated for the implementation of a fair and transparent work allocation system.

This system is designed to prevent employees from being inadvertently sidelined and ensures that all associates have equal access to challenging and career-defining projects. Through these measures, Nick aims to dismantle barriers to advancement and create a more inclusive atmosphere within the firm.

Nick's vision extends beyond the walls of his firm, as he seeks to open doors for diverse talent in the broader New Jersey legal market. His belief in the firm as the perfect platform to achieve this goal reflects his broader commitment to enhancing diversity and inclusion within the legal profession. By sharing his experiences and the lessons learned along his journey, Nick hopes to inspire other firms to adopt similar initiatives, thereby contributing to the creation of a more equitable and supportive legal community across New Jersey and beyond. ”

Diversity, Equity, and Inclusion (DEI) Challenges

For early career attorneys from diverse backgrounds, navigating the professional landscape in environments where DEI may not be prioritized presents a unique set of challenges and opportunities. Here are strategies and insights aimed at empowering these attorneys to carve out successful careers while also contributing to the gradual transformation of their workplaces toward more inclusive spaces.

Understanding Your Environment

- **Assess the Firm's DEI Climate:** Take stock of your firm's current stance on DEI. This understanding can help you navigate its culture more effectively and identify potential allies and resources within the organization.
- **Recognize Your Value:** Understand that your diverse background brings unique perspectives and strengths to your legal practice, enriching the firm's capability to address complex legal challenges and cater to a diverse clientele.

Empowering Yourself and Others

- **Build Your Network:** Cultivate relationships with peers, mentors, and allies who value DEI, both within and outside your firm. These connections can offer support, advice, and opportunities for collaboration and advancement.
- **Seek Out DEI Resources and Communities:** Engage with external legal associations and groups focused on supporting attorneys from diverse

backgrounds. These platforms can provide additional mentorship, advocacy, and a sense of belonging.

Advocating for Change

- **Start Small:** Initiate or participate in smaller, incremental DEI efforts, such as organizing informal discussions or sharing DEI-related resources and articles with colleagues. These small steps can foster awareness and open dialogues on DEI within your firm.
- **Be a Role Model:** Demonstrate the value of diversity and inclusion through your work ethic, collaboration, and interactions with colleagues and clients. Leading by example can influence the firm's culture and attitudes toward DEI over time.

Developing Resilience and Adaptability

- **Focus on Professional Development:** Invest in honing your legal skills and expanding your knowledge base. Excelling in your area of practice can help you build credibility and a strong professional reputation, which is crucial for career advancement.
- **Cultivate Emotional Intelligence:** Developing skills in empathy, self-awareness, and managing relationships can enhance your ability to navigate complex workplace dynamics and advocate for yourself and others effectively.

Creating Spaces for Inclusion

- **Form or Join Support Networks:** If formal DEI programs are lacking, consider forming or joining peer support networks within your firm. These can serve as safe spaces for sharing experiences, offering mutual support, and discussing strategies for professional growth and advocacy.
- **Propose DEI Initiatives:** As you gain experience and build relationships within your firm, look for opportunities to propose or contribute to DEI initiatives. Even small projects, such as a diversity-focused newsletter or a speaker series, can start meaningful conversations and gradually influence firm culture.

Seeking External Support

- **Professional Development and Continuing Education:** Use external resources for professional growth, including CLE courses focused on DEI, workshops, and conferences. This not only enriches your skill set but also connects you with a broader community committed to advancing DEI in the legal field.

- **Legal Advocacy and Support Organizations:** In cases where you face significant DEI-related challenges, seek advice and support from legal advocacy organizations. They can offer guidance, resources, and, if necessary, legal support to help you navigate and address these issues.

Embracing DEI as a Continuous Journey in the Legal Field

For early career attorneys and seasoned legal professionals alike, embedding DEI into the core of their practice isn't just ethical; it's strategic. DEI enriches the legal profession by fostering a more dynamic, innovative, and just legal community. Recognizing DEI as an ongoing journey is essential for personal growth and professional excellence.

Reflect and Reassess

Constant evaluation of DEI initiatives within your organization is crucial. This involves not just a superficial nod to diversity but a deep, meaningful commitment to cultivating an inclusive environment. Regular feedback sessions, DEI audits, and openness to change can help maintain momentum and ensure initiatives remain relevant and effective.

Celebrate Diversity

Actively celebrating the myriad backgrounds and accomplishments of colleagues and clients alike reinforces a culture of inclusion. Marking cultural events, acknowledging diverse historical contributions, and highlighting individual achievements can all contribute to a workplace where everyone feels valued and respected.

Actionable Steps for Legal Professionals to Implement and Advocate for DEI

Creating a Foundation for DEI

- **Leadership Commitment:** Advocate for and expect a clear, demonstrated commitment to DEI from your firm's leadership. This might involve initiating conversations, proposing the development of a DEI statement, or suggesting the allocation of resources toward DEI efforts.
- **Comprehensive DEI Policies:** Contribute to the development or revision of DEI policies. Offer to be part of a committee that reviews policies to ensure they're inclusive and promote equity across all levels of the organization.

Building DEI into the Institution's Fabric

- **Inclusive Recruitment Practices:** If you are in a position to do so, advocate for recruitment strategies that broaden the diversity of the candidate pool. This could involve suggesting partnerships with diverse legal associations or recommending training for hiring managers on inclusive practices.
- **Support and Development Programs:** Engage in or propose mentorship and sponsorship programs tailored to uplift underrepresented groups within your firm. Participating as a mentor or advocating for the creation of such programs can be a significant step toward enhancing DEI.

Fostering an Inclusive Culture

- **Ongoing Education and Training:** Participate in, or suggest, regular training sessions focused on unconscious bias, cultural competency, and inclusivity. Championing these initiatives can help cultivate a more understanding and respectful workplace.
- **Safe Spaces for Dialogue:** Advocate for the establishment of forums or discussion groups focused on DEI topics. Creating channels for open dialogue can facilitate understanding and collaborative problem solving.

Measuring and Evaluating DEI Efforts

- **Establish Clear DEI Metrics and Goals:** Encourage your organization to set measurable DEI objectives. Engage in the process by contributing to the development of these goals and participating in regular reviews to assess progress.
- **Continuous Improvement:** Advocate for DEI to be an ongoing priority, with regular assessments and adaptations based on feedback, research, and societal developments.

When to Consider Alternatives

Despite your best efforts, if your current organization's commitment to DEI does not align with your values, or if efforts to initiate change are met with resistance, it may signal that the environment is not conducive to your growth. In such cases, seeking opportunities within organizations that not only value but actively pursue inclusivity might be the more fulfilling path. Remember, your talents, perspectives, and commitment to justice are highly valued in the legal field—finding an environment that appreciates and nurtures those qualities is crucial for your professional satisfaction and success.

By actively engaging in DEI efforts, regardless of your role within the legal sector, you contribute to a more equitable, dynamic, and just legal profession.

Whether through advocacy, participation, or leadership, your actions can pave the way for meaningful change, benefiting not only your career but also the broader legal community.

Navigating Career Transitions and Social Justice Advocacy: The Journey of Laura Marquez-Garrett

Attorney, Social Media Victims Law Center

Laura Marquez-Garrett's career trajectory is a testament to their commitment to leveraging their legal expertise for broader societal impact. A graduate of Harvard Law School, Laura embarked on their legal journey with a focus on complex litigation matters and business disputes. Over two decades, they honed their skills, especially in the niche area of electronic discovery, becoming a recognized expert in navigating the complexities of data in legal disputes. At their previous firm, they were instrumental in founding and leading the firm's innovative electronic discovery practice group, serving as special discovery counsel for clients and law firms alike.

Their expertise in electronic discovery and their passion for equity and social justice propelled them to take on leadership roles, including serving as Hiring Partner and cochair of the DEI committee. Laura's relentless drive and their ability to marry their legal acumen with their advocacy for social justice have been hallmarks of their career.

In February 2022, Laura made a significant career shift, joining the Social Media Victims Law Center. This move was driven by their desire to address the harms inflicted by social media platforms, particularly on children. At the Social Media Victims Law Center, Laura aims to hold social media companies accountable, using their extensive legal experience to navigate the emerging challenges of social media litigation. Their transition from a secure position in a traditional law firm to a role that focuses on pioneering legal battles against powerful tech entities underscores their commitment to making a tangible difference in society through their legal work.

Evaluating Career Happiness and Making Bold Choices

Laura's approach to their career has always been deeply introspective, guided by a personal philosophy that places happiness and fulfillment at the forefront of their professional decisions. This reflective mindset became particularly pronounced following the passing of their father.

It was a pivotal moment that led them to initiate an annual tradition of career evaluation every December, a practice aimed at ensuring their professional path remained aligned with their core values and aspirations. This process of taking stock was not just about assessing their achievements over the past year but also about questioning whether their career choices continued to bring them joy and satisfaction.

The tradition of annual reflection eventually led Laura to a bold decision that would significantly alter their career trajectory. Feeling the need for a fresh start and driven by a desire to reassess their commitment to the legal profession, they made the radical choice to quit their job, sell their house, and move to Seattle. This decision was not taken lightly; it was a testament to their belief in the importance of being true to oneself and the pursuit of a career that not only challenges but also brings happiness. Laura's move to Seattle was a leap into the unknown, a step away from the security and familiarity of their previous job into a space where they could explore what truly mattered to them in their professional life.

Laura's time in Seattle was transformative. It led them to a firm that, despite its lack of mentoring and diversity, served as a crucial stepping stone in their career. Their experiences there further solidified their understanding of what they sought in a workplace—mentorship, diversity, and a culture that resonated with their values. These insights eventually guided them to their tenure at Lane Powell, where they spent eleven years immersed in work they loved, surrounded by colleagues who shared their dedication to the law.

The Drive for Social Justice and Technological Innovation

Laura's career has been characterized by a dual commitment to social justice and the innovative use of technology in the legal field. This unique blend of interests has been a driving force behind their work, particularly in their specialization in electronic discovery. Laura has long believed in the power of technology to transform the legal landscape, especially in how data can be leveraged to streamline processes and uncover truths. Their early realization that "within electronic data, very few things are truly disputed" led them to advocate for the use of technology to access crucial information. This approach not only saves time and resources but also significantly reduces the need for trials, highlighting a more efficient path to justice.

At the heart of Laura's work is the conviction that litigation should not always be the default strategy for corporate clients. They emphasize the importance of attorneys prioritizing their clients' best interests, which often means exploring alternative solutions that are more aligned with their long-term goals. This perspective is particularly relevant in the context of electronic discovery, where the strategic use of data can often lead to early resolution of disputes.

The transition to the Social Media Victims Law Center marked a significant shift in Laura's career, allowing them to merge their passion for social justice with their expertise in technology. Here, they have been able to take on the emerging challenges of social media litigation, a field that demands a deep understanding of data and its implications. Laura's work in this realm is driven by a commitment to holding social media companies accountable for the harms they cause, particularly to children. This effort is emblematic of their broader goal to use their legal skills and technological acumen to make a tangible difference in society. Through their pioneering work, Laura exemplifies how attorneys can lead the way in adapting to new legal landscapes, ensuring that their practices not only remain relevant but also serve the greater good.

Challenges and Rewards of Social Media Litigation

Upon joining the Social Media Victims Law Center, Laura Marquez-Garrett found themselves at the forefront of an emerging and challenging area of law: social media litigation. Their work has since encompassed a range of high-profile cases, including those related to fentanyl deaths on Snapchat and the Buffalo massacre. These cases are not only legally complex but also deeply intertwined with societal issues, such as the opioid crisis and the radicalization of individuals through social media platforms. Laura's involvement in these cases has required a deep understanding of both the legal and technological aspects of social media, as well as a commitment to navigating the intricacies of holding powerful tech companies accountable.

One of the most significant challenges Laura faced was the Snapchat fentanyl cases, where they and their team took on the daunting task of proving the platform's role in the distribution of counterfeit pills leading to fatal overdoses. The gravity of these cases is underscored by their impact on public health, with fentanyl deaths contributing to a decline in life expectancy in the United States for the first time in two decades. Laura's work in this area is not just about legal victories; it is about addressing a public health crisis and seeking justice for families who have lost loved ones.

In addition to litigation, Laura has been actively involved in efforts toward legislation aimed at making social media platforms safer for users, particularly children. Their work on the Kids Online Safety Act (KOSA) exemplifies this commitment. Through meetings with senators and public speaking engagements, they have advocated for policies that would hold social media companies to higher standards of user protection. This legislative work, although challenging, represents an important avenue for creating long-lasting change beyond the courtroom.

The fulfillment Laura derives from their work in social media litigation is palpable. Despite the uphill battles and the resource disparities between their team and the tech giants they challenge, the progress made in these cases offers a sense of victory not just for their team but for society at large. It is a testament to the impact that determined legal advocacy can have in holding powerful entities accountable and protecting vulnerable populations from harm. Through their pioneering work, Laura demonstrates the profound difference that dedicated legal professionals can make in emerging fields of law, driven by a commitment to justice and societal well-being.

Finding a Home in Law and Making a Difference

Laura's journey in the legal profession has been marked by a constant search for a place where their work could have a meaningful impact on society. This quest led them to the Social Media Victims Law Center, a firm that stands out not just for its pioneering work in social media litigation but also for its distinctive firm culture. Laura describes it as "the most human law firm" they have ever encountered, a place where leadership genuinely values input from all members and where the firm's culture is deeply rooted in caring about the people it works with. This environment has been crucial for Laura, providing them with the support and freedom to pursue their passion for holding social media companies accountable for their impact on users.

For other lawyers seeking fulfillment in their careers, Laura's journey offers valuable insights. They emphasize the importance of leadership and culture in achieving professional satisfaction. A firm that listens, adapts, and genuinely cares for its people can provide a more fulfilling work environment, encouraging lawyers to invest their best efforts and creativity. Laura's advice is clear: find a place where you can truly make a difference, not just in the legal outcomes you achieve but in contributing to a culture that uplifts and supports everyone involved. This, they believe, is the foundation of a rewarding legal career.

Work–Life Balance and Personal Development: Strategies for Managing Professional Demands Alongside Personal Life and Well-Being

Striking a balance between professional aspirations and personal well-being emerges as a crucial element for sustained success and satisfaction in the legal profession. This necessity transcends mere time management; it's about constructing a life where work enriches rather than depletes, where personal development is not sidelined but seamlessly integrated into our professional growth. The following segments offer a comprehensive exploration of establishing work–life harmony, delving into effective boundary-setting, time management, and the pivotal role of continuous learning in personal and professional advancement. We'll examine strategies for navigating career transitions with grace, the significance of nurturing both professional and personal support networks, and the delicate art of balancing family life and relationships within the demanding sphere of legal practice. In addition, we focus on personal fulfillment, highlighting the importance of mindfulness, self-care, and adaptability—key components in crafting a fulfilling career that aligns with one's values and aspirations. Through this exploration, we aim to provide early career attorneys with the tools and perspectives necessary to thrive in the competitive landscape of business law, ensuring a career that is not only successful but also profoundly rewarding.

Establishing Work–Life Harmony

In the realm of business law, establishing work–life harmony is not just desirable; it is essential for long-term success and personal fulfillment. This balance allows attorneys to meet the rigorous demands of their profession while maintaining their health, relationships, and personal interests. As we delve into the concept of work–life balance, we focus on why it is particularly important for business lawyers and how achieving it can significantly enhance both professional performance and personal satisfaction.

Work–Life Balance and Setting Boundaries

Work–life balance represents the equilibrium where a person equally prioritizes the demands of one's career and the demands of one's personal life. For business lawyers, achieving this balance is crucial due to the unpredictable hours and high stakes inherent in their profession. Balancing these demands affects not only lawyers' personal lives but also their ability to serve their clients effectively.

Understanding the Importance

The nature of business law can lead to long workdays and a blurred line between office and home life, potentially resulting in burnout, stress, and decreased job satisfaction. Recognizing the importance of work–life balance is the first step toward healthier work habits and a more satisfying and sustainable career.

Setting and Maintaining Clear Boundaries

Setting clear boundaries between work and personal time is a critical aspect of achieving work–life harmony. This involves establishing specific work hours and communicating these to colleagues and clients to manage expectations effectively.

Actionable Steps to Achieve Balance and Set Boundaries

- **Prioritize and Organize:** Differentiate between urgent and important tasks. Prioritize critical work assignments while ensuring personal activities are also scheduled.
- **Communicate Boundaries:** Clearly communicate your work hours to your team and clients. Be consistent in enforcing these boundaries to help others respect your personal time.
- **Use Technology Wisely:** Use technology for efficiency but ensure to disconnect from work-related communications during personal time to fully unwind.
- **Advocate for Flexibility:** Seek flexible working arrangements, such as remote work or flexible hours, to better balance professional and personal commitments.
- **Incorporate Self-Care:** Make time for exercise, hobbies, and quality time with loved ones. These activities should be viewed as essential, not optional.
- **Learn to Say No:** It is important to recognize when to decline additional responsibilities that may disrupt your work–life balance. Saying no is a vital skill in maintaining your boundaries and well-being.

By understanding the importance of work–life balance and implementing practical strategies for setting clear boundaries, business lawyers can not only improve their own lives but also enhance their professional efficacy. Achieving this balance requires deliberate actions and consistent effort, but the benefits to both personal well-being and career success are immeasurable.

Time Management Techniques

Effective time management is pivotal for business lawyers who juggle client needs, case deadlines, and firm responsibilities. Mastering these techniques ensures you can meet professional obligations efficiently while carving out essential time for personal activities and rest. Here are several strategies to enhance your productivity and safeguard your personal time.

Prioritize Tasks

- **Categorize Tasks by Urgency and Importance:** Use tools such as the Eisenhower Box to decide on and prioritize tasks based on their urgency and importance. This method helps in focusing on what truly needs your attention each day.
- **Set Realistic Deadlines:** Assign realistic deadlines to tasks based on their priority. This helps manage your workload effectively, preventing last-minute rushes that can eat into your personal time.

Plan and Organize

- **Daily and Weekly Planning:** Allocate time each week to plan your tasks. Daily, spend a few minutes prioritizing tasks for the day. This practice helps in creating a balanced schedule that includes work tasks, personal activities, and breaks.
- **Use a Digital Calendar:** Leverage digital tools and calendars to schedule your tasks, meetings, and personal commitments. Set reminders for important deadlines and appointments.

Delegate and Outsource

- **Leverage Your Team:** Delegate tasks that can be handled by junior lawyers or paralegals. This not only helps in managing your workload but also aids in their professional development.
- **Outsource Noncore Activities:** Consider outsourcing tasks not central to your practice, such as administrative duties or certain research activities, to free up more time for client-focused work and personal pursuits.

Eliminate Distractions

- **Limit Email and Social Media Use:** Set specific times for checking emails and social media to avoid constant distractions throughout the day.

- **Create a Focused Work Environment:** Minimize interruptions by informing colleagues of your focused work periods. Use noise-canceling headphones or apps that limit distracting websites.

Practice Efficient Work Methods

- **Batch Similar Tasks:** Group similar tasks together to reduce the mental load of switching between different types of work. This can include dedicating specific blocks of time for client calls, case research, or document review.
- **Adopt the Pomodoro Technique:** Work in focused sprints of twenty-five minutes followed by a five-minute break. This method can enhance concentration and prevent burnout.

Reflect and Adjust

- **Weekly Review:** At the end of each week, review what you accomplished versus what was planned. Reflect on what worked well and what could be improved to make better use of your time going forward.
- **Adjust Strategies as Needed:** Be flexible with your time management techniques. What works well one week may need adjustment the next. Stay open to changing your strategies to find what best suits your evolving workload and personal life.

Personal Development for Legal Professionals

Personal development is a crucial aspect of building a rewarding career in business law. It encompasses continuous learning, skill enhancement, and career progression, all tailored to align with both professional ambitions and personal well-being. For legal professionals, investing in personal growth not only enhances their expertise and marketability but also contributes to a more balanced and fulfilling life.

Seeking Resources for Improvement

Continuous learning is not just a professional obligation; it is a personal growth strategy that contributes significantly to work–life harmony. For early career attorneys and those transitioning, integrating continuous learning with personal development and work–life balance can lead to a more satisfying career trajectory. Here's how to approach continuous learning with an eye on both professional enhancement and personal fulfillment:

Incorporating Learning into Daily Routines

Make Learning a Part of Your Lifestyle

Integrate educational activities into your daily or weekly routines in a way that doesn't detract from personal time. Podcasts, audiobooks, and industry news can be consumed during commutes or workout sessions, making learning both efficient and enjoyable.

Actionable Steps

- Subscribe to podcasts and newsletters that cover both business law topics and personal development themes.
- Set aside a specific time each week for reading or online courses, ensuring it's a time that complements your personal schedule.

Leveraging Technology for Flexible Learning

Use Online Resources

Take advantage of the flexibility offered by online courses, webinars, and virtual conferences. These resources allow you to stay informed and develop your skills on your own time, reducing the pressure to sacrifice personal commitments for professional development.

Actionable Steps

- Enroll in online courses that offer asynchronous learning options.
- Participate in virtual networks and discussion forums to engage with peers and mentors without geographic or time constraints.

Balancing Learning with Well-Being

Mindful Learning: Recognize when continuous learning enhances your well-being and when it might be contributing to burnout. It's important to balance the desire for professional growth with the need for rest and personal time.

Actionable Steps

- Regularly assess your learning activities to ensure they're contributing to your sense of accomplishment and well-being, not detracting from it.
- Practice time management techniques that allocate space for learning without overwhelming your schedule.

Integrating Learning with Career Goals

Align Learning with Career Aspirations

Use continuous learning as a strategic tool to open doors to new opportunities within business law that are better aligned with your work–life balance goals and personal values.

Actionable Steps

- Develop a personal learning plan that includes goals for both professional advancement and personal fulfillment.
- Seek mentorship or coaching to help align your learning efforts with your broader career and life objectives.

Career Progression

Career progression encompasses a myriad of pathways, each offering unique opportunities for growth, challenge, and personal fulfillment. As a lawyer representing companies, the avenues for advancement are diverse, including climbing the ranks in a law firm, making strategic lateral moves, or even launching your own private practice. Understanding and navigating these options effectively can lead to a rewarding career that aligns with your personal and professional goals.

Climbing the Ranks in a Law Firm

Developing Expertise and Building a Reputation

Excel in your current role by specializing in areas of business law that are in demand. Become the go-to expert in your niche, whether it's mergers and acquisitions, intellectual property, or another sector. Contributing to high-profile cases, publishing thought leadership pieces, and speaking at industry events can elevate your profile within and beyond your firm.

Actionable Steps

- Seek out challenging projects that align with your career goals and showcase your capabilities.
- Engage in continuous learning to deepen your expertise in your chosen specialization.

Making Strategic Lateral Moves

Expanding Your Horizons

Lateral moves to other firms or legal departments can offer new challenges, the chance to work in different areas of business law, or more favorable conditions for work–life balance. Research potential employers to find those that align with your career aspirations and personal values.

Actionable Steps

- Network within the legal community to learn about opportunities and gather insights about different organizations.
- Consider the culture, values, and growth opportunities of potential new workplaces.

Launching a Private Practice

Entrepreneurial Venture

Starting your own practice in business law allows for unparalleled autonomy in choosing the clients you serve, the cases you take on, and the balance you strike between work and personal life. This path requires a blend of legal expertise, business acumen, and entrepreneurial spirit.

Actionable Steps

- Develop a business plan that outlines your niche, target clients, and marketing strategy.
- Seek advice from mentors who have successfully launched their practices and consider partnerships with other lawyers to share resources and expertise.

Building a Portfolio Career

Diverse Professional Experiences

Some business lawyers choose to build a portfolio career, combining part-time roles, consultancy work, and board positions. This approach can offer variety, flexibility, and the opportunity to apply your legal skills in different contexts.

Actionable Steps

- Identify opportunities where your legal expertise can add value, such as consulting for start-ups or serving on the board of a nonprofit.
- Manage your time effectively to ensure that you can meet all your commitments without compromising on work quality or personal well-being.

Prioritizing Personal Goals and Values

Aligning Career Choices with Personal Life

As you consider your career progression, reflect on how each path aligns with your personal goals and values. Whether seeking work–life balance, financial security, or the satisfaction of entrepreneurial achievement, choose the route that best supports your overall well-being and fulfillment.

Actionable Steps

- Regularly evaluate your career progression in light of your personal aspirations and life circumstances.
- Be open to reevaluating your career path as your goals and values evolve over time.

Navigating career advancement in business law requires a proactive and strategic approach. By understanding the various pathways available, aligning your career moves with your personal and professional goals, and being prepared to adapt as opportunities arise, you can achieve a fulfilling and successful career representing companies in the dynamic field of business law.

Exploring Interests Outside Law

Embracing interests outside the realm of law is not merely an avenue for personal enjoyment; it is a pivotal component of cultivating a well-rounded and enriching life. For business lawyers, who often navigate a world defined by deadlines and intricate legalities, dedicating time to hobbies, interests, and volunteer work enriches not just their personal lives but also their professional interactions. Engaging in diverse activities makes you a more interesting, relatable individual, facilitating deeper conversations and connections with colleagues, clients, and prospects. This blend of professional acumen and personal interests can significantly enhance your appeal as a legal professional in the business world.

Broadening Perspectives

Diversifying Experiences

Immersing yourself in activities unrelated to law broadens your perspective, fostering creativity and innovation that can positively influence your legal practice. It offers new ways of thinking and problem solving, which can be applied to your work.

Actionable Steps

- Identify activities that spark joy or curiosity and commit to exploring them regularly.
- Set realistic goals for engaging in your hobbies or interests to ensure they are a source of relaxation, not another task on your to-do list.

Enhancing Social Connections

Building Relationships Beyond the Legal Community

Pursuing interests outside law helps you build relationships with a diverse group of people, enriching your social life and providing support networks outside of your professional circles.

Actionable Steps

- Join clubs, groups, or classes that align with your interests to meet like-minded individuals.
- Participate in community events or local projects to connect with people in your area.

Contributing to the Community

Volunteer Work

Engaging in volunteer work not only contributes positively to your community but also offers a sense of purpose and fulfillment. It allows you to give back, using your skills in meaningful ways outside of the corporate world.

Actionable Steps

- Research organizations or causes that resonate with you and explore how you can contribute, whether through pro bono legal work or other forms of volunteering.

- Consider volunteer opportunities that allow you to learn something new or share your passion with others, such as mentoring youth in your area of interest.

Personal Growth and Development

Cultivating Personal Interests

Developing skills and knowledge in areas outside of law contributes to your personal growth, making you a more well-rounded individual. It can also provide a sense of achievement and satisfaction that comes from learning and mastering new skills.

Actionable Steps

- Dedicate time each week to pursue personal interests, treating this time as nonnegotiable in your schedule.
- Be open to trying new activities, even those that might initially seem outside your comfort zone.

Finding Balance and Fulfillment

The Role of Nonwork Activities

Balancing the demands of a business law career with personal interests and activities is key to maintaining mental and emotional well-being. It helps prevent burnout and ensures that your career is part of a fulfilling life, not the entirety of it.

Actionable Steps

- Reflect on how you spend your time and consider adjustments to ensure a healthier balance between work and personal pursuits.
- Communicate with colleagues and family about your interests and how they contribute to your overall well-being, fostering understanding and support.

Investing in personal interests and community involvement not only contributes to your well-being but also sharpens your professional edge. Being well-rounded enriches your perspective, making you a more versatile and relatable lawyer who can connect with a broader spectrum of clients, colleagues, and prospects. This multifaceted approach to personal development is vital for crafting a balanced, enriching life that enhances your legal practice. Diversifying your experiences in and out of the legal world does not just make you a more interesting person; it makes you a better lawyer, equipped with a wider range of insights and problem-solving skills. By embracing hobbies and passions outside of work, you ensure that your career in business law is bolstered by a wealth of experiences, ultimately enriching every professional interaction and contributing to your overall effectiveness as an attorney.

Navigating Well-Being in the Legal Profession: Insights from Jennifer DiSanza

Executive Director, Institute for Well-Being in Law

Jennifer DiSanza brings a wealth of experience and a deep commitment to the well-being of those in the legal profession. With a foundational education in business from Miami University, Jennifer's academic journey led her to pursue further studies, earning a Master of Science in organization development and strategic human resources from Johns Hopkins University. Her quest for knowledge didn't stop there; she went on to obtain a Juris Doctor from the University of Maryland, equipping her with a comprehensive understanding of the law and its implications on society and individuals within the legal field.

Jennifer's passion for improving the legal profession's approach to well-being is evident in her career trajectory. She has spent over two decades working in student affairs at various ABA-approved law schools, where she focused on enhancing student experiences and well-being. Her work has not only impacted the students she directly interacted with but also contributed to broader discussions and initiatives aimed at making the legal education system more accessible, affordable, and supportive of students' and professionals' mental and emotional health. This dedication to fostering a healthier, more inclusive legal community sets the stage for the insights and stories she shares in the following sections.

Improving Student Well-Being

Throughout her career, Jennifer DiSanza has been deeply involved in enhancing the well-being and educational experiences of law students. Her journey into this field was not just a professional choice but a personal mission, born out of her own challenges as a law student. Jennifer's early realization that many students, like herself, were navigating the demanding law school environment without a clear playbook, especially those from nontraditional backgrounds or first-generation college students, fueled her dedication to student support services. This insight led her to significant roles in student affairs, where she could directly influence the student experience.

In her capacity as a law school dean of students, Jennifer worked closely with various organizations, including the Kentucky Office of Bar Admissions and the Dave Nee Foundation, to bring about meaningful change. These collaborations were aimed at creating a more supportive and understanding environment that acknowledges the unique pressures faced by law students. By partnering with these organizations, she was able to introduce programs and initiatives focused on mental health, financial wellness, and academic support. These efforts were not just about providing resources but about fostering a community where students felt seen, heard, and supported in their diverse needs and challenges.

Advice for Legal Professionals

One of the core insights Jennifer shares is the importance of aligning one's career with personal values and well-being. "The number one reason I heard students going to law school is because they want to help people. But the reality is public service jobs don't pay enough. Yet, what they really love doing is helping people better their lives," Jennifer notes. This highlights a common dilemma many face in the legal field: balancing financial obligations with the desire to make a meaningful impact.

She points out how the traditional path can lead to burnout and dissatisfaction, suggesting that "the future is looking at alternative work arrangements. There are people turning down the idea of the current partner track to have a better work–life balance." This advice is particularly relevant in a time when the legal industry is grappling with high levels of stress and mental health issues among professionals. Jennifer's own career trajectory, which includes roles that were not traditionally associated with a JD, showcases the versatility of a legal education and the breadth of opportunities available beyond conventional paths.

For students and early career attorneys, Jennifer's advice underscores the importance of practical experience and exploration. She encourages law students to "explore their options. Don't get stuck. Even if they know what they want to do, they may take a course and be like, 'I love this. This is what I want to do.'" This openness to experience can lead to a more fulfilling career path that aligns with one's interests and values, thereby supporting overall well-being.

Health and Well-Being

In the high-stakes environment of business law, the mental health and well-being of practitioners can often take a backseat, overshadowed by the demands of complex transactions and intricate legal challenges. However, acknowledging and addressing the mental health needs of those in the business law sector is crucial for fostering a sustainable and fulfilling career. This section delves into understanding the unique stressors faced by business lawyers, offers strategies for maintaining well-being amid the pressures, and highlights the critical role of support systems and resources in cultivating a healthier professional life.

Understanding the Unique Pressures

Business law practitioners navigate a demanding landscape marked by tight deadlines, high client expectations, and complex legal frameworks. Recognizing these pressures is the first step toward managing their impact on mental health. Key stressors include the following:

- **High-Stakes Environment:** The pressure to succeed in negotiations, transactions, and legal strategies where significant financial and business interests are at stake.
- **Constant Connectivity:** The expectation to be always available, leading to long work hours and blurred boundaries between professional and personal life.
- **Rapid Pace of Change:** Keeping abreast of legislative updates, regulatory shifts, and new business models adds to the mental load.

Action Steps for Recognizing Stressors

- **Self-Reflection:** Regularly take stock of your mental and emotional state. Acknowledge feelings of stress or burnout as valid signals that need attention.
- **Peer Discussions:** Engage in open conversations with colleagues about the pressures of the profession. Shared experiences can validate your feelings and provide collective strategies for coping.
- **Seek Feedback:** Regularly check in with mentors or supervisors to discuss workload management and expectations. Honest conversations can lead to more sustainable work practices.
- **Educational Workshops:** Participate in or organize workshops focusing on identifying and managing stressors specific to the legal profession. These can offer valuable tools and foster a supportive community.

The Impact on Mental Health

Understanding the direct correlation between these stressors and mental health is crucial. The effects can range from mild anxiety and stress to more severe conditions such as depression and burnout. Recognizing the signs early and taking proactive measures can mitigate long-term impacts and support a healthier work–life balance.

Action Steps for Addressing Mental Health

- **Mental Health Training:** Advocate for or engage in mental health training within your organization to better understand symptoms and interventions.
- **Professional Support:** Encourage the use of professional mental health resources, such as counseling or therapy, which can offer specialized strategies for managing stress and anxiety related to work.
- **Mindfulness Practices:** Incorporate mindfulness and stress-reduction techniques into your daily routine, such as meditation, exercise, or hobbies that detach you from work pressures.
- **Policy Advocacy:** Work toward or support initiatives within your organization that recognize and act upon the mental health needs of employees, such as flexible work policies, mental health days, and access to wellness programs.

By acknowledging the unique stressors faced in the business law sector and their effects on mental health, legal professionals and their organizations can take significant steps toward fostering a healthier, more supportive work environment. This proactive approach not only benefits individual well-being but also enhances the collective resilience and productivity of the legal community.

Strategies for Well-Being

Achieving a healthy work–life balance is essential for sustaining long-term well-being and career satisfaction in business law. Implementing strategies that prioritize personal time and wellness can significantly reduce stress and prevent burnout.

Action Steps for Work–Life Balance

- **Set Boundaries:** Clearly define your work hours and communicate them to your team and clients. Use do-not-disturb features on devices outside these hours to protect personal time.

- **Time Management:** Prioritize tasks and delegate when possible. Effective time management can free up time for rest and personal activities.
- **Regular Breaks:** Take short breaks throughout the day to disconnect and recharge, even if it is just a five-minute walk or a moment of mindfulness.
- **Vacation Time:** Use your vacation days fully. Taking time off is crucial for mental health and can lead to increased productivity when you return to work.

Embracing Mindfulness and Self-Care

Mindfulness and self-care practices are powerful tools for managing stress and enhancing overall well-being. They help maintain focus, reduce anxiety, and improve emotional regulation.

Action Steps for Mindfulness and Self-Care

- **Daily Mindfulness Practice:** Incorporate mindfulness exercises into your daily routine, such as meditation, deep-breathing exercises, or yoga, to help center your thoughts and reduce stress.
- **Physical Activity:** Regular exercise can significantly improve mental health. Find an activity you enjoy, whether it's a daily walk, cycling, or a fitness class, to incorporate movement into your routine.
- **Healthy Habits:** Ensure a balanced diet, adequate sleep, and hydration. These fundamental health practices can profoundly impact your mental and physical well-being.
- **Hobbies and Interests:** Engage in activities outside of work that bring you joy and fulfillment. Hobbies can serve as a creative outlet and provide a sense of accomplishment unrelated to your profession.

Support Systems and Resources

Creating a supportive and healthy work environment is essential for the well-being of legal professionals. Here is how to access and provide support systems and resources for mental health in the legal profession.

Establishing In-House Support

- **Employee Assistance Programs (EAPs):** Encourage the adoption of EAPs that offer confidential counseling services to employees facing personal or professional challenges.

- **Action Step:** Advocate for EAP implementation within your firm or legal department. If already available, ensure all team members are aware of and understand how to access these services.

Utilizing Professional Resources

- **Bar Association Wellness Programs:** Many bar associations now offer wellness programs, resources, and helplines specifically tailored for legal professionals.
    - **Action Step:** Identify wellness resources offered by your local or national bar association. Participate in wellness seminars or workshops they provide and share this information with colleagues.

Building a Supportive Community

- **Mentorship and Peer Support Groups:** Foster a culture of mentorship and create peer support groups within the legal community. These groups can offer a safe space for sharing experiences and strategies for coping with stress.
    - **Action Step:** Initiate or join a mentorship program or support group within your legal community. Regularly meet to discuss challenges and share coping mechanisms.

Promoting Mental Health Education

- **Mental Health Training and Workshops:** Provide training for all employees on mental health awareness, stress management, and resilience building.
    - **Action Step:** Organize or advocate for regular mental health training sessions. This could include inviting mental health professionals to conduct workshops or utilizing online resources and courses.

Encouraging a Culture of Well-Being

For early career attorneys, establishing a balanced approach to work and personal life is crucial. Here's how you can cultivate a culture of well-being within your professional life:

Personal Well-Being Initiatives

- **Self-Directed Well-Being Programs:** Take initiative by integrating personal well-being practices into your daily routine. This could include setting aside time for physical activity, mindfulness meditation, or pursuing hobbies that contribute to your overall mental health.

- **Practical Approach:** Explore and incorporate mindfulness apps or online fitness programs into your daily schedule. Designate specific times for these activities to ensure they become a consistent part of your routine.

Work–Life Balance Strategies

- **Managing Workload with Flexibility:** Strive for a work–life balance by setting clear boundaries between work hours and personal time. Use organizational tools and techniques to manage your workload efficiently, allowing for flexibility in your schedule.
    - **Practical Approach:** Prioritize your tasks and utilize digital tools for time management. Be proactive in communicating with your team about your availability and boundaries to ensure mutual respect for personal time.

Stress Management Techniques

- **Adopting Stress Reduction Practices:** Learn and apply stress management techniques such as deep-breathing exercises, short mindfulness breaks, or engaging in physical activities to mitigate the stress of high-stakes legal work.
    - **Practical Approach:** Integrate short mindfulness or breathing exercises into your workday, especially during high-pressure periods. Regularly assess your stress levels and adjust your coping strategies accordingly.

Fostering Professional Support Networks

- **Cultivating Supportive Relationships:** Build a network of colleagues and mentors who understand the unique pressures of business law. These relationships can provide emotional support, practical advice, and a sense of community.
    - **Practical Approach:** Seek out mentorship opportunities and actively participate in legal communities, both online and offline. Share experiences and strategies for well-being with peers to foster a supportive network.

Advocating for Your Needs

- **Communicating Your Well-Being Needs:** While early career attorneys may have limited influence on firm-wide policies, openly communicating your needs and advocating for work arrangements that support your well-being is essential.

- **Practical Approach:** When appropriate, discuss with your supervisor or HR the importance of flexibility, such as the possibility of remote work-days or adjusting work hours to accommodate well-being activities.

Advocating for Policy Changes: Cultivating a Healthier Work Culture

Early career attorneys face the challenge of navigating a work culture that often prioritizes professional demands over personal well-being. With expectations from peers and clients reinforcing a work-above-all-else mindset, advocating for policy changes within your organization becomes crucial for fostering a healthier work environment. Here's how you can contribute to this cultural shift:

Understanding the Need for Change

- **Acknowledge the Culture:** Recognize the prevailing expectations within the legal profession that can contribute to stress and burnout. It's important to understand how these expectations impact your mental health and professional satisfaction.
- **Initiate Conversations:** Start discussions with your peers about the need for a cultural shift toward better work–life balance. Sharing experiences and perspectives can help illuminate the widespread effects of the current work culture on well-being.

Advocating for Flexible Work Policies

- **Promote Flexibility:** Advocate for the adoption of policies that allow for flexible work hours and remote work options. Highlight how such flexibility can contribute to improved mental health and job satisfaction.
- **Propose Mental Health Days:** Suggest the introduction of mental health days as part of the organization's leave policy, emphasizing the importance of mental health care as part of overall health.

Creating an Open Environment for Mental Health

- **Encourage Open Dialogue:** Foster an environment where discussing mental health openly is encouraged and free from stigma. This can be achieved by participating in or organizing workshops and training sessions focused on mental health awareness.
- **Support Platforms for Discussion:** Help establish regular forums or support groups within your organization where colleagues can share their experiences and strategies for managing stress in a supportive atmosphere.

Managing Client Expectations

- **Educate about Boundaries:** Work toward setting clear expectations with clients regarding your availability and reasonable turnaround times. This involves educating clients on the importance of respecting work–life balance for their legal counsel.
- **Develop Communication Guidelines:** Assist in creating guidelines that outline how to communicate boundaries to clients effectively, ensuring they understand the importance of these policies for maintaining the quality of work and well-being of their legal team.

Leading by Example

- **Model Healthy Practices:** As you progress in your career, demonstrate the importance of maintaining a healthy work–life balance. Share your own practices and strategies for managing professional demands and personal well-being.
- **Support from Leadership:** Encourage senior members of your organization to lead by example. Their visible support for mental health initiatives and adherence to work–life balance policies can set a positive precedent for the entire organization.

Advocating for policy changes that support mental health and work–life balance is a proactive step toward cultivating a healthier work culture in business law. It involves challenging the status quo, promoting flexibility, fostering open discussions about mental health, setting healthy boundaries with clients, and leading by example. By contributing to these efforts, you can help shift the professional environment to one where success is measured not just by professional achievements, but by the well-being and satisfaction of its practitioners.

Navigating Healthcare Law and Innovation: Ariella Cohen Coleman

Healthcare Attorney, Nelson Hardiman

Ariella Cohen Coleman brings a distinctive blend of regulatory insight and healthcare law expertise to her role at Nelson Hardiman, where she specializes in navigating the complex landscape of health care and life sciences. With a background that marries deep regulatory knowledge with a strong foundation in healthcare policy, Ariella has established herself as a go-to attorney for clients facing the intricacies of FDA regulations and healthcare compliance. Her journey into law was driven by a personal connection to health care, sparked by her father's cancer diagnosis and further fueled by her own health challenges during law school. These experiences not only shaped her professional focus but also instilled a profound commitment to improving access to care and advancing healthcare innovation.

Navigating the FDA Landscape

Ariella's journey through the intricacies of FDA regulation has been marked by notable achievements, particularly her involvement in the Over-the-Counter (OTC) Drug Monograph Reform legislation. Her work in this area exemplifies the critical role attorneys play in shaping healthcare policy and ensuring that new and innovative products can reach the market. By offering technical assistance on draft legislation and engaging in negotiations with Congress, the FDA, and other stakeholders, Ariella contributed to crafting a legal framework that not only addresses current healthcare needs but also anticipates future challenges. This legislative effort was crucial in modernizing the OTC monograph system, thereby facilitating the introduction of safe and effective OTC products to consumers.

Navigating the FDA landscape requires a deep understanding of both the regulatory environment and the scientific advancements driving healthcare innovation. Ariella's approach to this complex field is rooted in her ability to bridge these two worlds. She has worked closely with clients developing cutting-edge diagnostics and therapeutic technologies, guiding them through a regulatory maze that often seems designed for a different era of health care. Her expertise has been particularly valuable in the context of telemedicine and direct-to-consumer services, areas that have seen rapid growth and transformation in recent years. In these cases, Ariella's strategic guidance has enabled clients to navigate regulatory uncertainties and bring their innovative solutions to the patients who need them.

Ariella's work extends beyond merely responding to existing regulations. She actively engages in the dialogue around regulatory reform, advocating for changes that will allow the healthcare sector to fully embrace technological advancements. Her efforts are driven by a recognition of the potential for innovation to improve patient care and a commitment to ensuring that regulatory frameworks support rather than hinder this progress. Through her work, Ariella not only addresses the immediate legal needs of her clients but also contributes to shaping a more dynamic and responsive regulatory environment for the healthcare industry.

A Personal Touch to Healthcare Law

Her journey into the legal field was significantly influenced by her father's cancer diagnosis, a pivotal moment that steered her toward a career focused on healthcare law. This personal connection to healthcare challenges has been a driving force in her pursuit of legal solutions that improve access to care and foster innovation in the healthcare industry. Ariella's own health journey, marked by chronic conditions and the quest for wellness, has imbued her with a unique perspective on the importance of well-being in achieving professional success. This belief led her to found The Wellness Esquire, an initiative aimed at shifting the legal culture to recognize the integral link between well-being and success. Through this platform, Ariella advocates for a more holistic approach to the practice of law, one that values the health and wellness of legal professionals as essential to their effectiveness and fulfillment in their careers.

Through her work, Ariella seeks not only to address the legal and regulatory challenges of the healthcare industry but also to inspire a cultural shift toward a more sustainable, health-oriented approach to the practice of law. ”

Building Support Networks

The support networks you build can significantly influence both your professional journey and personal well-being. These networks, encompassing mentors, colleagues, family, and friends, serve as pillars that sustain and propel you forward through challenges and successes alike. This section delves into the crucial role these support systems play in a lawyer's life and offers insights into nurturing these connections for a balanced and rewarding career.

Importance of Professional and Personal Support

Navigating the complexities of a career in business law requires more than just legal acumen and hard work. The support from professional peers and personal circles adds a vital dimension to your career, offering guidance, encouragement, and a sense of community that enriches your professional journey.

Professional Support: Mentors and Colleagues

Mentors and colleagues provide invaluable insights, advice, and opportunities for growth. A mentor, with their wealth of experience, can guide you through the intricacies of the legal profession, offering advice on career decisions, skill development, and navigating the workplace dynamics. They serve as a sounding board for your ideas and concerns, helping you to refine your professional path.

Actionable Steps

- **Seek Out a Mentor:** Actively look for mentorship opportunities within your firm or through professional associations. Do not hesitate to reach out to seasoned professionals whose career paths resonate with you.
- **Engage with Colleagues:** Build meaningful connections with your peers through collaboration on projects, participation in professional development activities, and social events. These relationships can offer support, friendship, and mutual professional growth.

Personal Support: Family and Friends

Although professional networks are invaluable, the role of family and friends in providing emotional support and a sense of balance cannot be overstated. They offer a respite from the pressures of the legal profession, reminding you of life's broader spectrum beyond work.

Actionable Steps

- **Communicate Openly:** Share your career aspirations, successes, and challenges with your loved ones. Open communication helps in building understanding and support for your professional commitments.
- **Prioritize Quality Time:** Despite a busy schedule, make time for family and friends. These moments of connection are crucial for maintaining a support system that sustains you through the ups and downs of your legal career.

Building robust support networks, both within and outside the legal profession, is crucial for navigating the challenges and opportunities of a career in business law. These networks not only provide guidance and encouragement but also contribute to a sense of belonging and well-being that is essential for long-term success and fulfillment.

Networking for Support

Networking for support is a critical strategy for attorneys looking to build both their professional careers and personal well-being. By engaging with professional associations and social groups, lawyers can create a robust support network that benefits them in various aspects of their lives. Here are some actionable steps and considerations for leveraging these networks effectively.

Engage with Professional Associations

- **Choose Relevant Associations:** Select professional associations that align with your area of expertise in business law, as well as those that cater to broader legal interests or personal values. This could include local bar associations, industry-specific groups, or affinity groups.
- **Active Participation:** Simply being a member is not enough. Actively participate in meetings, committees, and events. Volunteering for leadership roles or project initiatives can elevate your profile within these associations and deepen your connections.
- **Seek Mentorship Opportunities:** Many associations offer formal mentorship programs. Engaging as both a mentor and mentee can expand your support network, provide valuable guidance, and foster meaningful professional relationships.

Leverage Social Groups

- **Join Interest-Based Groups:** Beyond strictly professional networks, join groups based on hobbies, interests, or community service. These groups can offer respite from the pressures of law practice and opportunities to connect with individuals on a more personal level.
- **Legal Community Meetups:** Participate in informal gatherings or meetups with fellow lawyers outside of work settings. These can provide a relaxed environment to share experiences, offer support, and discuss challenges unique to the legal profession.

Build Personal and Professional Support Networks

- **Professional Support:** Your network should include a mix of peers, mentors, and legal experts who can offer advice, share opportunities, and provide insights on navigating the complexities of business law.
- **Personal Support:** Equally important are those who offer emotional support, understand the stresses of legal work, and can provide a listening ear or a much-needed break from professional responsibilities.

Utilizing Digital Platforms

- **Online Communities:** Take advantage of online forums, LinkedIn groups, and social media platforms tailored to legal professionals. These can be invaluable resources for advice, support, and staying informed about industry trends and events.
- **Virtual Events and Webinars:** Many associations and groups host virtual events that can be more accessible for busy attorneys. These events can be excellent opportunities for learning and networking without the need for travel.

Foster Reciprocal Relationships

- **Give Back:** Networking is a two-way street. Offer your expertise, support, and time to others in your network. This could involve providing informal mentorship, sharing job leads, or volunteering for initiatives within your associations or groups.

By strategically engaging with professional associations and social groups, attorneys can build a supportive network that enriches both their professional and personal lives. This approach not only aids in career development but also contributes to a more balanced and fulfilling career in business law.

From Big Law to Founding BBS: Heidi Bradley's Journey of Resilience and Innovation

Founding Attorney, Bradley Bernstein Sands

Heidi Bradley's journey into the legal profession began with a clear focus and determination that led her to become the founding partner of Bradley Bernstein Sands (BBS). Her academic path took her to Stanford Law School, a decision driven by her ambition to excel in the field of business law. Despite the financial challenges, Heidi chose Stanford for its prestige and the doors it would open in the legal profession, particularly in big law firms where she aspired to practice. This choice set the foundation for her legal career, emphasizing the importance of aiming for the highest standards from the outset.

After law school, Heidi joined an AmLaw 25 firm, where she honed her skills in commercial litigation. Her work, especially on significant antitrust and securities matters, not only deepened her expertise but also her passion for understanding businesses and their challenges. This period was marked by long hours and demanding work, which, while rewarding, sparked Heidi's contemplation on the pace of her professional life. Her desire for a change led her to Lane Powell, a move that offered her a semblance of work–life balance and the opportunity to further establish her reputation in the legal community. It was here that Heidi became an equity partner and co-led the litigation department, achievements that underscored her professional growth and leadership abilities.

However, the pivotal moment in Heidi's career came with the realization that she sought not just success but fulfillment in her work. This reflection prompted her decision to leave the security of established firms and venture into founding BBS. Her vision for the new firm was clear: to create a practice that not only excelled in business law but also offered a balanced life for its employees and a culture rooted in shared values and mutual respect. This bold step was a testament to Heidi's belief in self-determination and her commitment to building something that aligned with her ideals of what a law firm could be.

Legal Expertise and Approach

Heidi's approach to legal challenges is distinguished by her broad expertise and a keen focus on understanding her clients' businesses. As a general commercial litigator with a significant portion of her practice dedicated to antitrust issues, she has successfully navigated complex legal landscapes for her clients. Heidi's commitment to her clients goes beyond the surface level; she immerses herself in their business, aiming to identify and address their pain points. This deep understanding enables her to spot issues that may not be immediately apparent, ensuring that her clients receive comprehensive legal support.

One of the defining aspects of Heidi's practice is her ability to maintain a broad view while dealing with specialized areas of law. Her work in antitrust litigation, for example, has not only remained a constant in her career but has also allowed her to be recognized as a leading lawyer in this field. Despite the challenges of starting her own firm, Heidi's reputation and the relationships she built over the years have continued to attract significant antitrust cases. This success is a testament to her expertise and the trust clients place in her abilities.

Advice for Lawyers and Law Students

Heidi emphasizes the transformative power of saying "yes" to opportunities, a principle that has guided her own career trajectory. She credits much of her success to early experiences where she was thrust into challenging situations, such as arguing motions before a judge as a relatively junior associate. These opportunities not only built her credibility but also taught her the value of preparation and resilience. For Heidi, the willingness to take on tasks outside one's comfort zone is crucial. She advises young lawyers and law students to embrace opportunities, even when they entail fear and uncertainty. According to her, this mindset not only accelerates professional growth but also opens doors to further opportunities.

Beyond just saying "yes," Heidi stresses the importance of sponsorship over mentorship. In her view, having someone who not only advises you but actively advocates for you and places you in positions to succeed is invaluable. This form of support was pivotal in her early career and is something she now seeks to provide to others. For those looking to advance in their careers, finding and cultivating relationships with sponsors can be a key strategy. It's about more than just doing good work; it's about being seen doing good work and having that work recognized and rewarded by those in positions to help you grow.

When it comes to what Heidi looks for in associates, the qualities are clear: a willingness to tackle challenges head-on and an openness to learning from each experience. She seeks individuals who demonstrate a readiness to step into the unknown, backed by a commitment to thorough preparation and a drive to improve with each new task. For Heidi, perfection is not the expectation; rather, it's the courage to try and the determination to do one's best that matter most. This approach not only fosters personal and professional development but also contributes to a culture of growth and resilience within her firm.

Managing Career Transitions

Career transitions are not only inevitable but often necessary for personal growth and fulfillment. Whether it's taking a deliberate pause from work, pivoting to a new legal specialty, or planning for retirement, navigating these changes thoughtfully is crucial.

Approaching Sabbaticals and Breaks

Sabbaticals and breaks offer invaluable opportunities for personal development, rejuvenation, and exploring interests outside the realm of law. For business lawyers, these periods can be strategically used to enhance both personal life and professional capabilities. Here's how to make the most out of sabbaticals and breaks:

Planning Ahead

- Start planning early to ensure financial stability and smooth transition back to work. Inform your employer or clients well in advance, and delegate responsibilities to avoid any work disruptions during your absence.

Setting Clear Objectives

- Define what you aim to achieve, whether it's acquiring a new skill, volunteering, traveling, or spending quality time with family. Clear objectives help in making your time off more fulfilling and purposeful.

Professional Development

- Consider dedicating part of your break to professional development through online courses, attending workshops, or getting involved in pro bono work to keep your skills sharp and stay updated on legal trends.

Reconnecting with Personal Interests

- Use this time to pursue hobbies or interests you've been putting off. Engaging in activities unrelated to law can provide a fresh perspective and contribute to your overall well-being.

Planning for Reentry

- Before your break ends, prepare for a smooth transition back into professional life. Update your knowledge of any significant legal developments that occurred during your absence and reconnect with colleagues and clients.

Effectively utilizing sabbaticals and breaks not only contribute to your personal growth but can also enhance your professional life, making you a more rounded, energized, and focused lawyer upon your return.

Career Pivots

Making a career pivot within the realm of business law can open new avenues for professional fulfillment and better alignment with personal goals and lifestyle preferences. Here are strategic steps for smoothly navigating such transitions.

Self-Assessment

- Begin with a thorough self-assessment to clarify your interests, strengths, and what you seek in your new role. Consider how a pivot aligns with your long-term career objectives and personal aspirations.

Research and Education

- Conduct detailed research on the new area of law or role you're interested in. Identify the skills and knowledge required and pursue relevant education or certifications to bridge any gaps.

Leverage Existing Skills

- Highlight transferable skills that are valuable across different legal specializations, such as analytical thinking, negotiation, and client management. This demonstrates your adaptability and potential to contribute effectively in a new domain.

Networking

- Engage with professionals already working in the desired field through legal associations, seminars, and social platforms. Networking provides insights into the new area and can uncover opportunities that might not be advertised publicly.

Mentorship

- Seek mentors who have successfully navigated similar transitions. Their guidance can offer practical advice, emotional support, and perhaps even introductions to key contacts in your target field.

Strategic Volunteering or Pro Bono Work

- Gain hands-on experience in your new area of interest through volunteering or pro bono projects. This not only builds your portfolio but also demonstrates your commitment and passion for the field.

Communicate Your Transition

- Clearly communicate your transition plan to your current employer, if applicable, to ensure a smooth departure. Be transparent about your reasons for the change, maintaining professionalism and gratitude for the opportunities provided.

Be Patient and Persistent

- Career pivots often require time and patience. Stay committed to your new path, be open to learning, and adapt as necessary. Success in a new area of law or a different role might not be immediate but can be incredibly rewarding in the long run.

Navigating a career pivot within business law with strategic planning, continuous learning, and a strong network can lead to renewed professional enthusiasm and alignment with personal life goals.

Retirement Planning

For business lawyers, retirement planning is a crucial aspect of career strategy, encompassing both financial readiness and the transition into fulfilling post-legal activities. Here are some key considerations.

Financial Preparedness

- Start planning early by contributing to retirement savings plans and seeking advice from financial advisors to ensure a stable financial future.
- Consider the lifestyle you envision for your retirement and plan your savings accordingly to support it.

Exploring Post-Legal Interests

- Retirement offers an opportunity to pursue interests and activities you may not have had time for during your active legal career. Start exploring these interests while you're still working to make the transition smoother.
- Consider roles in teaching, consulting, or volunteer work within the legal community to stay engaged and contribute your expertise.

Transition Strategies

- Gradually reduce your workload and responsibilities as you approach retirement to adjust to the change in pace.

- Network with retired colleagues or join professional organizations focused on retired professionals to gain insights and support during your transition.

By integrating financial planning with personal fulfillment strategies, retirement can become not just an end to work but a new, vibrant phase of life, rich with opportunities for growth, learning, and giving back.

Personal Fulfillment and Happiness

In the pursuit of a successful career in law, it's easy to lose sight of what personal success and happiness mean on an individual level. The legal profession, with its inherent pressures and demands, often pushes lawyers to measure success by external benchmarks, such as career milestones, financial gains, or recognition by peers. However, true fulfillment extends beyond the confines of professional achievements. This section invites lawyers to reflect on their own definitions of success and happiness, encouraging a more holistic approach to personal and professional satisfaction. It explores how aligning career aspirations with personal values and engaging in activities that foster happiness can lead to a more balanced and rewarding life. Through this introspective journey, lawyers can discover practices and pursuits that not only enhance their well-being but also enrich their professional endeavors, leading to a deeply fulfilling career in law.

Personal Values and Professional Alignment

Understanding Personal Values

Begin by identifying your core values. What principles guide your life and work? Integrity, advocacy for justice, work–life balance, or continual learning might be among these foundational beliefs. Recognizing these values provides a compass for making career decisions that resonate with your true self.

Aligning Career with Values

Reflect on whether your current practice or the direction you're heading in business law aligns with these values. For example, if you value social impact, does your work contribute to societal change? Alignment creates a sense of purpose and satisfaction in your daily tasks.

Setting Personal and Professional Goals

Defining Success on Your Terms

Success might mean achieving work–life harmony, making a significant impact in a niche area of business law, or simply finding joy in your legal practice every day. Set goals that reflect these personal benchmarks rather than society's or the profession's expectations.

Short-Term and Long-Term Goals

Establish a mix of short-term achievements and long-term aspirations. This could range from completing a certification that broadens your expertise to setting up a practice that reflects your values and serves the community in a meaningful way.

Reflecting and Reassessing

Periodic Self-Reflection

Regularly take stock of your career and personal growth. Are you moving closer to your definition of success? What adjustments can you make to better align your career trajectory with your personal values and goals?

Reassessing Goals

Life's constants are change and growth. As you evolve, so too will your definitions of success and fulfillment. Be open to reassessing and adjusting your goals as necessary, ensuring they continue to reflect your values and aspirations.

Embracing Success in Its Many Forms

Recognize and celebrate success in its many forms. This might mean appreciating the balance you've maintained between work and family, the pro bono work that's changed lives, or the mentorship you've provided to younger attorneys.

By defining success on their own terms, lawyers can forge a path in business law that achieves not only professional excellence but also personal fulfillment. This holistic approach to career development ensures that your professional achievements are in harmony with your personal well-being and life's ambitions.

Creating a Personal Development Plan

Creating a Personal Development Plan is a proactive strategy for lawyers aiming to align their personal and professional growth with their long-term goals for work–life balance and personal fulfillment. This plan acts as a roadmap, guiding lawyers through the evolving landscapes of their careers and lives. Here's how to create and implement an effective personal development plan:

Defining Your Objectives

- **Personal Goals:** Reflect on what you value most in your personal life and how you envision your ideal work–life balance. Consider aspects like family, health, hobbies, and any other personal interests that contribute to your overall well-being.

- **Professional Ambitions:** Clearly define your career objectives, whether they involve ascending to a partnership, specializing in a niche area of business law, or achieving a better balance between work and personal life.

Assessing Current State

- **Skills Inventory:** Take stock of your current skills, expertise, and areas where you seek improvement. This includes legal knowledge, soft skills like communication and leadership, and any new areas of law you wish to explore.
- **Work–Life Balance Check:** Evaluate how well your current work arrangement supports your personal well-being and family life. Identify areas of conflict or imbalance that need addressing.

Setting Specific Goals

- **SMART Goals:** Make your objectives Specific, Measurable, Achievable, Relevant, and Time-bound. For example, aiming to complete a specialist certification in business law within the next year is a SMART goal.
- **Balance-Focused Goals:** Include goals that specifically address improving work–life balance, such as dedicating uninterrupted time for family or personal hobbies each week.

Action Plan

- **Steps for Achievement:** Break down each goal into actionable steps. If your goal is to become a thought leader in your specialty, steps might include writing articles, speaking at conferences, and engaging on professional social platforms.
- **Timeline:** Assign realistic timelines to each action step, ensuring there's a clear path to achieving your goals within the desired time frame.

Resources and Support

- **Identify Resources:** Determine what resources you'll need to achieve your goals, including educational programs, mentorship, networking opportunities, and personal support systems.
- **Seek Support:** Engage your professional network, family, and friends in your plan, seeking their support and guidance. This might involve finding a mentor, joining a study group, or involving your family in setting aside personal time.

Regular Review and Adaptation

- **Periodic Review:** Schedule regular reviews of your personal development plan, ideally every quarter. This allows you to assess progress, celebrate achievements, and make adjustments as needed.
- **Flexibility:** Be prepared to adapt your plan in response to new opportunities, challenges, or changes in your personal life. Flexibility is key to aligning your career with your evolving personal aspirations.

Creating a Personal Development Plan empowers lawyers to take charge of their career trajectory and personal growth. By aligning professional ambitions with personal well-being, lawyers can forge a fulfilling path that respects both their career aspirations and their life outside of work.

Navigating Ethics, Compliance, and Diversity: Insights from Monica Lopez Reinmiller

Head of Global Ethics & Compliance, Assistant General Counsel, Panasonic

Monica Lopez Reinmiller stands at the forefront of legal compliance and risk management, bringing over fifteen years of experience to her role as the Head of Global Ethics & Compliance and Assistant General Counsel at Panasonic. Her journey in the legal profession is marked by a deep commitment to ethics, having navigated complex compliance landscapes across a variety of sectors, including automotive, telecommunications, chemicals, technology, and business outsource services. Monica's educational background, with a JD from California Western School of Law and an MBA from Xavier University, has provided a strong foundation for her distinguished career. Licensed to practice in both California and Washington, she also holds a certification as a compliance and ethics professional, highlighting her specialized expertise in this area.

In her current role, Monica leads a multifaceted global compliance function that encompasses everything from internal investigations and ethical conduct training to enforcement matters and legal compliance risk assessments. Her work ensures that Panasonic operates within the bounds of legal and ethical standards, safeguarding the company's reputation and operational integrity. This role involves a significant amount of collaboration with various departments within the company, including procurement and contract negotiation teams, to address and mitigate potential risks related to trade compliance, conflicts of interest, and anti-bribery laws.

Beyond her professional responsibilities, Monica is deeply invested in fostering diversity and inclusion within the legal community. She is an active member of the Washington State Bar, contributing to the Diversity Committee and the Corporate Counsel Section's Executive Committee. Her commitment to social justice extends to her leadership of the in-house T-Mobile Pro Bono Committee and participation in the T-Mobile Legal Department's Diversity Inclusion & Equity Task Force. Through her pro bono work, Monica advocates for racial justice and equality, embodying her belief in the power of the legal profession to effect positive change in society.

Operational Aspects of Corporate Compliance

Monica's role requires her to navigate the intricate dynamics of corporate compliance, particularly in her interactions with procurement and contract negotiation teams. Her team's work is crucial in identifying and mitigating risks associated with trade compliance, conflicts of interest, and anti-bribery laws. "Our daily operations involve close collaboration with various departments to ensure that our transactions not only advance our business objectives but also comply with legal and ethical standards," Monica explains. This collaborative effort is essential in maintaining the integrity and reputation of the company in a complex global market.

The relationship between legal and procurement functions has evolved significantly, especially in response to the COVID-19 pandemic. The pandemic brought unprecedented supply chain disruptions, highlighting the need for increased engagement between these departments. Monica notes, "The pandemic tested our adaptability and forced us to rethink our strategies. Our legal team worked more closely with procurement to navigate the challenges, ensuring that our contracts and negotiations reflected the new realities of the market." This period of intense collaboration led to the development of more robust contract negotiation teams within procurement functions, a change that has enhanced the company's resilience against similar future disruptions.

Monica's approach underscores the importance of a proactive and collaborative legal strategy in today's business environment. By working hand in hand with procurement and other departments, her team plays a pivotal role in safeguarding the company against legal risks while ensuring that business operations remain uninterrupted and aligned with ethical standards. This synergy between legal and procurement functions not only addresses immediate challenges but also sets a foundation for long-term success in a rapidly changing global landscape.

Prioritization of Diversity in Legal Representation

Monica emphasizes the increasing importance of DEI in the legal profession, particularly in the selection of outside counsel by corporations. "As companies diversify their employee population and leadership ranks, there's a parallel expectation for their legal representation to reflect similar diversity," she states. This shift is not just about optics; it is rooted in the understanding that diverse teams bring a wealth of perspectives that can lead to more informed and nuanced decision-making processes. Monica points out that this trend is largely driven by clients who recognize the value of diverse perspectives in navigating complex legal and ethical landscapes.

In addition to advocating for DEI, Monica highlights the essential skills for anyone considering a career in her area of law. "Issue spotting, analysis, and reaching a conclusion are the bedrock of effective legal advice," she explains. These skills are particularly crucial for in-house counsel, who often serve as risk advisors to their companies. Unlike in a law firm setting where the focus might be more on legal theory, in-house counsel need to quickly identify potential legal issues, analyze their implications for the business, and provide actionable advice. Monica stresses that this ability to think on one's feet and offer practical solutions is what makes an in-house counsel invaluable to their organization.

Her insights underscore the evolving role of in-house legal teams in today's corporate world. Not only are they expected to safeguard the company against legal risks, but they are also at the forefront of promoting and implementing DEI initiatives within the legal profession. Through her work, Monica exemplifies how in-house counsel can be both protectors and pioneers, steering their companies through complex legal terrains while championing the cause of diversity and inclusion. ”

Charting Your Path: From Professional Development to Business Development

The journey to building a successful legal career is deeply intertwined with developing both interpersonal and business acumen—skills that are foundational not just for professional development but also for navigating the apprenticeship model prevalent in law firms. The ability to identify what you want, assertively pursue opportunities, and cultivate the necessary experience underpins the early stages of a lawyer's growth. Yet, beyond these steps, the mastery of building and fostering relationships stands as the cornerstone of both personal development and subsequent business development within the legal profession.

In the initial phases of their careers, attorneys must focus on internal networking, building credibility, and enhancing visibility within their firms or organizations. This process is critical, as the legal field often adheres to an apprenticeship model where learning is hands-on and mentorship is key. Attorneys who fail to develop these essential interpersonal and business skills may find themselves at a disadvantage, unable to secure the mentorship and opportunities necessary to become proficient practitioners.

As attorneys progress, the focus shifts from internal development toward external business generation, leveraging the same skills of relationship building, strategic visibility, and credibility enhancement to attract clients. This evolution from professional to business development is not merely a shift in focus but a continuation of using foundational skills in a broader context. The abilities to identify opportunities, build relationships, and strategically position oneself become equally crucial in attracting clients and growing a practice.

This comprehensive approach to career development in law underscores the importance of early investment in both legal and soft skills. It highlights the interconnectedness of professional development and business development, emphasizing that the foundational skills acquired in the pursuit of legal excellence also pave the way for success in client acquisition and practice growth. Understanding this dynamic not only propels attorneys forward in their careers but ensures a fulfilling journey in the legal profession, marked by continuous learning, meaningful relationships, and the realization of professional and personal goals.

Discovering Your Career Aspirations

Navigating the early stages of a legal career often feels akin to charting unknown territories, where the myriad of paths and practice areas offer both opportunities and challenges. It is here, in this exploratory phase, that the foundation for a fulfilling legal career begins to solidify. Understanding and harnessing one's career aspirations are pivotal, necessitating a keen sense of exploration and reflection.

Embracing Exploration

In the evolving landscape of the legal profession, every stage of your career offers a unique opportunity for exploration and discovery. Whether you're in the early years of your journey or considering a change later in your career, embracing this phase of exploration is crucial for identifying the practice areas and roles that align with your interests and leverage your strengths. Within a law firm, the possibilities for gaining varied experience are extensive, encompassing everything from engaging in different practice groups to participating in pro bono projects or internal committees.

Strategies for Exploration within a Law Firm

- **Seek Varied Assignments:** Regardless of your career stage, actively seek to work on cases from diverse practice areas. This direct exposure is invaluable for understanding the nuances and day-to-day realities of various legal specialties.
- **Participate in Pro Bono Work:** Engage in pro bono projects offered by your firm. These opportunities are not only personally rewarding but also allow you to delve into areas of law that may not be part of your standard workload, offering a broader perspective.
- **Join Internal Committees or Groups:** Involvement in committees related to technology, diversity and inclusion, or professional development can broaden your understanding of the legal profession and firm operations. These groups offer a platform for contributing to meaningful change within your firm while exploring new interests.
- **Mentorship and Shadowing:** Regardless of where you are in your career, seek out mentors in areas of law that intrigue you. If possible, arrange shadowing opportunities to gain deeper insight into their daily practices and decision-making processes. Conversely, offering mentorship can also provide fresh perspectives and reinvigorate your passion for the law.
- **Attend Firm-Wide Training and CLEs:** Take advantage of all learning opportunities provided by your firm, including CLE and internal training

sessions. These resources can significantly widen your knowledge base and introduce you to new areas of law.

- **Networking within the Firm:** Build relationships across departments and practice areas. Informal conversations with colleagues at different career stages can offer valuable insights into their specialties and provide guidance on navigating your own career path.

By actively engaging in the breadth of experiences available within your law firm, you enrich your legal expertise and make informed decisions about the direction of your career. This period of exploration is a critical step in discovering where your true passions lie, guiding you toward a more fulfilling and rewarding career in law, regardless of your current stage.

George Fatheree's Vision: Bridging Law and Impact through Innovative Solutions

Fintech Founder, Social Impact Entrepreneur, Trailblazing Attorney

George Fatheree's journey in the legal profession is a testament to how positions of influence within prestigious law firms can be harnessed to champion social change. Early in his career, George faced a pivotal moment that shifted his focus toward more purposeful work. The discovery of his son's rare neurological disorder prompted a reevaluation of his professional path, steering him away from the demanding travel schedule of consulting toward roles that offered a broader social impact. This introspection led him to public education reform, a field deeply personal to him, given his own educational background. However, his transition into the legal world was where he found a unique opportunity to blend his passion for social justice with his professional skills.

Upon joining a major law firm, George initially viewed his tenure as a short-term commitment, a means to hone his legal skills. Yet, he quickly realized the potential of leveraging the firm's resources, network, and intellectual capital to support causes close to his heart. This epiphany was not just about the logistical support a law firm could offer but also about the profound impact that skilled legal advocacy could have on social issues. Through pro bono work, board service, and volunteering, George was able to contribute significantly to various causes, from securing reparations for survivors of the Holocaust to supporting Black cultural and arts institutions. His dedication to pro bono work underscored the importance of building a strong foundation in legal skills and experience to effectively address critical social issues.

George's tenure in big law, much longer than he initially anticipated, was marked by a conscious decision to use his position for good. This decision was rooted in a belief that the practice of law could be a powerful tool for social change when aligned with purposeful intention. His work, particularly in cases like representing the Bruce family, exemplified how legal expertise could be used to rectify historical injustices and contribute to broader societal change. Through his journey, George Fatheree demonstrates how lawyers can leverage their positions within the legal profession not just to advance their careers but to make a meaningful impact on the world around them.

The Path to Purposeful Mentorship

George's perspective on mentorship and sponsorship within the legal profession sheds light on the nuanced dynamics that can significantly influence a lawyer's career trajectory. George distinguishes between mentorship and sponsorship, noting that while both are crucial, they serve different roles. A mentor provides guidance, shares knowledge, and offers advice to help navigate the complexities of the legal field. In contrast, a sponsor is someone who not only advises but also actively advocates for and invests in the mentee's career advancement. George was fortunate to have a sponsor early in his career who deliberately created opportunities for him, provided feedback, and ensured his accomplishments were recognized within the firm. This relationship underscored the transformative impact a sponsor can have, particularly in pivotal moments of a lawyer's journey.

George believes that for mentorship to be truly beneficial, it needs to be genuine and involve a mutual investment from both parties. George's approach to forming these relationships was based on a foundation of authenticity and a willingness to contribute. He shared stories of how he demonstrated his value to potential mentors, such as engaging in pro bono work that aligned with his mentors' interests or offering assistance in areas where they were passionate. This not only helped in building meaningful connections but also in fostering a sense of community and shared purpose within the firm.

George advocates for the idea that mentorship is a two-way street. He insists that mentees should also consider what they can bring to the table. Drawing on his own experiences, George highlights how he sought to understand his mentors' goals and challenges, and how he could support them. This approach not only enriched his learning experience but also solidified the relationships, making them more reciprocal and rewarding. Through his journey, George exemplifies how a thoughtful and intentional approach to mentorship and sponsorship can not only advance one's career but also contribute to a more inclusive and supportive legal community.

The Intersection of Passion and Profession: The Bruce's Beach Case

George's career has been marked by a commitment to using his legal expertise for social justice, a commitment that found its most profound expression in the Bruce's Beach case. This case wasn't just a legal challenge; it was a historic moment where George's passion for Black social justice and his expertise in real estate law converged to correct a century-old wrong. Representing the heirs of Charles and Willa Bruce, African American entrepreneurs who were unjustly deprived of their property through racially motivated eminent domain in the early twentieth century, George embarked on a three-year legal battle. His efforts culminated in the first-ever return of land to a Black family under such circumstances in U.S. history. This victory was not only a testament to George's legal acumen but also to his deep commitment to rectifying historical injustices.

Key to the success of the Bruce's Beach case was George's ability to leverage his network and relationships outside the immediate sphere of real estate law. His work across various sectors and his involvement in pro bono cases built a diverse network of contacts and allies. This network proved invaluable, providing insights and support that were crucial to navigating the complex legal, historical, and societal issues surrounding the case. George's approach underscores the importance of building and maintaining relationships across different fields, highlighting how such connections can amplify the impact of legal work, especially in cases that intersect with broader social issues.

George's involvement in the Bruce's Beach case exemplifies his belief in the power of intentionality and deliberate action in achieving career goals and making a tangible social impact. He views his career not as a series of random opportunities but as a purposeful journey toward using his skills and position to effect change. This case, among others, illustrates how George's strategic choices in pro bono work and board service, although sometimes challenging, have significantly accelerated his trajectory toward making meaningful contributions to society.

Building Community and Inclusivity in Law Firms

George's motto, "get your money's worth," reflects his advice to prioritize finding places that offer the best training and experience possible. He argues that the value of a legal career isn't just in the prestige or the salary but in the opportunities it provides for learning, growth, and impact. George encourages lawyers to follow up with coffee meetings and inquire about mentor relationships at potential firms to gauge if a place is a good fit. This proactive approach to career planning is aimed at ensuring that lawyers invest their time and efforts in environments that not only advance their professional skills but also align with their values and goals for social change.

George shares how creating inclusive opportunities for connection and support can significantly enhance the work environment, particularly for minority attorneys. In the current hybrid work landscape, where physical presence in the office is less common, George stresses the need for law firms to be intentional about fostering a sense of belonging and inclusivity. This involves not just formal diversity and inclusion initiatives but also creating spaces for authentic connections and support networks among attorneys. Through his own experiences, George illustrates how such communities can empower attorneys to navigate the challenges of the legal profession while contributing to a more equitable and inclusive industry.

Revolutionizing Home Ownership with ORO Impact

George's journey into the fintech space with the launch of financial technology company ORO Impact represents a significant leap toward addressing the wealth gap through innovative means. Recognizing the pivotal role of homeownership in wealth creation for most Americans, George identified a critical barrier: the challenge of accumulating sufficient funds for a down payment. This insight led to the creation of ORO Impact, a social impact venture designed to revolutionize access to down payment assistance, thereby dramatically increasing homeownership rates. The company partners with employers to offer their employees loans for down payments on homes, a strategy that not only benefits employees by making homeownership more accessible but also provides employers with a potent tool for attracting and retaining talent.

George believes deeply in the transformative power of homeownership, not just as a means of wealth accumulation but as a foundation for achieving a range of positive life outcomes, including better education, health, and general well-being. By facilitating access to homeownership, ORO Impact aims to make a profound impact on closing the wealth gap, one family at a time. George's venture into fintech with ORO Impact exemplifies his commitment to leveraging his expertise and resources to create equitable outcomes for all, further solidifying his role as a trailblazer in the intersection of law, social justice, and now, financial technology. ”

Reflecting on Experiences

Every role—from internships and clerkships to positions held in the midst of your career—offers invaluable insights for personal and professional growth. This is equally true for those contemplating a career change within the law. Reflecting on these experiences is crucial for anyone looking to refine their career direction, ensuring alignment with both personal interests and professional strengths, regardless of their career stage.

Leveraging Diverse Legal Experiences

Whether you're in the early stages of your career or considering a pivot to a new area of law, each experience is a building block for your career. For those exploring a change:

- **Engage Fully and Reflect:** Engage in your current role with a mindset geared toward learning and observation. Reflect on the aspects of your work that you find most fulfilling and those that you do not.
- **Seek Varied Experiences:** If possible, seek assignments across different practice areas or volunteer for pro bono projects outside your usual scope. This can provide clarity on what legal fields might align better with your evolving interests and skills.
- **Evaluate Interpersonal Dynamics:** Pay close attention to the types of people you interact with in different areas of law—clients, colleagues, and mentors. Consider which interactions energize you and which feel draining, as this can be a significant factor in career satisfaction.

For Those Considering a Career Change

Making a career change within the legal field requires introspection and strategic planning. Consider the following:

- **Assess Your Current Role:** Reflect on your current position and practice area. What aspects do you enjoy, and what are you seeking to change? Is it the subject matter, the client base, or the work–life balance?
- **Explore New Areas:** Utilize CLEs, seminars, and networking events to explore new legal fields. These can offer insights into the day-to-day realities of different practice areas.
- **Consider Work–Life Integration:** Reflect on how the demands of potential new areas of law align with your personal preferences and lifestyle. Each area of law comes with its own set of expectations and pressures, which should align with your work and life balance goals.

Refining Career Direction

Whether early in your career or contemplating a shift, reflecting on your experiences is key to navigating your path in the legal profession:

- **Identify Patterns:** Look for patterns in your work that consistently engage you. This could be specific types of legal problems, client interactions, or the pace and style of work.
- **Evaluate Alignment with Personal Values:** Consider how different areas of law align with your values and the impact you wish to make. This alignment can be a powerful motivator and source of satisfaction.
- **Adaptability and Preferences:** Reflect on how the workflow and pace in various areas of law fit with your personal work style and life. Understanding your preferences can guide you toward a more fulfilling career path.

Reflecting on your experiences, whether you're just starting out or considering a change, is more than a professional exercise—it's a journey of self-discovery. By taking into account how you enjoy working with the types of people typical to different areas of law, how the work itself resonates with you, and whether the workflow aligns with your personal preferences, you can make informed decisions that guide you toward a fulfilling career that harmonizes with both your professional aspirations and personal life.

Positioning for Success

Positioning for success within the legal profession requires a nuanced understanding of the delicate balance between honing one's craft and cultivating the relationships that will propel a career forward. This intricate dance between developing legal expertise and interpersonal acumen is not just beneficial but essential for those aiming to carve out a successful path in law. As attorneys navigate their careers, the ability to strategically position themselves—by developing a broad set of relevant skills, establishing a strong professional reputation, engaging in thoughtful career planning, and embracing thought leadership—becomes a critical determinant of their success.

The journey of a legal professional is marked by the continuous expansion of one's skill set, not only in legal knowledge but also in the soft skills that facilitate effective communication and relationship building. These skills are the bedrock upon which attorneys can build credibility and visibility, both within their organizations and in the broader legal community. As the focus of one's career shifts from mastering the intricacies of law to generating business and attracting clients, the importance of strategic positioning becomes ever more apparent. It is through this lens that we explore the multifaceted strategies that enable attorneys to not only excel in their current roles but also lay the groundwork for future opportunities, ensuring a career that is not only successful but also deeply rewarding.

Developing Relevant Skills

In the rapidly changing field of business law, success for attorneys now hinges on more than just legal expertise. Technological advancements and the shift toward remote work have reshaped the landscape, demanding a proactive approach to professional development. Attorneys must broaden their skill sets, embracing not only soft skills such as effective communication and negotiation but also technological proficiency to stay competitive and meet evolving client expectations.

Building and maintaining strong professional relationships is equally crucial, offering access to mentorship and growth opportunities. The onus is on attorneys to seek out and engage in learning opportunities beyond the traditional apprenticeship model, whether through formal training, mentorship, or practical experience. By doing so, they not only advance their careers but also contribute to the broader legal profession's evolution.

Essential Interpersonal Skills for Lawyers: Navigating the Apprenticeship Model

In the legal profession, deeply rooted in the apprenticeship model, the cultivation of interpersonal skills is not just beneficial—it's essential. Lawyers are expected to excel in the technical facets of their work and to master the art of communication, negotiation, and empathy. These skills are pivotal for unlocking mentorship opportunities, accessing valuable feedback, and nurturing relationships that are crucial for both learning and refining legal skills.

The Crucial Role of Interpersonal Skills in Legal Apprenticeship

Effective Communication

The foundation of a successful legal career is built on clear and effective communication. This skill allows lawyers to convey complex legal concepts in an accessible manner, ensuring their message is accurately received by clients, colleagues, and the courts. For junior lawyers, effective communication is the key to opening doors to meaningful interactions with senior attorneys, from whom they can gain invaluable insights, guidance, and constructive feedback.

Negotiation and Persuasion

Beyond the courtroom, the ability to negotiate and persuade is integral to every aspect of legal practice, including professional development. Lawyers who adeptly articulate their needs and aspirations are more likely to secure the mentorship and opportunities essential for their growth. This skill is equally important in the collaborative nature of legal work, where finding common ground and forging agreements are part of the daily routine.

Empathy and Understanding

Recognizing and empathizing with clients' needs is a recognized strength in legal practice, fostering trust and building lasting relationships. Similarly, showing empathy toward colleagues and mentors creates a supportive learning environment. Understanding the challenges and pressures faced by senior attorneys allows junior lawyers to approach them respectfully, facilitating the development of mentorship relationships.

Action Steps for Enhancing Interpersonal Skills

Seek Opportunities for Feedback and Practice

Engage in activities that offer practice and feedback on your communication and negotiation skills, such as mock trials, negotiation competitions, or legal seminars. Feedback from peers and mentors is crucial for identifying improvement areas and refining your approach.

Cultivate Relationships with Senior Attorneys

Actively build relationships with senior attorneys and partners by engaging in informal discussions, assisting on projects, or showing genuine interest in their career paths. These relationships are key to accessing apprenticeship opportunities and understanding how to navigate and contribute within the firm's hierarchy.

Participate in Professional Development Workshops

Enroll in workshops and seminars designed to enhance interpersonal skills, tailored specifically for lawyers. These programs address the unique challenges of communication and negotiation within the legal profession.

Embrace Empathy in Professional Interactions

Practice empathy in all professional interactions, actively listening, considering others' perspectives, and responding thoughtfully. Empathy improves relationships with clients and colleagues and deepens your understanding of the human elements in legal issues.

Broadening Understanding with Behavioral Insights and Persuasion Techniques

Understanding human behavior's psychological underpinnings can significantly impact legal practice. Exploring literature on psychology, persuasion, and human motivation offers deeper insights into decision-making processes, conflict navigation, and effective communication strategies. This knowledge is invaluable for developing approaches that resonate more personally with clients, judges, and opposing counsel, enhancing legal argument and negotiation effectiveness.

Personal Growth through Professional Coaching

Complementing theoretical knowledge with professional coaching provides a personalized development path. Coaches specializing in communication, negotiation, and leadership offer feedback and strategies applicable to daily legal tasks. This guidance helps lawyers refine their interpersonal skills, tackle specific challenges, and achieve career goals more effectively, leading to improved performance, client interaction confidence, and a more fulfilling legal career.

By prioritizing the development of essential interpersonal skills, lawyers can more effectively navigate the legal profession's apprenticeship model, securing the mentorship and experiences necessary for professional growth. These skills are foundational, not just complementary, to legal expertise, paving the way for a successful and rewarding legal career.

Legal Expertise: The Importance of a Proactive Approach

From the beginning of their careers, attorneys must proactively pursue their professional development, a responsibility that extends beyond any formal training provided by their firms or organizations. The legal field is constantly evolving, making it essential for every attorney to commit to lifelong learning and skill enhancement, regardless of their practice focus. This proactive approach involves seeking mentorship, participating in continuous legal education, and engaging in practical experiences. By taking charge of their professional growth, attorneys ensure they remain competent and competitive, ready to serve their clients effectively and contribute to the justice system.

Action Steps for Proactive Legal Expertise Development

Prioritize Continuous Learning

In the ever-evolving legal landscape, staying informed through CLE programs and specialized seminars is essential. These opportunities not only keep you abreast of the latest legal developments but also connect you with thought leaders in the field. They blend theoretical knowledge with practical insights, enhancing your legal acumen and approach to complex issues.

Actively Seek Mentorship

Mentorship is invaluable in the legal profession. Proactively seeking guidance from experienced attorneys enriches your practice with their knowledge and insights. Mentors provide advice on tackling legal challenges, offer case feedback, and share their professional wisdom. Remember, effective mentorship is based on mutual respect and a genuine desire to learn. Initiate conversations with potential mentors by asking focused questions to spark meaningful exchanges.

Embrace Feedback Opportunities

Constructive feedback is a cornerstone of professional growth. Actively pursue chances to have your work reviewed by seasoned attorneys, whether through formal evaluations or casual discussions. Approach feedback with an open mind, viewing it as a chance to refine your skills and enhance your legal understanding.

Contribute to Legal Writing and Research

Writing for legal journals, blogs, or firm publications deepens your grasp of specific legal matters. This process hones your analytical and communication skills, making you a more effective lawyer. Such contributions also increase your visibility, potentially opening doors to mentorship with attorneys who share your interests.

Engage in Pro Bono Work

Pro bono cases allow you to apply your legal knowledge to real-world scenarios, broadening your experience and serving the community. These cases often involve collaboration with more experienced lawyers, providing further mentorship opportunities and diversifying your legal expertise.

By embracing these proactive steps toward developing your legal expertise, you build a robust foundation for a rewarding legal career. This approach not only broadens your knowledge and skills but also ensures you're well prepared to tackle the complexities of legal practice with confidence and proficiency.

Technological Proficiency: Navigating the Digital Transformation in Law

In today's legal landscape, where technology plays a pivotal role in shaping the practice of law, maintaining technological proficiency is not just an advantage—it's a necessity. The rapid evolution of legal technology, from AI-powered legal research tools to blockchain for secure transactions, is revolutionizing how legal services are delivered. Being adept in these technologies enhances your efficiency, allowing you to handle tasks more swiftly and accurately, thereby freeing up time for more complex, high-value work. Moreover, leveraging technology can help you provide innovative solutions to your clients, setting you apart in a competitive market.

Action Steps for Enhancing Technological Proficiency

- **Engage in Continuous Learning:** Dedicate time to enroll in courses, webinars, or workshops that focus on emerging legal technologies. Many legal associations and tech companies offer training sessions designed to keep you up-to-date with the latest advancements in legal tech.
- **Hands-On Experimentation:** Actively experiment with different software tools and platforms. Whether it's a new case management system, document automation software, or AI for legal research, hands-on experience is invaluable. Consider setting up pilot projects within your firm to test these technologies in a controlled environment, allowing you to assess their impact on your practice.
- **Join Legal Tech Communities:** Become part of online forums or local groups dedicated to legal technology. These communities are great resources for learning about new tools, sharing experiences, and getting advice on integrating technology into your practice.

Integration of Skills: Crafting the Modern Attorney

The modern attorney is not defined solely by legal expertise, soft skills, or technological proficiency but by the integration of all these competencies. This comprehensive skill set enables you to navigate the complexities of today's legal environment effectively. It not only positions you for success in your current role but also prepares you for future challenges and opportunities. Moreover, this integration fosters the development of strong professional relationships, which are crucial for career advancement. By combining your legal knowledge with interpersonal skills and technological savvy, you become a more versatile and valuable asset to your firm and clients.

Action Steps for Skill Integration

- **Self-Assessment and Goal Setting:** Take time to reflect on your current skill set and identify areas for improvement. Consider how you can better integrate your legal knowledge, soft skills, and technological proficiency. Set specific, measurable goals for enhancing these areas and create a plan for achieving them.
- **Cross-Disciplinary Learning:** Actively seek out learning opportunities that bridge the gap between law, business, and technology. This could include attending conferences that cover the intersection of these fields, participating in interdisciplinary projects, or pursuing certifications that complement your legal expertise with business acumen or tech skills.
- **Networking and Collaboration:** Engage with professionals both within and outside the legal field. Networking with peers in business and technology can provide fresh perspectives and insights, enriching your understanding and approach to legal issues. Collaboration on projects can also offer practical experience in applying an integrated skill set to real-world challenges.

By committing to these action steps, you'll be well on your way to becoming a well-rounded attorney equipped for the demands of the modern legal profession. This holistic approach to professional development not only enhances your capabilities but also opens up new avenues for career growth and innovation in your practice.

Continuous Learning: Cara Esposito's Path from Legal Practice to Philanthropic Leadership

Executive Director of the Leonetti/O'Connell Family Foundation, Former Los Angeles County Deputy District Attorney

With a foundation in law, Cara Esposito has navigated a path that spans the realms of criminal justice, philanthropy, and education, showcasing the broad applicability of legal skills across sectors. Initially serving as a Los Angeles County Deputy District Attorney with a focus on Juvenile Prosecutions, Cara's professional journey took a significant turn when she transitioned to the role of Executive Director at the Leonetti/O'Connell Family Foundation.

Her academic background laid a solid foundation for her diverse career. Cara's pursuit of knowledge led her from obtaining a BA at Harvard University to a JD at Loyola Law School, reflecting her early dedication to understanding the intricacies of law. Recognizing the need for a deeper understanding of policy and administration, especially in the context of her evolving career goals, she furthered her education at USC's Price School of Public Policy. There, she earned both an MPA and a Doctorate in Policy Analysis and Planning. Her doctoral dissertation, which evaluated collaborative governance and the implementation of participative systems, particularly in service delivery, highlights her interest in the intersection of law, policy, and community well-being.

This educational journey has equipped Cara with a unique perspective that she brings to her current role. At the Leonetti/O'Connell Family Foundation, she has focused on funding innovative projects and initiatives aimed at improving the well-being of communities in Los Angeles County. Her transition from prosecuting juvenile cases to managing grants for community betterment is reflective of a broader vision: to utilize legal and policy expertise in crafting and supporting initiatives that have a tangible, positive impact on society. Through her work, Cara embodies the potential of legal professionals to drive change beyond the courtroom, influencing policy, education, and philanthropy.

The Importance of Emotional Equilibrium in Law and Leadership

Cara's experiences as a Deputy District Attorney and later as the Executive Director of a philanthropic foundation underscore the importance of maintaining emotional balance. This balance, Cara emphasizes, is crucial not only for effective decision making and advocacy but also for navigating the complexities of leadership. The ability to control one's emotional responses, she suggests, can significantly impact the outcomes of legal proceedings, the success of philanthropic initiatives, and the dynamics of team leadership.

Throughout her career, Cara encountered numerous situations that tested her emotional resilience. Transitioning from the structured environment of the DA's office to the fluid and often unpredictable world of philanthropy required a significant adjustment. In these moments, the importance of emotional equilibrium became strikingly clear. Cara notes that maintaining a steady emotional state allowed her to approach each challenge with clarity and purpose, ensuring that her decisions were driven by logic and strategic thinking rather than transient emotions. This approach was particularly beneficial in her philanthropic work, where the stakes involved the well-being of entire communities.

Cara's insights into emotional equilibrium extend beyond personal management to include its influence on team dynamics and leadership effectiveness. She observed that leaders who exhibit emotional stability tend to inspire greater confidence and loyalty among their teams. This stability creates a work environment where open communication, creativity, and innovation can thrive. For Cara, the ability to manage her emotions became a tool for fostering a positive and productive organizational culture, one that encouraged collaboration and collective problem solving.

In reflecting on her journey, Cara underscores the value of mindset and resilience in achieving professional success. The challenges she faced in her career transitions served as opportunities for growth, teaching her the importance of adaptability and emotional intelligence. By sharing her experiences, Cara provides a valuable lesson for aspiring legal professionals and leaders: that emotional equilibrium is not just a personal asset but a critical component of professional excellence and leadership. ”

Building a Professional Reputation

Building a professional reputation is a pivotal aspect of legal career development, acting as a catalyst for both internal progression within your firm and external recognition in the broader legal market. A strong, authentic professional identity not only aligns with your career aspirations but also attracts the kind of work and clients you are most passionate about. Here's how to build and communicate a professional reputation that sets you apart:

Crafting Your Professional Identity

Your professional identity is a blend of your legal expertise, personal values, and career aspirations. It's essential to define what sets you apart from others in your field and how you want to be perceived by colleagues, clients, and the broader legal community.

Action Steps

- Reflect on your strengths, interests, and the values you want to embody in your professional life.
- Develop a clear narrative that communicates your unique approach to law, your specialization areas, and how you add value to clients and colleagues.

Building a Reputation Inside Your Firm

Establishing a strong reputation within your firm is foundational for early career development. It involves demonstrating your legal acumen, reliability, and ability to contribute positively to the team's success.

Action Steps

- Seek out challenging assignments that align with your career goals and showcase your capabilities.
- Volunteer for cross-departmental projects to broaden your exposure and build relationships with senior attorneys.
- Actively seek feedback from peers and superiors to continually refine your skills and approach to work.

Building a Reputation in the Marketplace

As your career progresses, extending your professional reputation beyond the confines of your firm becomes increasingly important. This external recognition facilitates business development opportunities and positions you as an expert in your field.

Action Steps

- Engage in thought leadership by publishing articles, speaking at conferences, and participating in industry panels related to your area of specialization.
- Utilize professional networking platforms like LinkedIn to share your insights and connect with peers, potential clients, and industry influencers.
- Get involved in professional associations, not only to network but also to contribute to the advancement of your field through committee work or leadership roles.

Ensuring Authenticity

The cornerstone of a strong professional reputation is authenticity. Your professional identity should be a true reflection of who you are, your values, and how you wish to impact the legal profession.

Action Steps

- Ensure that your public communications, whether on social media, professional publications, or speaking engagements, consistently reflect your genuine interests and professional values.
- Build authentic relationships with colleagues, mentors, and clients by being transparent about your goals and how you aim to achieve them.

By strategically crafting and communicating your professional identity, you not only distinguish yourself in a competitive legal market but also lay the groundwork for a fulfilling career aligned with your aspirations. Remember, building a reputation is an ongoing process that evolves with your career. Remaining true to your authentic self while adapting to the changing dynamics of the legal profession ensures that your professional reputation continues to open doors to new opportunities and successes.

Emphasizing Thought Leadership and Visibility

Emphasizing thought leadership and visibility is a strategic method to enhance your professional reputation and establish your authority within the legal community. This approach involves sharing your knowledge, insights, and perspectives on relevant topics, thereby positioning yourself as a go-to expert in your field. Here is a detailed guide on leveraging thought leadership and visibility for career growth.

Writing as a Visibility Tool

Writing on niche subjects boosts your credibility and reinforces your expertise. Through professional writing—including blog posts, white papers, client alerts, newsletters, and articles—you demonstrate a deep understanding of your practice area, attracting clients and business opportunities. Writing not only grows your audience but also strengthens your digital profile, essential for when prospective clients search for your expertise online.

Actionable Steps

- Choose topics that resonate with your ideal client and are related to the work you seek.
- Collaborate on thought leadership pieces with colleagues, clients, or complementary professionals to expand your reach.

- Consider third-party publications for greater impact, selecting those respected by your target audience.
- Use your writing to maintain contact with your network, providing valuable content that keeps you top of mind.

Speaking Engagements for Enhanced Visibility

Speaking engagements, including podcasts, webinars, panels, and live presentations, offer a platform to share your expertise and connect with a wider audience. These opportunities not only improve your oral communication skills but also significantly boost your professional credibility.

Actionable Steps

- Speak on topics that align with your professional aspirations and appeal to your target clients.
- Seek speaking opportunities at industry conferences or through professional organizations where your target audience is likely to be present.
- Partner with other professionals for presentations to combine expertise and networks.
- Utilize speaking engagements to foster existing relationships and build new connections.

Maximizing Conference Attendance

Conferences provide a unique opportunity to network, gain industry insights, and showcase your expertise. Making the most of these events involves strategic planning before, during, and after attendance.

Actionable Steps

- Before the event, reach out to contacts and speakers, expressing your interest in their sessions and arranging meetups.
- During the conference, actively participate in discussions and social events to make new connections and reinforce existing ones.
- After the event, follow up with new contacts on LinkedIn and share your learnings or experiences with your network.

Leveraging Technology for Visibility

The digital age offers myriad tools for lawyers to enhance their visibility and establish thought leadership. Social media platforms, legal technology forums, and webinars are just a few channels through which lawyers can share their insights and connect with a global audience.

Actionable Steps

- Regularly engage with your online network by sharing articles, commenting on discussions, and participating in webinars.
- Use social media analytics to understand what content resonates with your audience, tailoring your strategy accordingly.

Building a professional reputation through thought leadership and visibility is a powerful strategy for lawyers at any stage of their career. By sharing your knowledge and engaging with your professional community, you not only contribute to the legal field but also pave the way for future opportunities, client engagements, and a fulfilling career in law.

Steering Career Success in Corporate Law: Insights from Natalie Logan

Chief Legal Officer, Accession Risk Management Group

After graduating cum laude from Boston University School of Law, Natalie Logan began her career at an international law firm in Boston, where she honed her skills in corporate law with a focus on private equity transactions. Her talent and dedication soon led her to a significant opportunity in San Francisco, where she was instrumental in expanding the firm's private equity practice. This period of her career was not just about geographical relocation but also about deepening her expertise and impact in the field of corporate law.

The next pivotal move in Natalie's career came when she transitioned to Kirkland & Ellis, earning a partner role that further solidified her reputation as a skilled advisor in corporate, M&A, and securities matters. Her tenure at Kirkland was marked by her proactive approach to client management and her ability to navigate complex legal landscapes. However, it was her willingness to embrace challenges and her capacity to build strong professional relationships that set the stage for the next chapter of her career.

Natalie's transition from private practice to an in-house role at Risk Strategies and One80 Intermediaries, now Accession Risk Management

Group, was a significant leap, positioning her at the helm of the organization's legal and compliance functions. As Chief Legal Officer, she brings a decade of experience in corporate law to her role, coupled with a strategic vision for legal and risk management that supports the company's growth and governance. Her journey from the courtrooms of Boston to the executive suites exemplifies a career built on a foundation of legal acumen, strategic thinking, and an unwavering commitment to excellence in the legal profession.

Embracing Challenges and Opportunities

Natalie's career trajectory is a testament to her belief in embracing challenges and seizing opportunities, even when they involve stepping into roles that others might shy away from. Early in her career, she demonstrated this philosophy by volunteering for tasks that were perceived as difficult or undesirable. This approach not only allowed her to build a diverse skill set but also positioned her as a go-to professional willing to tackle complex issues. One particularly defining moment came when she raised her hand to work on the private equity side of a real estate transaction, a move that would lay the groundwork for her future.

Handling challenging situations and difficult personalities was another area where Natalie excelled. Her experience managing a particularly tough chief financial officer (CFO) is a case in point. Despite the CFO's reputation for being hard to work with, Natalie saw it as an opportunity to demonstrate her capabilities. By taking on this challenge, she not only succeeded in building a strong working relationship but also cemented her reputation as a resilient and effective negotiator. This relationship would later become a pivotal factor in her career.

Natalie's journey underscores the importance of not just accepting challenges but actively seeking them out. Her willingness to engage with difficult tasks and her ability to navigate complex interpersonal dynamics have been instrumental in her career advancement. It's a powerful reminder that stepping out of one's comfort zone and tackling the tasks that others avoid can lead to significant opportunities and pivotal professional relationships.

Navigating Firm Dynamics for Career Advancement

Natalie's approach to navigating the dynamics of a high-powered law firm environment underscores the importance of not just doing good work but also being strategic about one's visibility and engagement within the firm. At Kirkland, she quickly realized that building a solid reputation from the outset was crucial. This meant not only delivering high-quality work but also being proactive in seeking out opportunities to contribute beyond her immediate assignments. Her strategy included engaging in ancillary work across different practice groups, which allowed her to broaden her expertise and visibility within the firm. This proactive approach was about more than just expanding her legal knowledge; it was a deliberate effort to position herself as a versatile and invaluable asset to the firm.

Natalie's commitment to understanding the broader business context of her clients' legal issues was another key aspect of her strategy for career advancement. She made it a point to get involved in complex deals and to participate in investment committee meetings with partners. This not only deepened her understanding of her clients' goals and investment strategies but also demonstrated her willingness to go beyond the traditional role of a legal advisor. By doing so, Natalie was able to offer more comprehensive and strategic advice, aligning legal guidance with business objectives.

Becoming a Trusted Advisor: Understanding the Business

Transitioning to an in-house role, Natalie emphasized the transformative power of understanding the business landscape in which legal decisions are made. She pointed out that applying the law effectively often requires more than just a theoretical grasp of legal principles; it necessitates a deep understanding of the business's operational, strategic, and financial dimensions. For Natalie, this meant dedicating time to learn about the industries her company operates in, thereby equipping herself to offer not just legal advice but strategic business insights as well. This approach allowed her to become a trusted advisor, capable of framing legal advice in a way that resonates with business objectives and challenges.

Natalie's experience highlights the importance of lawyers being able to communicate in the language of business. She found that legal risks are often better understood and addressed when framed in the context of their impact on the business. This skill became particularly valuable in discussions with nonlegal colleagues, enabling her to steer conversations toward solutions that mitigate legal risks while advancing business goals. Her ability to translate complex legal concepts into actionable business strategies has been a key factor in her effectiveness as a Chief Legal Officer. ”

Strategic Career Planning

Strategic career planning is an essential process for any professional aiming to achieve success and fulfillment in their career. It involves a thoughtful and deliberate approach to defining your career objectives and outlining the steps necessary to reach them. This process is particularly crucial in the legal profession, where the path to career advancement can be highly competitive and complex. Strategic career planning encompasses setting both long-term and short-term goals, and developing a comprehensive roadmap to achieve these goals. This roadmap should consider various factors, including further education, gaining relevant experience, building strategic relationships, increasing your visibility within the legal community, obtaining certifications, and making calculated career moves.

Setting Long-Term and Short-Term Goals

- **Long-Term Goals:** These are the overarching objectives you aim to achieve in your career. They define who you want to be working with and what you want to be doing in the future. Long-term goals might include becoming a partner at a law firm, establishing your own practice, specializing in a particular area of law, or transitioning into a legal role within a specific industry or sector.
- **Short-Term Goals:** These are the milestones that will help you progress toward your long-term goals. Short-term goals are more immediate and can be achieved within a shorter time frame. They might include passing a certification exam, completing a significant case, building a network of mentors and peers, or gaining experience in a specific legal area.

Creating a Roadmap to Achieve Your Goals

- **Further Education:** Determine if pursuing additional degrees or specialized legal education will enhance your expertise and make you more competitive in your desired career path. This might include LLM programs, business courses, or other legal specializations.
- **Experience:** Identify the types of legal cases, projects, or roles that will provide you with the necessary experience to advance your career. Seek opportunities that align with your long-term goals and offer valuable learning experiences.
- **Relationships and Involvement:** Cultivate relationships with mentors, colleagues, and professionals within and outside the legal field. Get involved in legal associations, committees, or community organizations to expand your network and increase your visibility.

- **Visibility Activities:** Engage in activities that raise your profile within the legal community and beyond. This could include publishing articles, speaking at conferences, participating in legal forums, or contributing to community service projects.
- **Certifications:** Research and pursue relevant certifications that will bolster your credentials and expertise in your chosen area of law.
- **Career Moves:** Strategically plan your career moves, whether it involves transitioning to a new firm, starting your own practice, or exploring alternative legal careers. Consider how each move aligns with your long-term objectives and what it offers in terms of growth and development.

Strategic career planning is an ongoing process that requires regular reflection and adjustment as your goals, interests, and the legal landscape evolve. By setting clear objectives, creating a detailed roadmap, and taking proactive steps toward your goals, you can navigate your legal career with purpose and direction, ultimately achieving the success and satisfaction you seek.

Cultivating Key Relationships

Whether it's mentors who provide guidance, peers who offer support, or clients who trust in your expertise, the network you build is foundational to your career's growth and success. This chapter delves into the art and science of nurturing these essential connections. From identifying valuable contacts to maintaining and deepening these relationships over time, we explore strategies that enable legal professionals to create a robust network. Cultivating key relationships is not just about expanding your professional circle; it's about fostering meaningful interactions that can lead to opportunities, mentorship, and collaborations, ultimately enriching your legal career and personal development.

Identifying Helpful People

In the journey of building a successful legal career, identifying and connecting with influential people is a pivotal step. These are the mentors, colleagues, peers, and industry leaders who can offer invaluable feedback, guidance, opportunities, and support. Here's how you can approach this crucial task:

Recognizing Your Valuable Supporters

Advocates within your professional network or the broader legal community play a pivotal role in shaping your career trajectory. These individuals not only inspire and challenge you but also facilitate access to opportunities for growth and development. Identifying these key figures involves the following:

- Reflecting on Past Interactions: Think about individuals who have offered you insightful advice or constructive feedback that has significantly impacted your career progression.
- Identifying Skills or Experiences You Desire: Pinpoint specific skills or experiences you aim to acquire and seek out individuals who excel in these areas. These supporters can offer guidance, mentorship, and practical insights to help you achieve your goals.
- Researching Industry Leaders: Investigate thought leaders within your fields of interest who are recognized for their contributions, innovative solutions, and authoritative insights.

Building and Bolstering Relationships

The foundation of a successful legal career often lies in the strength and quality of your professional relationships. Building and nurturing these connections is essential for both personal growth and career advancement. Here's how to cultivate these vital relationships:

- **Initiate Meaningful Engagements:** Reach out to those you admire or wish to learn from with specific questions or topics of discussion. This could be related to their published work, a recent case, or their career path. Genuine curiosity and a willingness to learn can open doors to valuable conversations.
- **Offer Value:** Relationships are a two-way street. Think about how you can contribute to the relationship, whether it's through sharing your own insights, offering support on a project, or connecting them with other professionals in your network. Showing that you're also a resource can strengthen these bonds.
- **Mentorship and Sponsorship:** Seek mentors who can provide personalized advice and guidance based on their own experiences. In addition, identify potential sponsors—those who can advocate for you and open doors to opportunities within and outside your organization.
- **Participate in Professional Associations:** Joining legal associations or groups related to your area of expertise can put you in touch with like-minded professionals. Active participation, such as serving on committees or speaking at events, can enhance your visibility and lead to meaningful connections.
- **Maintain and Deepen Existing Relationships:** Don't overlook the importance of deepening relationships with current colleagues, mentors, and peers. Regular check-ins, updates on your progress, and expressions of gratitude can keep these relationships strong and supportive.
- **Leverage Social Media and Online Platforms:** Platforms like LinkedIn offer a space to connect with professionals globally. Engage with content

posted by your valuable supporters, share your own achievements and learnings, and participate in discussions to keep these connections active and mutually beneficial.

Building a network of valuable supporters requires consistent effort and genuine engagement. By approaching each interaction with sincerity and a mindset of mutual benefit, you can develop a support system that not only aids in your current professional development but also paves the way for future opportunities and successes.

Building a Litigation Career: Patricia Brum's Guide to Strategic Adaptability

Partner, Snell & Wilmer

Born and raised in Brazil, Patricia Brum embarked on her academic journey at the Universidade de Brasilia, where she pursued a degree in International Relations and International Business. Her quest for knowledge and expertise later led her to the United States, where she completed her MBA at the University of Southern California. Patricia's academic achievements culminated in her graduation from Southwestern University School of Law, where she distinguished herself by graduating first in her class.

Starting her career at Ernst & Young, she gained invaluable experience in international trade, which provided her with a solid foundation in the complexities of global business practices. Her career trajectory took her through significant roles in the private sector, including a managerial position at a building material company and a stint as a judicial extern in the United States District Court, Central District of California. These experiences honed her skills and deepened her understanding of both the procedural and substantive aspects of law, particularly in the realm of business litigation.

Today, Patricia is recognized not only for her legal acumen but also for her commitment to fostering DEI within the legal profession. Her work in defending companies against consumer claims under various acts, coupled with her advocacy for the LGBTQ+ community, has earned her accolades.

Passion for Litigation and Overcoming Challenges

Patricia's journey into the world of litigation was fueled by an intellectual curiosity and a passion for the procedural nuances of the legal system. She found herself drawn to litigation over transactional law, intrigued by the opportunity to delve into case law and craft compelling narratives in court. For Patricia, litigation was not just about arguing a case; it was about telling a story that is both persuasive and grounded in law, finding unique angles that others might overlook. This approach to litigation, combining creativity with rigorous legal analysis, was what set her on the path to becoming an accomplished litigator.

Despite her strong academic record and evident passion for the field, Patricia faced initial disappointment when she was not immediately recruited by a big law firm after graduating from law school. This setback, however, did not deter her. Instead, it offered valuable insights into the challenges faced by foreign-trained lawyers and those with perceived disadvantages in the highly competitive legal market. Patricia's advice to others in similar situations is proactive and strategic: reach out to firms ahead of on-campus interviews (OCI), make personal connections, and leverage any perceived disadvantage by finding others who have turned similar challenges into assets.

This phase of Patricia's career also underscored the importance of resilience and adaptability. She emphasizes the value of starting one's career at a boutique law firm, where she gained a wealth of experience in entertainment and homeowners association law, despite not initially being drawn to these areas. This experience, she reflects, was instrumental in shaping her litigation skills and broadening her perspective on the diverse opportunities within the legal profession.

Strategic Career Moves and Reputation Building

Early in her career, Patricia made the choice to start at a boutique law firm, a decision that provided her with a broad range of experiences and a solid foundation in litigation. This environment allowed her to take on significant responsibilities early on, fostering a deep understanding of the procedural aspects of litigation and corporate structures. Patricia views this period as critical in shaping her as a litigator, emphasizing the value of diverse experience in developing a well-rounded skill set.

Her reputation within the legal community was built through a combination of hard work, strategic positioning, and a willingness to go above and beyond. Patricia volunteered for tasks that others might overlook, understanding that every opportunity was a chance to learn and demonstrate her capabilities. She committed herself to writing at least eight articles a year and participated in presentations to some of the largest financial institutions in the United States. This not only showcased her expertise but also her ability to convey complex legal issues in an accessible manner. By doing background research and contributing to cases without the expectation of immediate recognition or billing credit, she cemented her status as a reliable and knowledgeable attorney among her peers.

Business Development and Technology in Law

Patricia's approach to business development is as thoughtful and strategic as her approach to litigation. She has always been intentional about the type of work she wants to pursue, recognizing early in her career the importance of focusing on areas that not only interest her but also align with the firm's needs and the evolving landscape of the law. This mindfulness led her to walk away from easier, "low hanging fruit" work, choosing instead to invest her energy into developing a reputation in more challenging and rewarding areas. By identifying gaps within her firm and the broader legal market, Patricia positioned herself as an expert in niche areas, such as consumer class action defense, that were of growing importance to her clients and her firm.

Patricia's fascination with the intersection of technology and law highlights her forward-thinking and innovative mindset. She is captivated by how new technologies can raise complex legal questions that require novel solutions. For instance, the legal challenges posed by advancements in AI and privacy issues related to online consumer behavior are areas where Patricia has found the law to lag behind technological progress. This gap presents both a challenge and an opportunity for legal professionals to rethink traditional legal frameworks and adapt to the digital age. Patricia's work in these areas demonstrates not only her expertise but also her ability to navigate uncharted legal territories, making her an invaluable asset to her firm and her clients.

Building and Bolstering Relationships

Cultivating meaningful professional relationships is pivotal for career growth in business law. Authenticity and a service mindset are key to initiating and nurturing these connections. Here's how to approach this with intentionality:

Initiating Authentic Connections

- **Identify Common Ground:** Begin by finding shared interests or goals. This could be a similar legal specialty, shared alma mater, or mutual professional acquaintances. Common ground serves as a solid foundation for a meaningful connection.
- **Reach Out Genuinely:** When you contact someone for the first time, make sure your communication is personalized and genuine. Mention why you're reaching out to them specifically, referencing a piece of their work or an achievement that genuinely impressed you.

Nurturing Relationships with a Service Mindset

- **Offer Value before Asking for Anything:** One of the best ways to deepen a professional relationship is by offering help or value without expecting anything in return. This could be as simple as sharing an article relevant to their work or offering insights into a mutual interest.
- **Be a Connector:** Look for opportunities to introduce your contacts to others in your network who might help or collaborate with them. Being a connector not only adds value to your relationships but also strengthens your network.

Effective Networking

- **Participate in Industry Events:** Attend conferences, seminars, and other events related to your field of interest. These are great opportunities to meet new people and engage in meaningful conversations.
- **Engage in Social Media Professionally:** Platforms like LinkedIn are powerful tools for maintaining visibility and engaging with your professional network. Share your achievements, comment on others' posts, and contribute to discussions to keep your connections alive and active.

Mentorship and Sponsorship

- **Seek Mentors and Be One:** Mentorship is a two-way street. Seek out mentors who can guide you and be open to mentoring others. Sharing your knowledge and experience can be incredibly rewarding and can foster deep, lasting relationships.
- **Identify Potential Sponsors:** Look for individuals who are not only mentors but can also act as sponsors—those who can advocate for you and open

doors to opportunities within your field. Building trust with these individuals can catalyze significant career advancements.

Authenticity Is Key

- **Be Yourself:** Authenticity resonates. Be honest about your aspirations, challenges, and interests. Genuine interactions are more memorable and form the basis of strong relationships.
- **Listen Actively:** Show genuine interest in what others have to say. Active listening demonstrates respect and facilitates a deeper understanding of the other person's perspectives and needs.

Adopting a Service Mindset

- **Focus on Giving Back:** Whether it's through providing mentorship, sharing opportunities, or simply offering a listening ear, approaching professional relationships with the intention to serve enriches both your career and personal life.

Building and bolstering relationships in the business law sector, grounded in authenticity and a service mindset, not only enhances your professional journey but also contributes to a supportive, collaborative legal community. Remember, the most impactful relationships are those rooted in mutual respect, shared values, and a genuine desire to support one another's growth.

From Colleagues to Clients

Transitioning relationships from a focus on professional development to business development is a critical shift that occurs as attorneys progress in their careers. This evolution requires a nuanced approach, where understanding client needs and building trust become paramount. Here's how to navigate this transition effectively:

Understanding Client Needs

- **Deep Listening:** Truly understanding client needs begins with active listening. This involves paying attention to not just what is said but also what is left unsaid, picking up on concerns, goals, and the context behind a client's legal issues.
- **Anticipate and Address:** Beyond listening, anticipate your clients' needs based on your understanding of their business and legal landscape. Offering proactive advice and solutions can set you apart as a trusted advisor.

Building Trust

- **Consistency in Quality:** Deliver consistently high-quality work. Reliability in meeting deadlines and providing thorough, well-researched advice builds confidence in your capabilities.
- **Personal Integrity:** Be transparent and honest in all your dealings. Integrity forms the bedrock of trust and is crucial for long-term relationships with clients.
- **Adapt Communication Style:** Tailor your communication to match the client's preferences, whether they appreciate detailed legal briefs or succinct summaries. Effective communication reinforces understanding and trust.

Transitioning Relationships

- **Shift Perspective:** As your career progresses, shift your perspective from viewing colleagues purely as peers in professional development to potential clients or referrers of business. This means broadening the scope of your interactions to include discussions about business challenges and legal needs.
- **Leverage Existing Relationships:** Use your established relationships within your network as a foundation. Introduce the idea of providing legal services in areas you know are relevant to their business needs or where they've expressed interest in the past.
- **Offer Value:** Before pitching your services, offer valuable insights or advice related to their industry or specific legal challenges they might face. Demonstrating your expertise and value upfront can facilitate a smoother transition to discussing your legal services.

Cultivating Business Development Skills

- **Networking with Purpose:** Attend industry events, conferences, and seminars not just for learning but with the aim of networking and identifying potential client opportunities. Approach these with a mindset of how you can help others, rather than what you can gain.
- **Seek Feedback and Referrals:** After successfully delivering on a client's project, don't hesitate to seek feedback. Satisfied clients are often willing to refer you to others if you've built a strong, trust-based relationship.

Transitioning from colleagues to clients is a nuanced process that emphasizes the importance of understanding client needs, building trust, and effectively communicating your value. By focusing on these areas, attorneys can successfully navigate the shift toward business development, ensuring a thriving practice that benefits from strong, lasting client relationships.

Joanna Boisen's Blueprint: Advancing Legal Careers through Pro Bono Commitment

Chief Pro Bono and Social Impact Officer, Davis Wright Tremaine

Joanna Boisen's journey in the legal profession is a testament to her commitment to serving communities in need and her belief in the power of pro bono work to effect change. Before joining Davis Wright Tremaine (DWT) as the firm's first chief pro bono and social impact officer, Joanna carved out a niche for herself as a partner and chair of the tax-exempt organizations group at a leading law firm in Seattle. Her passion for pro bono work was not just a side project; it was central to her professional identity. Joanna was instrumental in founding and developing an award-winning pro bono program that gained national recognition for its impact and innovation.

Her transition to DWT marked a significant milestone in her career, allowing her to take her commitment to pro bono work to a new level. In her current role, Joanna leads and oversees the firm's nationwide pro bono department, creating entrepreneurial and novel flagship initiatives. She focuses on procuring cutting-edge, high-impact matters that aim to change the world for the better. Joanna maintains her own pro bono practice as well, with a particular focus on serving BIPOC (Black, Indigenous, and People of Color) communities, Holocaust survivor reparation litigation, domestic violence advocacy, and income-eligible nonprofits. Through her work, Joanna embodies the belief that legal professionals have a duty to leverage their skills and resources to serve those who are most in need.

Joanna's motivation for dedicating her career to pro bono work is deeply personal. Coming from a low-income immigrant family, she understands the challenges faced by communities struggling to navigate the complex legal system. This background has fueled her drive to ensure that access to justice is not a privilege reserved for the few but a fundamental right available to all. By leading by example, Joanna hopes to inspire a new generation of lawyers to integrate pro bono work into their careers, not only as a way to give back to the community but also as a means of professional development and personal fulfillment.

Evolution of Pro Bono Work in the Legal Industry

Joanna has witnessed a significant transformation in the legal industry's attitude toward pro bono work. She notes that there has been a fundamental shift in mindset, with pro bono now seen as a crucial element of a law firm's contribution to society. This change is reflected in the growing number of professional pro bono positions, from a few dozen to hundreds in recent years. Joanna's observation underscores the increasing importance law firms place on social responsibility and community impact, a stark contrast to the situation two decades ago when pro bono work was often considered optional or peripheral.

The significance of a firm's commitment to pro bono work extends beyond its impact on communities; it has become a vital factor in attracting and retaining talent. Joanna points out that law students and lateral hires now evaluate potential employers based on their pro bono programs, asking sophisticated questions about the nature and extent of the firm's community engagement. This trend indicates a growing expectation for law firms to demonstrate a genuine, impactful commitment to pro bono work, not just in word but in deed.

Professional Development Benefits of Engaging in Pro Bono Work

Joanna draws a compelling parallel between pro bono legal work and medical residency, underscoring the unparalleled opportunity for hands-on learning and skill development that pro bono offers to lawyers, especially those in the early stages of their careers. She points out a notable gap in traditional legal training, where new lawyers often spend their initial years focused on tasks like discovery without much direct courtroom or negotiation experience. Pro bono work, according to Joanna, fills this gap by allowing young lawyers to represent clients in court, engage in negotiations, and develop crucial advocacy skills, much like medical residents who learn by doing, working directly with patients.

One illustrative story from Joanna's career involves a partner at her firm who, as an associate, took on what was deemed an unwinnable pro bono case. Despite the challenging odds, the experience allowed him to apply and hone his legal skills in a real-world setting, ultimately leading to a surprising victory. This story not only highlights the professional growth that can come from pro bono work but also showcases the potential for young lawyers to make meaningful contributions to their clients' lives while building confidence in their abilities as advocates.

Joanna emphasizes that pro bono work is not just about giving back to the community; it's also a strategic investment in a lawyer's professional development. Through her initiatives, she has created avenues for lawyers to engage in meaningful pro bono work that aligns with their interests and career goals, fostering a culture of continual learning and improvement. This approach not only benefits the lawyers and their clients but also strengthens the firm's commitment to social responsibility and community impact.

Joanna's Advice and Vision for the Future of Pro Bono in the Legal Profession

Joanna offers a piece of advice to early career attorneys and law students, emphasizing the dual benefits of pro bono work. She advocates for viewing pro bono not just as a moral obligation but as a critical component of a lawyer's professional development. Joanna underscores that engaging in pro bono work exposes lawyers to diverse legal issues and client interactions that they might not encounter in their regular practice areas. This exposure, she argues, accelerates the development of practical skills and deepens legal understanding, enriching the lawyer's professional experience and enhancing their ability to serve clients effectively.

In closing, Joanna envisions a future where pro bono work is seamlessly integrated into the fabric of legal practice, with every lawyer recognizing the value of contributing to the community not just as an add-on but as an essential part of their professional identity. She encourages lawyers at all stages of their careers to seek out pro bono opportunities, not only to give back to the community but also to enrich their own legal practice and personal growth. Through this lens, pro bono work emerges as a powerful tool for building a more just society while simultaneously advancing the legal profession. ”

From Professional Development to Business Development

The transition from honing professional development skills as an associate to mastering business development as a seasoned attorney is a natural progression in a legal career. This evolution leverages the foundational skills learned early on: identifying the type of work you are passionate about and the people you enjoy working with, building credibility and visibility within your firm, and cultivating relationships inside your organization that provide valuable feedback, guidance, and opportunities. As you progress, these very skills become instrumental in being successful at building a practice that aligns with your interests and goals. Now, the focus shifts toward using your developed skills in credibility, visibility, and relationship building to not only attract work from partners but also forge a practice that is both rewarding and fulfilling. This journey emphasizes the importance of transitioning the skills acquired during your early career into strategies for building and nurturing a client base that resonates with the practice you enjoy.

The Evolution of Your Career Focus

The journey through a legal career witnesses a pivotal shift in focus. Initially, the primary aim is to secure the right job and work on cases that align with your interests and strengths. However, as you progress, this emphasis naturally transitions toward attracting clients and securing work that not only resonates with your expertise but also fuels the growth of your practice.

First Priority: Securing the Right Job and Cases

In the early stages, your focus is on building a solid foundation:

Developing Legal Expertise: Gaining experience in preferred areas of law and honing your legal skills.

Building Internal Relationships: Establishing connections with colleagues and mentors who can provide guidance and opportunities to work on meaningful cases.

Second Priority: Building Credibility and Visibility

As you gain experience, the goal shifts to making yourself known both within and outside your firm:

Enhancing Professional Reputation: Through consistent performance and contribution to your legal community, you start to build a name for yourself as a reliable and skilled attorney.

Increasing Visibility: Engaging in thought leadership, networking, and visibility activities that highlight your expertise and attract attention from potential clients and partners.

Third Priority: Attracting Clients and Securing Work

With a solid foundation and a growing reputation, you begin to focus on business development:

Expanding Client Base: Utilizing your established network and reputation to attract clients looking for the specific legal services you offer.

Securing Meaningful Work: Positioning yourself to not only attract any clients but those whose cases and projects are most aligned with your personal and professional goals.

Continuous Evolution

Throughout your career, this shift from internal development to external growth is guided by continuous learning and adaptation. The skills and relationships you've nurtured over the years become your greatest assets in building a practice that is not only successful but deeply satisfying.

The evolution of your career focus from securing the ideal role to becoming a magnet for clients and engaging work underscores the dynamic nature of legal careers. It highlights the importance of adaptability, strategic relationship building, and maintaining a lifelong commitment to professional development.

Leveraging Your Network for Business Development

The progression of a legal career involves a gradual but significant shift toward business development. One of the most effective tools in this transition is leveraging your existing network. The relationships you've established with colleagues, mentors, and industry contacts can be instrumental in generating business opportunities, referrals, and strategic collaborations.

Harnessing Established Relationships

Identifying Opportunities: Actively seek out ways in which your network can open doors to new business opportunities. This might involve direct referrals, introductions to potential clients, or collaboration on projects that align with your expertise.

Maintaining Engagement: Keep your network informed of your professional developments and areas of focus. Regular updates, through newsletters or personal communications, ensure that you stay top of mind when opportunities arise.

Strategic Networking for Growth

Targeted Outreach: Focus your networking efforts on individuals and organizations that are most likely to require your legal services. This targeted approach ensures that your networking is both efficient and effective.

Offering Value: Approach networking with a mindset of offering value rather than seeking immediate gains. Share insights, offer assistance, and be a resource to your contacts. This service-first approach builds trust and strengthens your relationships.

Fostering Collaborations

Partnerships with Peers: Look for opportunities to collaborate with peers on cases, publications, or events. These partnerships not only expand your exposure but also showcase your ability to work well with others, a valuable trait for potential clients.

Industry Collaborations: Engage with professionals outside the legal field but within your niche or target market. These collaborations can lead to a deeper understanding of your clients' needs and position you as an integral part of the industry.

Referral Strategies

Cultivating Referral Sources: Identify and nurture relationships with individuals who are in a position to refer clients to you regularly. This includes not just fellow lawyers but also accountants, financial advisors, and other professionals who serve your target market.

Reciprocity: Be proactive in referring business to others in your network where appropriate. This reciprocity not only strengthens your relationships but also encourages others to think of you when they encounter someone in need of your services.

Leveraging your network for business development is a nuanced art that balances strategic outreach with genuine relationship building. By utilizing the connections you've built over the years and focusing on providing value, you can effectively generate new business opportunities, referrals, and collaborations that propel your career forward. This approach ensures that your transition from focusing on professional development to emphasizing business development is both seamless and successful.

Strategies for Effective Business Development

Effective business development in law is about more than just attracting new clients; it's about building a sustainable practice through strategic marketing, strong client relationships, and continuous growth. Here's how you can effectively develop your business in the legal sector.

Understand Your Client Base

- Identify Your Ideal Client: Clearly define who your ideal clients are, including their industry, legal needs, and how you can uniquely address those needs. This understanding will guide your marketing efforts and service offerings.
- Client Needs Analysis: Regularly engage with current and potential clients to understand their challenges and business and legal needs. This proactive approach ensures that your services remain relevant and valued.

Marketing Your Legal Services

- Content Marketing: Share your expertise through articles, webinars, and newsletters that address common legal issues faced by your target clients. This not only showcases your knowledge and creates resources for clients and prospects but also helps in Search Engine Optimization (SEO), improving your visibility and ranking on search engines, making you more discoverable online.
- Social Media Presence: Use platforms such as LinkedIn to share insights, comment on industry trends, and participate in discussions. A strong social media presence can enhance your visibility and establish you as a thought leader in your field.

Building and Enhancing Client Relationships

- Personalized Service: Offer customized advice and solutions tailored to each client's specific situation. Personalized service fosters trust and loyalty, encouraging repeat business and referrals.
- Regular Communication: Keep clients informed about their cases, changes in the law that may affect them, and any other information that demonstrates your commitment to their success. Consistency in communication is key to maintaining strong relationships.

Networking and Referrals

- Leverage Existing Relationships: Tap into your professional network for introductions and referrals. Maintaining strong relationships with colleagues, peers, and mentors can lead to new business opportunities.
- Attend Industry Events: Participate in conferences, seminars, and other events related to your practice area. These are excellent opportunities for networking, learning about new developments, and showcasing your expertise.

Offering Value beyond Legal Advice

- Educational Workshops and Seminars: Host or participate in events that educate clients and prospects on legal issues, trends, and preventive strategies. This adds value to your relationships and positions you as a helpful resource.
- Client Feedback: Regularly seek feedback from clients on your services and their overall experience. Use this feedback to continuously improve and adapt your offerings to meet their needs better.

Continuous Learning and Adaptation

- Stay Informed: Keep abreast of the latest trends, technologies, and legal developments that affect your practice area. Being knowledgeable and forward-thinking is attractive to clients looking for top-tier legal representation.
- Adapt and Innovate: Be open to adapting your business development strategies as the market and your clients' needs evolve. Innovation in service delivery, client engagement, and marketing can set you apart in a competitive legal market.

Implementing these strategies requires a consistent effort and a focus on long-term relationship building. By prioritizing your clients' needs, leveraging your network, and continuously improving your offerings, you can develop a thriving legal practice that not only attracts but retains business.

Deborah Knupp's Blueprint for Authentic Growth in Legal Business Development

Managing Director, GrowthPlay

Deborah Knupp has spent the last three decades at the forefront of business development, working closely with leaders across various industries, including legal, manufacturing, accounting, and financial services. Her unique approach intertwines sales methodologies with human resources insights to foster cultures rooted in accountability and integrity. This approach champions the concept of selling as an act of service, emphasizing the establishment of authentic relationships and prioritizing the needs of others in problem solving.

Deb's journey into the legal sector was motivated by a desire to address the unique challenges law firms face in business development and to dismantle the negative stereotypes often associated with lawyers. By applying her comprehensive sales and human resources expertise, she aims to help lawyers not only excel in their professional lives but also thrive as individuals. Through her work, Deb aspires to cultivate an environment where lawyers are empowered to build fulfilling careers by harnessing the power of genuine connections.

Tackling Negative Stereotypes

Deb is acutely aware of the negative stereotypes that often shadow the legal profession. Lawyers, as she notes, are frequently the butt of jokes and are subjected to a socially accepted bias that can be both aggressive and demeaning. This external perception, coupled with the inherent nature of legal work—which often focuses on identifying risks and protecting against downsides—can foster a mindset that is antithetical to building positive, authentic relationships. According to Deb, this risk-averse attitude often translates into a scarcity mindset among lawyers, where the focus is on playing not to lose rather than seeking opportunities to connect and build.

The challenge, as Deb sees it, is not just about changing how lawyers are perceived by society but also about transforming how lawyers view their own roles and the possibilities for connection within their profession. The stereotypes and biases serve as barriers, making it difficult for lawyers to approach their work with an abundance mindset—an outlook that sees possibilities for growth, connection, and positive outcomes. This scarcity mindset can lead to a defensive posture, where arrogance and bravado become shields against criticism, further alienating lawyers from potential relationships that could enrich their professional and personal lives.

Deb believes that helping lawyers to thrive as human beings is a critical part of overcoming these stereotypes and mindset challenges. By focusing on the human aspects of legal work and emphasizing the importance of authentic relationships, lawyers can begin to see their profession in a new light—one that values service, connection, and positive impact. This shift is essential not only for individual lawyers but for the legal profession as a whole. As Deb points out, lawyers play a crucial role in all significant commercial, educational, financial, and political endeavors. By empowering lawyers to build genuine relationships and approach their work with an abundance mindset, the potential for positive change and impact is immense.

The Importance of Relationships in Career Development

Deb emphasizes the crucial role of understanding individual career aspirations within the legal profession, particularly the nuanced desires of lawyers when it comes to their paths toward partnership. She observes that law firms often operate under traditional expectations and career trajectories, which might not align with the evolving aspirations of newer generations entering the field. By advocating for a dialogue that is open, curious, and transparent, Deb suggests that law firms can better align their structures and opportunities with the genuine career goals of their lawyers. This approach not only fosters a culture of growth but also ensures that the aspirations of individual lawyers are met with understanding and support.

Deb underscores the importance of fostering a culture within law firms where generational differences are acknowledged and leveraged, rather than seen as barriers. By encouraging dialogue that bridges the gap between different generations within the firm, law firms can create an environment where mutual understanding and mentorship flourish. This not only aids in the professional development of younger lawyers but also enriches the firm's collective knowledge and adaptability. In such an environment, relationships become the cornerstone of career development, enabling lawyers at all stages of their careers to navigate their paths with clarity and confidence.

Authentic Relationships as a Teachable Skill

Deb firmly believes that the ability to build authentic relationships is not an innate talent reserved for a select few but a skill that can be systematically taught and developed. This perspective is particularly relevant in the legal profession, where the cultivation of genuine connections can significantly impact business development outcomes. According to Deb, the process of developing business in law is predictable when the right building blocks are in place. By focusing on actionable steps and consistent efforts, lawyers can demystify the often daunting task of business development, turning it into a structured and manageable process.

Deb introduces practical strategies for building these relationships, emphasizing the importance of persistence and thoughtful engagement. She notes that, on average, it takes seven to fourteen interactions before a potential client is ready to engage in business, a statistic that underscores the necessity of perseverance in relationship-building efforts. Lawyers are encouraged to think creatively about how they can provide value at each touchpoint, whether through sharing insights, making introductions, or extending invitations to events that align with the interests of the person they're seeking to connect with. These actions, rooted in genuine interest and service, are the building blocks of the authentic relationships that drive successful business development in law.

GrowthPlay's Three Currencies of Authentic Relationships

Deb introduces a pivotal concept from GrowthPlay's revenue acceleration framework that centers on the three universal concepts crucial to building authentic relationships: revenue, relationships, and reputation. This framework encourages a shift in perspective, urging lawyers to view business development not merely as a means to generate revenue but as an opportunity to serve others. By adopting this service-oriented mindset, lawyers can engage in business development activities that are not only more aligned with their professional values but also more likely to result in meaningful and lasting connections.

The first currency, revenue, is the most obvious and tangible outcome of successful business development efforts. However, Deb emphasizes that focusing solely on revenue can limit the potential of professional relationships. Instead, she advises lawyers to broaden their perspective and recognize the value of the other two currencies: relationships and reputation. Relationships refer to the network of connections that lawyers build over time, which can become sources of referrals, collaboration, and support. Reputation, on the other hand, encompasses the lawyer's standing within the legal community and with clients, which is built through consistent, high-quality service and ethical practice.

By prioritizing these three currencies, lawyers can approach business development in a way that fosters authenticity and mutual benefit. For instance, when lawyers engage with potential clients or colleagues, they should focus on how they can add value to the other person's work or life, rather than viewing the interaction merely as a step toward securing a new client or project. This might involve sharing relevant insights, making meaningful introductions, or simply offering support without an immediate expectation of return. Such acts of service not only contribute to building a positive reputation but also deepen relationships, creating a foundation for sustainable business growth.

In essence, Deb's framework challenges the traditional view of sales and business development as purely transactional activities. By embracing the three currencies of revenue, relationships, and reputation, lawyers can transform their approach to business development, making it a more fulfilling and effective component of their professional practice. This shift not only benefits the individual lawyer but also contributes to the broader goal of humanizing the legal profession and fostering a culture of service and authenticity. ”

Specialization, Business Acumen, and Technology

Specializing in Business Law

Navigating the vast expanse of business law, attorneys are presented with a plethora of pathways each leading to unique specializations such as mergers and acquisitions, bankruptcy, corporate law, and intellectual property. The journey to finding a niche within this complex landscape is not just about identifying an area of law that resonates with personal interests and strengths; it's also about understanding and aligning with the evolving needs of the market. This alignment is crucial, as it not only ensures professional fulfillment but also positions attorneys to meet the demands of their clients more effectively.

Specialization within business law offers the opportunity to delve deeper into specific legal realms, becoming an expert in areas that are both personally compelling and critically needed in the market. As legal professionals embark on this journey, they encounter various challenges and rewards, navigating through market trends, client needs, and continuous learning paths. The process of specializing is a strategic endeavor that requires careful consideration, guidance, and an openness to evolving alongside the legal field. Through this specialization, attorneys can achieve a heightened level of expertise, credibility, and professional satisfaction, making a significant impact within their chosen domains.

Finding Your Niche

The journey to establishing a niche within the realm of business law can initially appear overwhelming, particularly for new lawyers or those contemplating a pivot in their legal careers. The early years often necessitate a degree of flexibility, accepting a variety of assignments that may not directly align with one's ultimate interests. However, the deliberate pursuit of a specialized area not only enhances your professional trajectory but also positions you as a sought-after expert. This section revisits the process of finding your niche, incorporating key factors to consider that can guide your decision making and strategic planning.

Reflecting on Personal Interests and Strengths

The cornerstone of identifying your niche lies in introspection—understanding what genuinely captivates you within the vast landscape of business law. Reflect on the aspects of your education and early career experiences that have been most engaging. Whether it was a particular course in law school, an internship, or a specific type of case, these experiences can serve as indicators of where your interests and strengths lie. Documenting your reactions and preferences toward different tasks can provide clarity over time, helping you to discern the areas that resonate most deeply with you.

Considering Key Factors for Niche Selection

When navigating toward your niche, several critical factors should guide your decision making:

- **Favorite Matters to Work On:** Identify the legal issues or case types that you find most fulfilling. A niche that aligns with your passions will keep you motivated and engaged.
- **Market Opportunities:** Explore niches with growing demand due to emerging markets, legislative changes, or evolving industries. Future growth potential is a crucial consideration.
- **Client and Referral Partner Fit:** Assess the types of clients and referral partners you connect with best. A niche that caters to these groups can foster strong relationships and a steady stream of business.
- **Profitability:** Evaluate the financial aspects of different niches. Higher billing rates and the potential for premium fees can make certain specializations more lucrative.
- **Market Stability:** Choose a niche with long-term viability. It is essential to select an area with a stable and growing demand for legal services.
- **Delegation Opportunities:** Consider whether aspects of the niche work can be delegated or outsourced, allowing you to focus on higher value tasks.
- **Leveraging Reputation and Connections:** Utilize your existing network and reputation to establish yourself quickly within your chosen niche.

Aligning Interests with Market Realities

While you may not have full control over the assignments you receive early in your career, it's important to remain adaptable and attuned to the legal market's evolution. Engage in professional development opportunities related to your areas of interest, such as specialized CLEs, legal associations, and writing on relevant topics. These activities not only build your expertise but also signal your specialization interests to colleagues and mentors.

Navigating and Adapting within Your Chosen Path

As you gain more autonomy in your career, make strategic choices that align with your identified niche. Volunteer for relevant projects, seek mentorship from established professionals in the field, and network within your specialty. Remember, the path to finding and establishing a niche is not always linear. Stay open to exploration and be prepared to pivot as new opportunities and interests emerge.

In summary, identifying and developing a niche in business law is a strategic process that involves a deep understanding of your personal interests, an assessment of market opportunities, and a commitment to aligning your career path with these elements. By carefully considering these factors and remaining adaptable, you position yourself for a fulfilling and distinguished career as a recognized expert in your chosen area of specialization.

Building a Niche Practice: Gabriela Sanchez's Strategy for Success

Shareholder, Senior Living & Long-Term Care Team Co-chair, Lane Powell

Gabriela Sanchez stands out in the legal profession as the Co-chair of the Senior Living & Long-Term Care Team at Lane Powell, where she has built a distinguished career by addressing the complex challenges faced by long-term care, senior housing, and home health and hospice providers. With a focus on compliance, regulatory, and risk management advice, Gabi has become a trusted advisor in the senior living and long-term care industry. Her approach is characterized by a blend of pragmatism and dedication, aimed at helping clients navigate the intricate legal landscape they face.

Her journey into the legal field was not a straightforward one. Gabi's entry into senior living and long-term care law was serendipitous, starting with a chance involvement with a senior living facility client. This experience piqued her interest and led her to specialize in an area that is both challenging and rewarding. Over the years, Gabi has represented clients in a wide array of matters, from resident transfers and compliance issues to disputes with residents and their families. This breadth of experience has not only deepened her understanding of the field but also solidified her commitment to her clients.

Beyond her direct work with clients, Gabi is deeply involved in the broader legal and professional community. She serves as Chair of the American Health Lawyers Association Post-Acute and Long-Term Services (PALS) Practice Group, is a Board Member of the Oregon Health Care Association, and participates on its Legal Committee. In addition, she holds a board position at a prominent continuing care retirement community. These roles underscore her commitment to the senior living and long-term care sector and reflect her standing as a thought leader and advocate for best practices within the industry. Gabi's work is driven by a passion for making a tangible difference in the lives of her clients and their residents, showcasing a career that is both impactful and inspiring.

Discovering a Niche in Senior Living and Long-Term Care Law

Gabi's foray into senior living and long-term care law was a blend of serendipity and proactive choice. Initially practicing creditors' rights and bankruptcy law at a respected firm in Eugene, Oregon, her legal career took an unexpected turn when she was presented with an opportunity to work with a senior living facility. Despite having no prior experience in this niche, Gabi volunteered to take on the case. This decision marked the beginning of her journey into a field that was still burgeoning at the time, with few lawyers specializing in it. Her curiosity and willingness to learn propelled her forward, as she delved into the intricacies of the business and its legal needs, particularly focusing on billing practices.

This initial engagement not only sparked Gabi's interest in the senior living and long-term care sector but also highlighted her potential to the general counsel of the firm. Recognizing her dedication and the unique perspective she brought to the table, the client followed her when she moved to Portland for personal reasons, solidifying her role as an indispensable asset. Over the years, what started as an accidental assignment evolved into a successful and fulfilling career. Gabi developed a comprehensive understanding of the industry, expanding her expertise to cover various aspects of operations and business alongside the legal challenges.

Gabi's story underscores the importance of being open to new opportunities, even those that seem daunting or outside one's comfort zone. Her experience illustrates how a single case can not only redefine a lawyer's career path but also contribute significantly to a niche field. Through her journey, Gabi has become a prominent figure in senior living and long-term care law, offering a testament to the power of curiosity, adaptability, and the willingness to embrace unexpected opportunities.

The Importance of Skills, Networking, and Mentorship

Gabi emphasizes that success in senior living and long-term care law hinges on a set of core skills: curiosity, creativity, patience, tenacity, good listening, and being readily available to clients. These traits, she points out, are crucial in navigating the complexities of the field. For Gabi, curiosity and creativity are about finding innovative solutions to the unique challenges her clients face, while patience and tenacity are necessary for dealing with the often slow-moving regulatory environment. Being a good listener helps her understand the nuances of each case, and availability ensures that clients feel supported throughout their legal journeys.

Networking and mentorship have played pivotal roles in Gabi's career. She shares that her entire career trajectory has been significantly shaped by networking, recounting how each of her job opportunities came through connections made within the legal community. From securing her first position through a recommendation from a judge to landing her current role at Lane Powell through a persuasive conversation with the firm's president, Gabi's story illustrates the power of building and maintaining professional relationships. She advises emerging legal professionals to put themselves out there, emphasizing that networking is about not just being in the right place at the right time but making the most of every opportunity.

Building a Book of Business and Advocating for Change

Gabi underscores the significance of cultivating a personal book of business as a foundational step toward achieving autonomy and influence within the legal profession. She highlights how being a successful rainmaker, someone who is adept at attracting and retaining clients, not only secures one's position within a firm but also amplifies their voice when advocating for systemic changes. According to Gabi, establishing a robust portfolio of clients and cases is akin to mastering one's destiny in the legal field. It creates a scenario where the firm values your contribution so significantly that it opens doors to discussions about structural changes, diversity, and inclusion efforts that might otherwise be overlooked.

Achieving success and becoming an indispensable asset to a firm, Gabi notes, provides a unique platform for advocating change. She emphasizes the importance of using one's position and influence to champion diversity and inclusion within the legal industry. Gabi points out that real, long-term change in the profession requires more than just occupying roles; it necessitates participation in decision-making processes, leadership, and governance. She advocates for leveraging success to ensure that firms not only listen but are motivated to act because they understand the value you bring to the table.

Gabi stresses the importance of mentoring as a tool for fostering the next generation of leaders who can continue to push for positive changes within the legal landscape. She believes that helping others to succeed, guiding them in developing their own client base, and encouraging them to aim for leadership positions are crucial steps in ensuring the legal profession becomes more inclusive and reflective of the society it serves. Gabi's approach is rooted in the belief that structural changes in the industry are best achieved by those who have navigated its challenges successfully and are in positions to influence policy and practice from within. Through her work, Gabi exemplifies how success in one's career can be leveraged to not only achieve personal goals but also advocate for a more equitable and inclusive legal profession. ”

Market Needs and Specialization

Navigating the intricacies of market needs and specializing accordingly is fundamental for legal professionals seeking to make a significant impact in the business law arena. This segment underscores the importance of understanding both current and prospective market trends in business law, alongside grasping the diverse needs of clients across various specializations.

Analyzing Current and Future Market Trends in Business Law

Staying abreast of market trends is crucial for legal professionals aiming to specialize in business law. This entails not just a passive observation but an active analysis of how global economic shifts, technological advancements, regulatory changes, and societal movements influence the demand for legal services. For instance, the rise of digital commerce has heightened the need for expertise in cybersecurity and data privacy law. Similarly, global environmental concerns have bolstered the demand for specialists in environmental law and sustainable business practices. By analyzing these trends, legal professionals can identify burgeoning areas of law that align with their interests and expertise.

Understanding Client Needs in Different Specializations

Equally important to analyzing market trends is the ability to understand and anticipate the needs of clients within these specializations. Each area of business law serves a unique client base, with specific challenges, goals, and expectations. For example, start-ups may require guidance on venture capital and intellectual property protection, while multinational corporations may need assistance navigating international trade laws. By deeply understanding the nuances of client needs within a chosen specialization, lawyers can tailor their services to offer more value, thereby establishing themselves as indispensable advisors in their field.

Pathways to Specialization

Navigating the path to specialization within the field of business law involves a multifaceted approach, combining formal education and certifications, practical experience, and the strategic use of mentorship and professional networks. This comprehensive strategy not only equips legal professionals with the necessary knowledge and skills but also guides them in identifying and refining their niche areas.

Education and Certifications Relevant to Business Law Specializations

The foundation of any legal specialization is a robust understanding of the law, which begins with a law degree. However, to carve out a niche in business law, additional education and certifications can be invaluable. For instance, an LL.M. in a specific area such as Tax Law, Corporate Law, or Intellectual Property can provide a deeper understanding and a competitive edge. In addition, certifications from recognized legal organizations in areas like compliance, cybersecurity law, or financial regulations can further demonstrate expertise and commitment to a specialization. These educational pursuits signal to potential employers and clients alike a lawyer's dedication and proficiency in their chosen field.

Gaining Practical Experience through Internships, Clerkships, and Early Career Roles

While formal education lays the groundwork, practical experience is where theoretical knowledge is applied and honed. Internships and clerkships offer invaluable opportunities for law students and new graduates to immerse themselves in the real-world workings of business law. These experiences provide a glimpse into various specializations, helping individuals to identify areas that resonate with their interests and strengths. Furthermore, early career roles serve as a critical phase for young lawyers to start building their specialization. Taking on projects and cases in desired niche areas, even if they constitute a small portion of the workload initially, can gradually steer a career toward full specialization.

The Role of Mentorship and Professional Networks in Finding and Refining One's Niche

Mentorship and professional networks play pivotal roles in the journey toward specialization. Mentors, with their wealth of experience and insights, can offer guidance, advice, and sometimes even opportunities to engage with niche areas of interest. They can help navigate the complexities of the legal profession, provide feedback on career strategies, and introduce mentees to key contacts within their specialization. Similarly, professional networks, whether formed through legal associations, conferences, or even social media platforms, can offer support, resources, and opportunities for collaboration and growth. Engaging with these networks allows for the exchange of ideas, staying updated on industry trends, and potentially discovering untapped areas of specialization.

Building Expertise in Your Chosen Area

Building expertise in your chosen area of business law specialization is a journey that goes beyond the foundational knowledge acquired through education and initial practical experiences. It involves a deep dive into the nuances of your field, a commitment to staying abreast of the latest developments, and actively contributing to the scholarly and practical understanding of your specialization. This section focuses on strategies specifically tailored to deepening your expertise.

Deepening Legal Knowledge through Advanced Studies and Research

To truly excel in your chosen specialization, consider pursuing advanced studies or engaging in research. This could involve enrolling in an LL.M. program focused on your area of interest, such as International Business Law, Environmental Law, or Intellectual Property Law. Alternatively, participating in research projects, whether independently or as part of an academic or professional team, can provide deeper insights into specific legal issues and contribute to your development as an expert.

Specialized CLE

While general CLE courses are essential for maintaining your license and staying updated, specialized CLE offerings can be instrumental in building expertise. Seek out CLE programs that delve into advanced topics within your specialization.

These programs often feature experts discussing cutting-edge legal issues, emerging trends, and complex case studies, providing a wealth of knowledge that can enhance your understanding and skills.

Engaging in Professional Writing and Publication

Writing articles, case commentaries, or even a book on topics within your specialization not only contributes to your learning but also helps solidify your expertise. The process of writing requires thorough research and analysis, deepening your understanding of the subject matter. Publication in respected legal journals, blogs, or industry publications also contributes to the body of knowledge in your field and establishes your credibility as an expert.

Active Involvement in Specialized Legal Forums and Think Tanks

Participation in forums, working groups, or think tanks focused on your area of specialization offers a platform for deep intellectual engagement with complex legal issues. These groups often bring together leading practitioners, academics, and policymakers to discuss, debate, and develop solutions to current challenges in the field. Active involvement in these settings not only enhances your knowledge but also allows you to contribute to the evolution of legal practice in your specialization.

Learning from Complex Cases and Client Engagements

Finally, one of the most effective ways to build expertise is through hands-on experience with complex cases and client engagements. Seek opportunities to work on challenging projects that push the boundaries of your current understanding. Each case or project is a learning opportunity, offering insights into the practical application of legal principles, client needs, and innovative problem-solving strategies.

Building expertise in your chosen area of business law specialization requires a proactive and multifaceted approach. By engaging deeply with your field through advanced studies, specialized CLE, professional writing, involvement in legal forums, and tackling complex cases, you can develop a profound understanding and skill set that sets you apart as an expert in your field.

Challenges and Rewards of Specialization

Specializing in a specific area of business law not only enhances your expertise and credibility but also significantly impacts your marketing efforts, client relationships, and overall career satisfaction. This section revisits the challenges and rewards of specialization, incorporating the benefits of niche marketing and how it contributes to a successful legal practice.

Navigating the Challenges of Becoming a Specialist

Although the journey to specialization is rewarding, it presents unique challenges:

- **Selecting a Niche:** Deciding on a specific area of specialization requires careful consideration of your interests, market demand, and long-term career goals. It is a balance between following your passion and recognizing where you can make the most significant impact.
- **Maintaining Relevance:** Specialized fields, especially those influenced by technology or global trends, can evolve quickly. Staying informed and adaptable is crucial to maintaining your relevance and expertise.
- **Building a Specialized Client Base:** Initially, attracting clients within a niche may be challenging. It requires targeted marketing strategies and demonstrating the unique value you bring to your specialization.
- **Avoiding Overspecialization:** There is a risk of becoming too narrowly focused, which could limit your adaptability if market demands shift. Balancing deep expertise with a broad understanding of related areas is key.

The Rewards of a Focused Practice: Enhanced Marketing and Career Fulfillment

Specialization in business law brings numerous rewards that extend beyond personal fulfillment to tangible benefits for your practice:

- **Differentiation:** Specializing allows you to stand out in a crowded market. Your unique expertise makes it easier for potential clients to understand why they should choose you over a generalist.
- **Expertise and Credibility:** Deep knowledge in a specific area builds your credibility, positioning you as a trusted authority. This reputation enhances your relationships with clients, colleagues, and referral sources.
- **Enhanced Client Relationships:** A focused niche enables you to deeply understand your clients' specific needs and challenges, allowing for tailored solutions and personalized service. This leads to stronger relationships and higher client satisfaction.
- **Targeted Marketing:** Specialization streamlines your marketing efforts. You can focus on communicating your expertise to a specific audience, making it easier to attract clients who are seeking your specialized services.
- **Increased Referrals:** A well-defined niche makes you memorable and builds a strong referral network. Professionals are more likely to refer clients to you when they encounter someone in need of your specific expertise.

- **Efficiency and Effectiveness:** Focusing on a niche streamlines your workflow, increases efficiency, and leads to higher quality work, enhancing client satisfaction.
- **Higher Billing Rates:** As a recognized authority, you can command higher billing rates. Clients are often willing to pay a premium for specialized expertise.
- **Reduced Competition:** Specializing reduces competition from generalists, allowing you to position yourself as the go-to expert in your niche.
- **Long-Term Growth Potential:** Becoming a leader in your field opens doors to high-profile cases, speaking engagements, and other prestigious opportunities, offering significant growth potential.
- **More Fulfilling Practice:** Working in a niche that aligns with your passions leads to a more rewarding career, allowing you to make a meaningful impact and enjoy greater job satisfaction.

Although specialization in business law comes with its set of challenges, the rewards—ranging from targeted marketing advantages and increased referrals to higher billing rates and a more fulfilling practice—make it a compelling strategy for legal professionals. By carefully selecting a niche, staying adaptable, and leveraging targeted marketing strategies, lawyers can navigate these challenges successfully and reap the significant benefits of specialization.

Bobby Moore: Navigating the Complexities of International Tax Law with Resilience and Innovation

Partner in North America Tax Practice Group and the Former Managing Partner of the Miami office, Baker McKenzie

Robert "Bobby" Moore's path into the realm of tax law was not a straightforward journey but rather a series of discoveries and decisions that gradually led him to his current specialization. Initially attracted to the broad field of law for its intellectual challenges and societal impact, Bobby's entry into law school was marked by curiosity and an openness to explore various legal disciplines. It was during his first year that he stumbled upon tax law, a field that hadn't been on his radar initially. The complexity and the critical thinking it required resonated with him deeply. He recalls, "I did really well at it and said, well, maybe I'm good at this." This early success and enjoyment in tax law courses encouraged him to delve deeper into the subject.

As Bobby navigated through law school, he strategically shaped his experience around tax law and related business law classes, such as securities law. His proactive approach included taking on internships at the Department of Justice's Civil Tax Division and the Security Exchange Commission, further solidifying his interest in the field. However, the journey wasn't without its challenges. The job market at the time of his graduation was less than ideal, leading him to heed the advice of a cherished professor to pursue an LL.M. in taxation. This decision to specialize further was a turning point. "Suddenly it all clicked," Bobby explains, reflecting on his time at the University of Florida, where he not only excelled academically but also found the doors to previously closed opportunities beginning to open.

This phase of Bobby's educational journey underscores the importance of perseverance, mentorship, and the willingness to take calculated risks. His decision to pursue an LL.M. in taxation, despite the financial and personal challenges it entailed, was driven by a genuine passion for the field and the desire to excel. This narrative serves as a testament to the idea that finding one's niche in the legal profession often requires exploration, dedication, and sometimes, a leap of faith.

The Road to Employment

Bobby's journey to securing employment after law school was fraught with uncertainty and setbacks, illustrating the unpredictable nature of the job market and the vital role of resilience. Initially setting his sights on a boutique firm in his hometown of Charlotte, North Carolina, he felt confident about his prospects there, given his top-of-the-class status and local roots. However, despite a lengthy interview process and seeming alignment with the firm's needs, he was ultimately passed over for a candidate with no apparent ties to Charlotte. This rejection, particularly stinging due to his personal connections to the area and his high academic standing, served as a harsh introduction to the competitive and often unpredictable job search process.

Undeterred by this setback, Bobby reassessed his strategy, broadening his search to include cities in Florida, where he was completing his LL.M. Despite numerous interviews and some interest from midsized firms, he found these opportunities lacked the focus on tax law he was seeking. It was a chance email to a partner at a major firm in Miami that turned the tide. The partner's prompt and encouraging response, although not a job offer, opened the door to an interview and, eventually, a position at Baker McKenzie. This opportunity, which Bobby described as his "dream job," came about through a blend of timing, persistence, and the willingness to reach out directly to potential employers, underscoring the importance of networking and taking initiative in the job search process.

Bobby's experience highlights that the path to employment in the legal field can be circuitous and filled with unexpected turns. His story is a testament to the power of resilience, the importance of networking, and the need to remain open to opportunities, even in less traditional or anticipated locales. Through rejection and uncertainty, Bobby's persistence and proactive approach to job hunting ultimately led him to a fulfilling career in international tax law, serving as a valuable lesson for law students and early career attorneys navigating their own paths.

The Essence of Enjoyment and Challenge in Work

For Bobby, the key to a fulfilling career lies in the intersection of enjoyment and challenge. He reflects on his nearly two decades in tax law with a sense of satisfaction, noting, "I can't even tell you if I ever had a day where I was really dreading going to work." This sentiment is rooted in the dynamic nature of tax law—a field that constantly evolves and requires a deep engagement with new legal landscapes. For Bobby, the appeal of tax law is in its complexity and the intellectual rigor it demands. This has kept him motivated and interested, ensuring that his workdays are rarely monotonous.

Bobby's enthusiasm for his work is particularly evident when he discusses tax planning. He likens the process to solving a Rubik's cube, where aligning different pieces to solve a complex problem brings a sense of accomplishment and excitement. This analogy highlights the creative aspect of tax law, which Bobby finds both fun and intellectually stimulating. He contrasts this with other areas of law that did not spark the same interest for him, emphasizing the importance of finding a field that not only challenges but also captivates.

The essence of Bobby's career satisfaction also lies in the impact of his work. Whether it's structuring deals for multinational corporations or navigating the intricacies of international tax planning, the tangible outcomes of his efforts provide a continuous source of fulfillment. This blend of intellectual challenge, creativity, and real-world impact has been crucial in keeping his passion for tax law alive. Bobby's experience underscores the importance for aspiring lawyers to seek out areas of law that not only challenge them but also align with their interests and values.

Advice for Aspiring Lawyers

Bobby's guidance for those at the beginning of their legal careers is both practical and philosophical. He underscores the importance of exceeding expectations and actively seeking opportunities to grow. "Doing more than you're asked to do is crucial," he states, emphasizing that merely fulfilling tasks will not set one apart in the competitive legal landscape. This proactive approach not only enhances one's skill set but also signals a genuine commitment to the profession and a desire for excellence. Bobby's own career, marked by a willingness to engage deeply with his work and continuously expand his expertise, serves as a testament to this advice.

Mentorship and feedback emerge as other critical components in Bobby's advice to aspiring lawyers. He encourages seeking out mentors actively, noting that building a network of guidance and support can significantly impact one's career trajectory. "Mentors can provide invaluable insights and open doors that you might not even know exist," he explains. In addition, he stresses the importance of being open to feedback, viewing it not as criticism but as a vital tool for growth and improvement. This mindset of learning and adaptability is crucial for navigating the complexities of the legal field.

Finally, Bobby advises maintaining a long-term perspective on one's career. He reminds us that a legal career spans decades, and early setbacks or challenges are merely temporary. "Don't be afraid to try new things or switch practices if you're not finding fulfillment," he suggests. This willingness to adapt and explore different areas of law can lead to a more satisfying and successful career. Bobby's journey, marked by curiosity, resilience, and a constant pursuit of engagement and challenge, illustrates the rich possibilities that await those who approach their legal careers with openness, dedication, and a forward-looking mindset.

Business Skills for Lawyers: The Importance of Financial Literacy, Business Understanding, and Client-Centric Approaches

Understanding Business Fundamentals

In today's complex legal environment, lawyers are not only expected to provide legal advice but also to understand the business context in which their advice will be applied. This understanding begins with mastering the fundamentals of business, including financial literacy and the basic concepts and terminology that underpin the business world. This foundational knowledge is crucial for lawyers aiming to offer comprehensive counsel and build stronger relationships with their clients.

The Necessity of Financial Literacy for Lawyers

Financial literacy is essential for lawyers across all specializations, not just those directly involved in financial law. A basic understanding of financial principles enables lawyers to interpret financial documents, assess the financial health of a business, and understand the economic implications of legal decisions. This competency allows lawyers to offer advice that not only addresses legal concerns but also supports the client's overall business objectives. For instance, in mergers and acquisitions, understanding the financial statements of the entities involved is crucial to evaluating the deal's viability and structuring agreements that maximize value for clients.

Basic Business Concepts and Terminology Every Lawyer Should Know

To effectively communicate with clients and other professionals in the business world, lawyers must be conversant in the language of business. This includes understanding basic concepts such as the following:

- **Profit and Loss (P&L) Statements:** These documents provide a summary of the revenues, costs, and expenses incurred during a specific period. They are essential for assessing a company's financial performance.
- **Balance Sheets:** Balance sheets offer a snapshot of a company's financial condition at a specific point in time, detailing assets, liabilities, and shareholders' equity.
- **Cash Flow Statements:** These statements track the flow of cash in and out of a business, highlighting its operational, investing, and financing activities.

- **ROI:** ROI measures the gain or loss generated on an investment relative to the amount of money invested. It is a key indicator of the efficiency and profitability of an investment.
- **Market Capitalization:** This term refers to the total market value of a company's outstanding shares of stock. It is calculated by multiplying the company's share price by its total number of outstanding shares.

In addition to these financial concepts, lawyers should familiarize themselves with business terminology related to their clients' industries. This might include specific jargon used in technology, health care, real estate, or any other sector relevant to their practice.

Understanding business fundamentals is not just about acquiring knowledge; it is about applying this knowledge to enhance legal practice. Lawyers who are financially literate and well-versed in business concepts can better serve their clients, offering advice that is both legally sound and strategically aligned with business goals. This dual competency fosters trust, strengthens client relationships, and positions lawyers as indispensable advisors in the business decision-making process.

Jacques L. Moye: Blending Finance and Law for Expertise in M&A and Real Estate Transactions

Member, Clark Hill

Jacques L. Moye's career trajectory is a compelling example of how diverse professional experiences can enrich one's capabilities in the legal domain. Initially embarking on a career as a certified public accountant (CPA) at a Big 4 accounting firm, Jacques developed a robust foundation in finance and business operations. His interest in law was piqued through exposure to complex case studies involving financial fraud and misappropriation of assets, where he noticed the pivotal roles played by lawyers and accountants in navigating corporate transactions. This realization led him to pursue a dual expertise, aiming to make himself as marketable and versatile as possible.

After acquiring significant experience and obtaining his CPA designation, Jacques decided to deepen his expertise by transitioning into law. He attended law school in the evenings while working in government auditing, a period he describes as challenging but ultimately rewarding. His unique blend of skills in both accounting and law has positioned him as a valuable advisor in the fields of mergers and acquisitions, private equity, and real estate transactions. Jacques' journey from accounting to law exemplifies the importance of interdisciplinary knowledge and the advantage of possessing a diverse skill set in today's complex legal landscape.

Mergers, Acquisitions, and Real Estate: A Dual Focus

Jacques' involvement in the legal field spans a broad spectrum, with a significant focus on M&A as well as real estate law. His early years in the profession saw him deeply engaged in large transactions, including asset acquisitions and sales, alongside complex stock deals and joint venture transactions. These experiences, which involved representing both buyers and sellers in multimillion and billion-dollar deals, provided Jacques with an in-depth understanding of the dynamics and intricacies of corporate law. His work did not stop at corporate transactions; Jacques also played a pivotal role in private equity work, facilitating the raising of capital for investment in companies and real estate projects across the United States.

His transition into real estate law was somewhat serendipitous, stemming from his work with national real estate developers. This shift saw his practice evolve to include the representation of clients in the acquisition of office buildings, hotels, and the development of commercial retail centers and malls. Jacques' unique position, with a foot in both the corporate and real estate legal worlds, allowed him to manage comprehensive agreements that typically require the expertise of both a real estate lawyer and a corporate lawyer. This dual capability is particularly advantageous in real estate transactions involving complex financing structures, where Jacques' ability to understand and navigate both the real estate and corporate aspects streamlines the process for his clients.

Jacques strongly advocates for aspiring lawyers interested in real estate law to gain corporate experience and vice versa. His rationale is grounded in the belief that understanding the broader context of transactions, including the financial and structural components, significantly enhances a lawyer's ability to provide comprehensive and effective counsel. This advice is not just theoretical but is based on Jacques' own experiences where his corporate background enabled him to handle all aspects of real estate deals, including those typically outsourced to corporate specialists. This integrated approach not only simplifies transactions but also offers clients a more coherent and efficient service, highlighting the value of interdisciplinary knowledge in the legal profession.

The Value of a Business Background in Law

Jacques underscores the significance of having a business background, especially in accounting, for those looking to forge a career in corporate law or M&A. He shares an illustrative example from his practice where his accounting expertise directly contributed to a more favorable outcome for a client. In one instance, Jacques was able to leverage his deep understanding of financial statements to negotiate a higher purchase price during a transaction. His ability to analyze balance sheets and income statements in detail allowed him to identify undervalued aspects of the company being acquired, thereby arguing for a higher valuation. This example not only highlights the practical benefits of possessing technical skills but also showcases how such skills can lead to tangible advantages in negotiations.

Beyond the technical, Jacques also emphasizes the importance of soft skills and energy in the legal profession. He believes that the ability to communicate effectively, build relationships with clients, and understand their needs is as crucial as having a strong technical foundation. Jacques's approach to law is client-centered, focusing on building trust and ensuring that his clients feel valued and understood. This combination of technical prowess and interpersonal skills has been key to his success and longevity in the field.

Jacques advises aspiring lawyers to cultivate a mindset of continuous learning and adaptation. The legal landscape is constantly evolving, with new laws and regulations shaping the practice. Having the energy and motivation to stay informed and adapt to these changes is essential. Jacques' own career, marked by a transition from accounting to law and a continuous expansion of his areas of expertise, exemplifies the benefits of embracing change and seeking out new challenges. This blend of technical skills, soft skills, and a proactive attitude forms the foundation of a successful career in law, according to Jacques.

Developing Financial Literacy

For lawyers, developing financial literacy is not merely an enhancement to their skill set; it's a critical component of their professional development. This literacy empowers them to interpret key financial documents accurately and conduct financial analysis from a legal perspective, enabling them to understand a client's business more deeply. This section delves into the essential financial documents lawyers should be familiar with and outlines how financial analysis can be applied in legal practice.

Key Financial Documents and Their Interpretations

- **Profit and Loss (P&L) Statements:** Also known as income statements, these documents are fundamental for understanding a company's revenue, costs, and expenses over a specific period. Lawyers need to interpret these statements to assess a company's operational efficiency and profitability, which can be crucial in cases involving financial disputes, mergers, or acquisitions.
- **Balance Sheets:** A balance sheet provides a snapshot of a company's financial condition at a particular moment, detailing its assets, liabilities, and shareholders' equity. For lawyers, understanding a balance sheet is essential for evaluating a company's solvency, financial stability, and the implications of these factors on legal strategies.
- **Cash Flow Statements:** These statements track the movement of cash in and out of a business, offering insights into its liquidity and cash management practices. Lawyers can use this information to gauge a company's ability to meet its short-term obligations and fund its operations, which is particularly relevant in bankruptcy or restructuring cases.
- **Equity Statements:** Also known as statements of shareholders' equity, these documents detail changes in the ownership interest of a company's shareholders over time. They provide insights into the company's dividend policy, issuance of new shares, and other equity-related activities, which can be pertinent in shareholder disputes or corporate governance issues.

Financial Analysis for Lawyers: Understanding a Client's Business from a Financial Perspective

Financial analysis involves interpreting the data contained in financial documents to make informed judgments about a company's financial health and future performance. For lawyers, this analysis is not about making investment decisions but about understanding the financial implications of legal actions and advising clients accordingly.

- **Ratio Analysis:** Lawyers can use financial ratios, such as the debt-to-equity ratio, current ratio, and return on equity, to assess a company's financial health. These ratios can provide insights into a company's leverage, liquidity, and profitability, informing legal strategies in various contexts, from litigation to corporate transactions.

- **Trend Analysis:** By examining financial statements over multiple periods, lawyers can identify trends in a company's performance. This can be crucial for understanding the impact of past events or decisions on a company's financial health and anticipating future challenges or opportunities.
- **Benchmarking:** Comparing a company's financial metrics with those of its peers or industry standards can offer valuable context. This analysis can help lawyers understand a client's competitive position and the legal implications of industry-specific risks and opportunities.

Developing financial literacy enables lawyers to view their clients' legal issues through a financial lens, enhancing their ability to provide comprehensive advice that considers both legal and business implications. By mastering the interpretation of key financial documents and applying financial analysis techniques, lawyers can deepen their understanding of a client's business, leading to more informed legal strategies and stronger client relationships. This financial acumen is a powerful tool in the lawyer's tool kit, facilitating a more holistic approach to legal practice.

Business Understanding and Client-Centric Approaches

Possessing a deep understanding of your client's business model and industry is not just beneficial—it's imperative for delivering high-quality, relevant legal services. This comprehension enables lawyers to anticipate the needs and challenges their clients face, tailoring their advice to not only address legal issues but also support business objectives. Coupled with a client-centric approach, this understanding fosters stronger relationships, enhances client satisfaction, and ultimately contributes to the success of both the client and the legal practice.

The Importance of Understanding Your Client's Business Model and Industry

A client's business model and industry context significantly influence their legal needs and the potential risks and opportunities they face. For example, a technology start-up will have different priorities and legal concerns than a manufacturing company. Understanding the specific dynamics, regulatory environment, and competitive landscape of your client's industry allows you to provide more nuanced and strategic legal advice.

This understanding is crucial for several reasons:

- **Anticipating Legal Needs:** By knowing the ins and outs of a client's business, lawyers can proactively identify potential legal issues before they become problems, offering preventive advice and solutions.
- **Strategic Decision Making:** Lawyers can contribute to strategic business decisions by advising on the legal implications of various options, helping clients navigate complex choices with confidence.

- **Risk Management:** An in-depth understanding of a client's business and industry enables lawyers to better assess and manage risks, advising on compliance, regulatory issues, and potential legal challenges.

Strategies for Adopting a Client-Centric Approach in Legal Practice

A client-centric approach focuses on understanding and meeting the client's needs and expectations, ensuring that the legal services provided are not only of high quality but also relevant and valuable to the client. Here are strategies to adopt this approach:

- **Active Listening and Communication:** Engage in active listening to truly understand your client's concerns, objectives, and expectations. Clear and open communication helps build trust and ensures that you are aligned with your client's goals.
- **Tailored Legal Solutions:** Customize your legal advice and solutions to fit the specific context and needs of your client's business. Avoid one-size-fits-all approaches and consider the unique aspects of each client's situation.
- **Accessibility and Responsiveness:** Be accessible and responsive to your clients. Timely responses and the willingness to be available when needed demonstrate your commitment to their success.
- **Feedback and Improvement:** Regularly seek feedback from your clients on your services and their satisfaction. Use this feedback to continuously improve and adapt your approach to better meet their needs.

Adopting a client-centric approach, underpinned by a thorough understanding of your client's business model and industry, is essential for modern legal practice. It enables lawyers to provide advice that is not only legally sound but also strategically aligned with the client's business objectives. This approach strengthens client relationships, enhances the value of legal services, and positions lawyers as trusted advisors who play a key role in their clients' success.

Insights and Perspectives in Corporate Immigration Law and Legal Profession: Dustin O'Quinn

Shareholder, Immigration Team Chair, Lane Powell

Dustin O'Quinn has established himself as a distinguished figure in the realm of immigration law, advising a broad spectrum of employers ranging from start-ups to Fortune 100 corporations. With a keen focus on industries such as health care, technology, design, higher education, and finance, Dustin's expertise encompasses the development of immigration programs for emerging companies, guiding them through corporate structuring, fundraising, and investor relations. In addition, he offers strategic counsel to large corporations navigating the immigration implications of mergers, acquisitions, I-9 compliance, and government audits.

His legal acumen extends to representing employers in less common visa classifications, including those for investors, individuals of extraordinary ability, religious workers, and maritime immigration matters. This breadth of experience underscores Dustin's ability to navigate the complex landscape of immigration law with a nuanced understanding of its application across various sectors.

Currently serving as the Shareholder and Immigration Team Chair at Lane Powell, Dustin's role involves steering the firm's direction in immigration law and ensuring that it remains at the forefront of legal practice in this area. Through his work, Dustin O'Quinn exemplifies the blend of technical expertise and approachable professionalism that defines successful practice in the dynamic field of immigration law.

Advice for Young Lawyers and Law Students

Dustin's own professional journey illustrates the unpredictable twists and turns a legal career can encompass. After law school, he faced the challenge of entering a job market that had suddenly contracted, leaving him without an immediate position in big law—a sector many assume to be the most lucrative and prestigious path in the legal field. "I only had one basket. I put all my eggs in the big law basket," he recalls, acknowledging the narrow focus that initially guided his career aspirations. This experience taught him the value of flexibility and resilience, qualities that would prove instrumental in his eventual success.

His first role at a small immigration firm in San Antonio, Texas, marked a pivotal moment in his career. It was an opportunity that many might have overlooked, but for Dustin, it was a chance to dive into the field of immigration law—a sector he had always been interested in but had set aside in pursuit of big law opportunities. This position not only allowed him to gain invaluable hands-on experience but also opened doors to larger firms and more complex immigration cases. "That open-mindedness was, I think, so important," he reflects on his decision to embrace an opportunity outside of his initial expectations. Through this experience, Dustin underscores the importance of being receptive to the opportunities that come one's way, regardless of how they measure up to preconceived notions of success in the legal field.

Billing Structures and Business Models in Corporate Immigration Law

In the world of corporate immigration law, billing practices significantly influence the delivery of services, client relationships, and the operations of law firms. Dustin sheds light on the prevailing billing structures within this specialized field, highlighting the distinction between fixed fees and hourly billing. Large clients, particularly those with extensive immigration needs, often work with large immigration firms on a fixed fee basis. This model provides predictability for both the firm and the client, facilitating the management of large volumes of cases with efficiency. "Corporate immigration is vastly fixed fees for the very large clients," Dustin explains, emphasizing the practicality of this approach for handling high-volume immigration work.

However, the scenario shifts when dealing with smaller clients or cases that require a more detailed analysis and strategic planning. In these instances, hourly billing becomes more common, as it allows for a tailored approach to each case. Dustin points out the necessity of this flexibility, stating, "Immigration is just not one size fits all anymore," underscoring the importance of adapting billing practices to the specific demands of each case. This adaptability ensures that the firm can provide comprehensive service while accurately compensating for the time and effort invested in each client's unique situation.

Despite recognizing the merits of both billing models, Dustin also acknowledges the challenges and inefficiencies they present. The fixed fee model, while beneficial for managing large volumes of work, can lead to rate suppression and potentially compromise the quality of service if not carefully managed. On the contrary, the billable hour model, although it allows for greater flexibility in billing, can be perceived as promoting inefficiency and can be psychologically taxing for legal professionals. Dustin candidly shares his concerns about the billable hour system, describing it as "soul crushing" and expressing a preference for billing methods that better align with delivering value to clients.

Through his insights, Dustin O'Quinn highlights the nuanced considerations that law firms must navigate in structuring their billing practices. Whether opting for fixed fees or hourly billing, the ultimate goal remains the same: to provide effective legal services that meet the needs of clients while ensuring the sustainability and integrity of the firm's operations. In navigating these billing structures, Dustin's approach underscores the importance of flexibility, transparency, and a steadfast commitment to client service in the ever-evolving landscape of corporate immigration law.

Mentorship, DEI, and AI in the Legal Profession

Dustin shares a personal story about how mentorship played a crucial role in his career development, emphasizing the importance of finding mentors who can offer guidance and insight. "I'm a firm believer in carefully and professionally asking for what you want," he says, recounting a time when he proactively sought speaking opportunities, leading to increased visibility and connections with experienced lawyers, sponsors, and mentors. This initiative not only expanded his professional network but also positioned him as a thought leader in the field of immigration law.

On the topic of DEI, Dustin highlights the undeniable business case for DEI in corporate immigration law. He notes that diverse teams yield better results, as they bring varied perspectives that challenge each other, leading to more creative and effective outcomes for clients. "It's been proven by countless consulting firms and studies that diverse teams yield better results," Dustin remarks, underscoring the value of incorporating diverse perspectives in business and legal strategies.

Looking toward the future, Dustin discusses the anticipated impact of AI on the practice of business law, particularly in immigration. He predicts that AI will revolutionize aspects of pricing, billing, and corporate culture, making processes more efficient but also challenging traditional models. "AI will change the way we think about billing and pricing," he explains, suggesting that the legal profession must adapt to these technological advancements to stay competitive and meet clients' evolving needs. Dustin's insights into mentorship, DEI, and AI underscore his forward-thinking approach to law, highlighting the importance of adaptability, inclusivity, and innovation in shaping a successful legal career.

Enhancing Client Relations and Business Development

Building and maintaining strong client relationships are central to the success of any legal practice. Effective communication and relationship-building techniques, coupled with leveraging business understanding, can significantly enhance client relations and open new avenues for business development and networking. This section explores strategies that go beyond the basics, focusing on innovative ways to deepen client connections and use business insights for growth, ensuring the content complements rather than duplicates previous sections.

Techniques for Effective Client Communication and Relationship Building

- **Personalized Communication:** Tailor your communication style and methods to match each client's preferences. Some clients may prefer brief email updates, while others might value more in-depth discussions via video calls. Personalizing your approach shows respect for their time and working style.
- **Proactive Updates and Insights:** Don't wait for clients to reach out with questions or concerns. Proactively provide updates on their cases and share relevant insights that might impact their business. This could include sending briefs on recent legal developments or industry trends that could affect their operations.
- **Client Education:** Offer to conduct workshops or seminars for your clients on legal topics relevant to their business. This not only reinforces your role as a trusted advisor but also provides added value to your clients by enhancing their understanding of legal issues.
- **Transparent Processes:** Be clear about your legal processes, timelines, and fees. Transparency builds trust and helps manage client expectations. Consider using client portals or other technology tools that allow clients to track the progress of their cases in real time.

Leveraging Business Understanding for Business Development and Networking

- **Industry-Specific Networking:** Participate in networking events, conferences, and seminars relevant to your clients' industries. This not only helps you stay informed about industry trends but also positions you as an engaged and knowledgeable legal professional among potential clients.
- **Content Marketing:** Use your business understanding to create and share content that addresses the specific challenges and questions of businesses in your client's industry. This could be through blog posts, newsletters, or social media content. Tailored content marketing can attract new clients who are seeking legal advice that aligns with their business needs.
- **Strategic Partnerships:** Build strategic partnerships with other professionals and firms that serve your clients' industries, such as accountants, consultants, and financial advisors. These partnerships can provide mutual referral opportunities and enhance the range of services you can offer to your clients.
- **Client Feedback Mechanisms:** Implement structured mechanisms for collecting and analyzing client feedback, focusing on their satisfaction with

your services and their evolving business needs. Use this feedback to refine your approach and identify new business development opportunities.

- **Customized Business Solutions:** Offer legal services that are packaged as business solutions, addressing not just the legal issue but also the business implications. For example, if you're advising a client on compliance, consider how this impacts their operational efficiency and risk management strategies. This approach demonstrates a deep understanding of your client's business and can differentiate your services in a competitive market.

By employing these advanced techniques for client communication and leveraging your business understanding for development and networking, you can enhance client relations and drive the growth of your legal practice. These strategies emphasize the importance of being not just a legal advisor but a strategic business partner to your clients.

Building a Business-Savvy Legal Practice

In the rapidly evolving legal landscape, building a business-savvy legal practice is no longer optional—it's essential. A legal team that possesses not only legal expertise but also a deep understanding of business principles and acumen can significantly enhance a law firm's value proposition. This section explores the multifaceted benefits of cultivating a business-savvy legal team, including gains in efficiency, innovation, and competitive advantage, and the importance of leaning on experts in various areas to achieve these goals.

The Benefits of a Business-Savvy Legal Team

- **Efficiency:** A legal team with strong business acumen can operate more efficiently by understanding the broader business implications of legal decisions. This understanding allows for streamlined processes, better allocation of resources, and more effective management of client expectations. Efficiency not only reduces costs but also improves client satisfaction by delivering value more quickly and effectively.
- **Innovation:** Business-savvy legal teams are better positioned to innovate in their service delivery. By understanding the market dynamics and challenges their clients face, they can develop innovative legal solutions that address these challenges head-on. This might include offering alternative billing models, leveraging technology to provide more accessible services, or developing specialized expertise in emerging areas of law that are critical to their clients' business success.

- **Competitive Advantage:** In a crowded legal market, a business-savvy approach can differentiate a law firm from its competitors. Clients are increasingly looking for legal advisors who not only understand the law but also grasp the nuances of their business and industry. By demonstrating a deep understanding of business principles and applying them in legal practice, a firm can position itself as a preferred partner for clients seeking strategic legal counsel.

Leaning on Experts in Various Areas

Building a business-savvy legal practice often requires going beyond the traditional boundaries of legal training and expertise. It involves the following:

- **Cross-Disciplinary Collaboration:** Encourage collaboration between lawyers and professionals from other disciplines, such as finance, technology, and marketing. This cross-pollination of ideas can lead to more comprehensive and innovative legal solutions that address all aspects of a client's business.
- **Continuing Education:** Invest in ongoing education and training for your legal team in key business areas. This could include workshops on financial literacy, seminars on industry-specific trends, or courses on business strategy and management.
- **Hiring Diverse Talent:** Consider hiring or partnering with professionals who bring a blend of legal and business expertise to the team. This could include individuals with MBAs, experience in business consulting, or backgrounds in industries relevant to your clients.
- **Utilizing External Consultants:** When necessary, don't hesitate to bring in external consultants with deep expertise in specific business areas. These experts can provide valuable insights and guidance on complex issues, helping your legal team navigate unfamiliar territory.
- **Fostering a Culture of Business Curiosity:** Cultivate an environment where lawyers are encouraged to think beyond the legal aspects of a case and consider the business implications. This can involve regular discussions about business news, case studies that highlight the intersection of law and business, and incentives for lawyers who demonstrate strong business acumen.

Building a business-savvy legal practice is a strategic investment that can pay dividends in terms of efficiency, innovation, and competitive positioning. By embracing business principles, leaning on experts in various areas, and fostering a culture of continuous learning, law firms can enhance their ability to serve clients effectively and navigate the complexities of the modern business world.

Calvin Cheong: Innovating Business Growth in Emerging Companies and Venture Capital

Director of Client Development—Emerging Companies and Venture Capital, Holland & Knight

Calvin Cheong stands at the forefront of client development and strategic growth in the legal profession, particularly within the realms of Emerging Companies and Venture Capital practices. As the Director of Client Development at Holland & Knight, based out of the firm's Century City office in Los Angeles, Calvin brings over two decades of experience to the table. His work is centered on spearheading initiatives that not only expand the firm's reach within the tech industry but also enhance the range of business-related services provided to clients. His role involves a deep commitment to connecting high-growth companies at all stages with the necessary strategic partners, human capital, and growth equity to fuel their advancement.

Educationally, Calvin's background is as diverse as his professional experience. He holds a Bachelor of Science from the University of Maryland, complemented by specialized programs that have honed his skills in negotiation and leadership from Harvard Law School, corporate strategy from the University of Chicago, and venture capital from the University of California, Berkeley. This rich educational tapestry has equipped him with the insights and analytical skills necessary to navigate the complex landscape of business law and client development.

Before joining Holland & Knight, Calvin had already made significant strides in the legal and business development sectors, holding top roles at global law firms. Calvin's unique approach to client development, combined with his extensive experience and educational background, positions him as a pivotal figure in the legal profession. His focus on the tech industry and emerging companies not only highlights the evolving nature of legal services but also underscores the importance of strategic, client-focused initiatives in fostering growth and success.

Innovative Client Development Approach

At his previous firm, Calvin recognized a gap in the traditional legal service model, particularly in how firms managed relationships with their clients. "At the end of the day, as a founder, I want to know, what else does your firm offer me? What insights, what additional services, what network connectivity?" he reflected. This question led to the conceptualization and implementation of the Value-Added Services program. Calvin's vision was to create a 360-degree relationship management strategy that extended beyond the standard scope of legal services, incorporating additional support in marketing, PR, and HR for clients. This approach aimed to provide a more comprehensive support to clients, ensuring that their needs were met in a holistic manner.

The impact of this innovative program on client satisfaction and firm growth was significant. "When you're paying $1,000 an hour, your expectation is that you're going to get best in class legal counsel," Calvin explained, highlighting the importance of exceeding these expectations by offering something more. By focusing on what additional value the firm could provide, Calvin was able to foster deeper, more meaningful relationships with clients. This not only enhanced client satisfaction but also contributed to the firm's growth by setting it apart from competitors. The program demonstrated that understanding and addressing the broader needs of clients could lead to greater success for both the clients and the firm.

Calvin's work showcased his ability to think innovatively about client development. By identifying and addressing a critical need for more comprehensive client support, he was able to implement a program that significantly benefited both the clients and the firm.

Calvin's Unique Role at Holland & Knight

In his current role, Calvin has taken a comprehensive approach to client development, focusing on the firm's Emerging Companies and Venture Capital practices. His strategy involves a multifaceted engagement with businesses, aiming to connect them with essential resources such as strategic partners, human capital, and growth equity. Calvin leverages his extensive background in capital markets, start-ups, economic development, and professional services to guide these companies through their growth phases. His work is instrumental in creating effective go-to-market strategies, uncovering business expansion opportunities, and providing actionable insights through market and competitive analysis.

Calvin's approach to capital raising advisory is particularly noteworthy. Although Holland & Knight is not a registered broker-dealer or an investment bank, Calvin emphasizes the firm's robust relationships within the venture capital and private equity communities. This network, built on years of experience and pattern recognition, enables him to assist companies in refining their brand messaging, narratives, and pitches. The goal is to facilitate meaningful introductions to investors, some of whom are firm clients, while others are external investors. This strategic advisory extends beyond mere introductions; it involves a deep dive into the companies' business plans, operational strategies, and market positioning to identify opportunities and potential hurdles.

Furthermore, Calvin utilizes Holland & Knight's extensive platform to offer a wide range of resources to clients. This includes access to marketing and communications, public relations, performance and talent management, professional development, and human resources. For instance, if a growing company needs to implement DEI programs, Calvin and his team can provide non-billable resources to advise on best practices and connect them with external contractors or vendors. This holistic approach not only ensures that clients receive top-notch legal counsel but also benefits from the firm's comprehensive support in navigating their growth and development challenges.

Through these strategic initiatives, Calvin has significantly contributed to enhancing Holland & Knight's service offerings to emerging companies and venture capitalists. His work underscores the importance of not just legal expertise but also a deep understanding of the business landscape and the ability to provide value-added services that support clients' broader business objectives.

Insights and Advice for Early Career Attorneys

One piece of advice Calvin emphasizes is the importance of genuinely understanding your clients' businesses. "There's nothing worse than going to a pitch meeting and the first question you hear from an attorney is, 'Tell me about what you do,'" Calvin notes. He advocates for a proactive approach, where attorneys should enter meetings already well-versed in their client's industry, challenges, and goals. This level of preparation not only positions you as a trusted advisor but also demonstrates your commitment to their success.

Strategic networking is another area Calvin highlights as crucial for career development. He shares an example from his own experience, where building relationships across the tech and venture capital sectors has been instrumental in his role. "By virtue of pattern recognition, we can help companies refine their brand messaging, their narrative, and their pitches," he explains. This ability comes from not just meeting but understanding and connecting with a wide array of stakeholders in the industry. For Calvin, networking isn't just about expanding your contact list; it's about building meaningful relationships that can provide value both to you and to those you connect with.

Calvin's advice to aspiring legal professionals is clear: understand your clients deeply, invest in strategic networking, and commit to lifelong learning. These principles have guided him through a successful career in business law, and they offer a solid foundation for those looking to make their mark in this challenging yet rewarding field.

Technology and Legal Practice: Navigating Technological Advancements

Technology plays a pivotal role in shaping the way legal practitioners develop their skills and learn, the way legal services are delivered, and how legal practices operate. From AI and cybersecurity to document automation and data analytics, technological advancements are transforming the field, offering both opportunities and challenges. This section, D3, delves into the critical aspects of technology in legal practice, providing insights into how attorneys, especially those in the early stages of their careers, can navigate these changes effectively.

Understanding the tech landscape is essential for modern legal professionals who aim to enhance their practice, safeguard client information, and maintain a competitive edge. Through exploring AI's role in legal tasks, cybersecurity essentials, the use of legal tech tools for efficiency, and the ethical considerations of technology use, this section offers a comprehensive guide to integrating technology into legal practice. In addition, it highlights the importance of continuous learning to keep pace with technological change, the career advantages of tech proficiency, and ways to cultivate innovation in legal work.

As we embark on this exploration of Technology and Legal Practice, we emphasize the transformative impact of technology on the legal profession and underscore the necessity for attorneys to adapt, innovate, and thrive in this dynamic environment.

The Journey of Pankaj Raval: From Social Justice to Legal Innovation

Founder of Carbon Law

Pankaj Raval's journey into the legal profession was significantly influenced by his early passion for social justice, a flame that was ignited by reading Mahatma Gandhi's *The Story of My Experiments with Truth*. This seminal moment in his teenage years not only shaped his desire to make a tangible impact in the world but also led him to see the law as a potent vehicle for change. His leadership roles, spanning from high school to law school, where he led various clubs and organizations, further cemented his commitment to making a difference. This drive was not confined to academic or extracurricular leadership; Pankaj also explored creative avenues, notably in dance and graphic design, showcasing a multifaceted approach to his interests and talents.

Before embarking on his legal education, Pankaj spent a transformative year in India with Indicorps, an experience that immersed him in grassroots social work. Working in the slums to teach music and English, advocating for fishermen's rights against corporate land seizures, and tutoring Tibetan monks in English, Pankaj lived and breathed the essence of service. This period was not just about the work done on the ground; it was a profound journey of personal growth, living modestly and forming lasting bonds with those committed to giving without expectation. The hardships faced and the simplicity of life in these communities left a lasting imprint on him, reinforcing his belief in the power of service.

Returning to the University of Arizona for law school, Pankaj found himself at a crossroads, trying to reconcile his deep-seated desire to help with the theoretical and often abstract nature of legal studies. However, his involvement in a clinic for start-ups during his third year provided a glimpse into how law could be applied to assist entrepreneurs and small businesses directly. This experience was instrumental in shaping his future path, laying the groundwork for his commitment to serving businesses and entrepreneurs through his legal practice. Through these diverse experiences, Pankaj Raval's path to law was marked by a consistent theme: a dedication to service and social justice, informed by a tapestry of leadership, creativity, and transformative real-world experiences.

Embracing Change and Innovation in Legal Practice

Pankaj's aspirations initially aligned with the conventional trajectory many law students envision: securing a position in a large, prestigious law firm. However, the economic downturn in 2009 drastically altered the landscape for many new graduates, including Pankaj. The widespread loss of job offers from big law firms forced him to reconsider his path. Reflecting on this period, Pankaj not only acknowledged the disillusionment but also recognized it as a pivotal moment that steered him toward a more fulfilling career. He found solace and opportunity in a smaller firm environment in Tucson, where he could engage directly with clients and develop his legal skills in a more hands-on, practical manner. This experience underscored the importance of balance in his professional life, a principle that would guide his future decisions.

The move to Los Angeles marked a significant shift in Pankaj's career. Despite the daunting prospect of entering a saturated market, he was driven by a desire to work in entertainment law, fueled by previous experiences and personal connections in the industry. His early days in Los Angeles were characterized by relentless networking and a willingness to leverage his unique skills, such as graphic design, to add value in unconventional ways. This proactive approach not only helped him secure opportunities but also laid the groundwork for his own practice. Pankaj's entrepreneurial spirit was evident as he navigated the challenges of starting and growing a law firm, driven by a commitment to serve the creative and business communities.

Innovation has been a cornerstone of Pankaj's legal practice, particularly in how he structures his services and billing. Moving away from the traditional hourly billing model, he embraced flat fees and subscription pricing, reflecting a broader trend toward transparency and predictability in legal costs. This approach not only aligns with the needs of his entrepreneurial clientele but also represents a shift in the legal industry toward more client-centered service models. In addition, Pankaj's openness to technology and AI underscores his belief in the evolving role of lawyers. While acknowledging the transformative potential of these tools in streamlining tasks and enhancing efficiency, he maintains that the core of legal practice—strategic advising and building trust with clients—remains indispensable. Through these innovative strategies, Pankaj has not only adapted to change but has actively shaped a practice that reflects his values and vision for the future of law.

Building a Network and a Name in a New City

After settling in Los Angeles, Pankaj faced the immense challenge of establishing himself in a city brimming with legal professionals. Without the security of a job offer in hand, he embarked on a journey of strategic networking and skill leveraging, which would ultimately lay the foundation for his own law firm. Pankaj reached out to contacts, new and old, for meetings over coffee or lunch, making it a point to meet with someone three to four times a week. His approach wasn't just about expanding his professional network; it was about being transparent with his intentions and asking directly for what he wanted—opportunities in transactional law and, later, clients for his own firm.

Pankaj's unique background in graphic design and his personal interests, such as meditation, played a crucial role in differentiating him in a crowded market. His ability to offer more than just legal expertise, helping a bankruptcy lawyer with website design, for example, showcased his multifaceted skills and willingness to add value in unconventional ways. This approach not only helped him secure initial work but also fostered a spirit of collaboration and partnership with other professionals. Pankaj's engagement with various networking groups and his active participation in a meditation group led to significant connections, including close friendships and professional relationships that resulted in a steady flow of referrals.

The value of giving without expecting immediate returns was a principle that Pankaj embraced wholeheartedly. By focusing on building genuine relationships and offering help where he could, he cultivated a network of peers and clients who trusted him and were willing to support his burgeoning practice. This approach, rooted in generosity and clear communication, enabled Pankaj to establish a name for himself in Los Angeles and build a client base from the ground up. Through persistence, clarity of purpose, and a willingness to give, he navigated the challenges of entering a new city's legal landscape and laid the groundwork for what would become a thriving law firm.

The Future of Law and Advice for Aspiring Lawyers

Pankaj acknowledges the transformative potential of AI and technology in the legal profession, emphasizing that while they introduce efficiencies, the essence of legal practice as a strategic and trust-based advisor remains unchanged. He highlights the rapid advancements in AI, noting its capacity to streamline tasks that traditionally consumed significant time. However, Pankaj firmly believes that the nuanced understanding and strategic guidance a lawyer provides cannot be replicated by technology. This blend of innovation and timeless professional values, he suggests, will shape the future of legal practice, where lawyers leverage technology to enhance their service while focusing on the core advisory role that defines their relationship with clients.

For law students and early career attorneys, Pankaj offers practical advice drawn from his own experiences. He stresses the importance of building a strong network, starting in law school, and continuing to nurture those connections throughout one's career. He recounts how relationships formed during his education and early professional life have been invaluable, leading to opportunities and mutual support. Furthermore, Pankaj champions the value of practical experience, particularly through participation in clinics and real-world client interactions, which he found more educational than theoretical study. These experiences, he suggests, are crucial in developing the skills necessary to navigate the complexities of legal practice.

Reflecting on the broader implications of the pandemic on work and life goals, Pankaj observes a significant shift toward reassessing priorities and embracing flexibility in work arrangements. He notes the legal profession's adaptation to remote work and the increased interest in finding a balance between professional aspirations and personal well-being. Pankaj encourages aspiring lawyers to remain open to change, to continuously evaluate their goals, and to seek paths that align with their values and desired lifestyle. ”

Understanding the Tech Landscape in Legal Practice

The intersection of technology and legal practice is not just a passing trend; it's a fundamental shift in how legal services are conceptualized, delivered, and improved upon. As we delve into the various facets of this intersection, it's crucial to understand that while specific technologies will evolve, the underlying principles of adaptability, efficiency, and innovation remain constant. This section aims to equip legal practitioners, especially those early in their careers, with the knowledge and mindset to navigate and leverage technological advancements in their practice.

The legal field is increasingly influenced by technological advancements such as AI, cybersecurity measures, and a plethora of digital tools designed to streamline legal operations. For early career attorneys, familiarizing themselves with this tech landscape is not just about keeping pace with current trends; it's about understanding the potential of technology to transform legal practice fundamentally. This understanding forms the foundation for leveraging technology to enhance service delivery, improve client satisfaction, and develop innovative legal solutions.

AI's Role in Modern Legal Tasks

AI is reshaping the way legal tasks are approached, offering tools for legal research, case analysis, and contract management that significantly enhance efficiency and accuracy. For new attorneys, integrating AI tools into their practice isn't just a means to an end; it's a strategic move that can provide a competitive advantage. Strategies for effective integration include identifying repetitive tasks that can be automated, using AI for data-driven insights in case strategy, and staying informed about the latest AI developments relevant to the legal field.

Cybersecurity Essentials for Legal Professionals

In an era where data breaches are increasingly common, the importance of cybersecurity in protecting client confidentiality and ensuring data integrity cannot be overstated. Legal professionals must adopt practical cybersecurity measures, including secure communication channels, data encryption, and regular security audits, to safeguard their practice and client information. Understanding the basics of cybersecurity is not just a technical skill but a professional responsibility in the digital age.

Enhancing Efficiency with Legal Tech Tools

A myriad of legal tech tools exists to streamline case management, automate document handling, and facilitate client communication. The key to effectively leveraging these tools lies in selecting and adopting solutions that align with your practice area, workflow, and client needs. Tips for successful technology adoption include evaluating tools based on their potential to improve efficiency, seeking feedback from peers, and considering the scalability of solutions as your practice grows.

Ethical Considerations in Technology Use

The use of technology in legal practice comes with its own set of ethical considerations, including concerns around AI, data privacy, and the security of client information. Navigating these ethical implications requires a thorough understanding of professional responsibility guidelines and a commitment to ethical conduct in all technological endeavors. Guidelines for ethical technology use include maintaining client confidentiality, ensuring the accuracy of automated processes, and being transparent with clients about the use of technology in their cases.

Keeping Pace with Technological Change

The pace of technological change in the legal sector is rapid, making continuous learning and adaptation essential for legal professionals. Approaches for staying updated include engaging with legal tech communities, participating in online courses and webinars, and attending industry conferences. Resources for legal tech education are plentiful, offering opportunities for skill development and networking with like-minded professionals.

Advancing Your Career with Tech Proficiency

Developing tech proficiency is not just an asset—it's a necessity for those looking to advance their careers and stay ahead of the curve. The integration of technology in legal practice has opened up new avenues for specialization, from cybersecurity law to legal data analytics, and has fundamentally changed the way legal services are delivered. To truly excel and differentiate oneself in this environment, legal professionals must cultivate a blend of technical skills, an innovative mindset, and a commitment to continuous learning.

Embracing a Tech-Savvy Legal Identity

Positioning yourself as a tech-savvy legal professional involves more than acquiring a set of technical skills; it requires embracing an identity that reflects a deep understanding of how technology can enhance legal practice. This identity is characterized by the following:

- **Curiosity and Openness to Innovation:** A genuine interest in emerging technologies and their potential applications in the legal field drives continuous exploration and learning.
- **Adaptability:** The legal tech landscape is constantly changing, with new tools and platforms emerging regularly. Being adaptable means staying flexible and open to adopting new technologies as they become relevant to your practice area.
- **Collaborative Mindset:** Technology often breaks down traditional silos within organizations and across the legal industry. A tech-savvy legal

professional recognizes the value of collaboration with IT professionals, data scientists, and other nonlegal experts to develop and implement tech-driven solutions.

Building Technical Skills and Knowledge

Developing tech proficiency requires a strategic approach to building your technical skills and knowledge. Key areas to focus on include the following:

- **Legal Tech Tools and Platforms:** Familiarize yourself with the most widely used legal tech tools, such as case management software, e-discovery platforms, and contract analysis tools. Understanding the capabilities and limitations of these tools is essential.
- **Data Analytics and Visualization:** The ability to analyze and interpret legal data can significantly enhance case strategy and client advice. Skills in data analytics and visualization can set you apart in a data-driven legal world.
- **Cybersecurity and Privacy:** With increasing concerns about data breaches and privacy violations, knowledge of cybersecurity practices and privacy laws is crucial. This is especially true for professionals working in areas like cybersecurity law and data protection.
- **Blockchain and Smart Contracts:** As blockchain technology finds more applications in legal contexts, such as smart contracts and intellectual property management, understanding its principles and potential legal implications is valuable.

Leveraging Resources for Continuous Learning

The journey to tech proficiency is ongoing, requiring a commitment to continuous learning. Resources to support this journey include the following:

- **Online Courses and Certifications:** Many platforms offer courses specifically designed for legal professionals looking to enhance their tech skills. These can range from introductory courses on legal tech to advanced certifications in data analytics or cybersecurity.
- **Legal Tech Conferences and Webinars:** Attending industry conferences and webinars is a great way to stay informed about the latest trends and innovations in legal tech. These events also offer networking opportunities with other tech-savvy legal professionals.
- **Professional Networks and Communities:** Joining legal tech communities, both online and offline, can provide valuable insights, support, and collaboration opportunities. These communities often share best practices, tools, and strategies for integrating technology into legal practice.

By embracing a tech-savvy identity, building technical skills, and leveraging resources for continuous learning, legal professionals can significantly advance their careers and meet the evolving demands of legal clients. The journey toward tech proficiency not only enhances your ability to deliver superior legal services but also positions you as a forward-thinking leader in the legal industry.

Cultivating Innovation in Legal Practice

Encouraging innovation and a forward-thinking mindset is crucial for legal professionals seeking to engage with legal tech trends proactively. Initiatives for fostering a culture of technological adoption and innovation within legal teams and organizations can include setting up innovation labs, hosting hackathons, and encouraging interdisciplinary collaboration. Cultivating innovation is about more than just adopting new tools; it's about reimagining the delivery of legal services in the digital age.

The transformative impact of technology on the legal profession underscores the necessity for attorneys to adapt, innovate, and thrive amid these changes. By engaging proactively with technological advancements, early career attorneys and those transitioning within business law can position themselves for career growth and success. The future of legal practice is inextricably linked with technology, and embracing this reality is key to developing a dynamic, efficient, and client-focused legal practice.

Cybersecurity and Privacy Law: Insights from Melissa Ventrone

Shareholder, Cybersecurity, Data Protection, and Privacy, Clark Hill

Melissa K. Ventrone stands at the forefront of addressing the multifaceted challenges that arise in the realm of cybersecurity, data protection, and privacy. Her leadership in the Cybersecurity, Data Protection, and Privacy practice at Clark Hill equips her with a pivotal role in guiding clients through the intricacies of the digital economy. Melissa's expertise is not limited to navigating current data security regulations such as the GDPR, CCPA (California Consumer Privacy Act), and HIPAA but extends to foreseeing and mitigating potential legal and security risks. This proactive approach ensures that clients not only comply with stringent regulatory requirements but also safeguard their most sensitive data.

Her background as a Marine Corps veteran brings a unique perspective to her professional endeavors. This experience instills in her a strategic approach to cybersecurity, emphasizing the importance of preparedness and resilience. By reviewing and enhancing data security policies and procedures, Melissa aids clients in developing comprehensive action plans. These plans are designed to establish compliance with a broad spectrum of laws and regulations while minimizing cyber risks.

Melissa's role exceeds the preventative measures, as she leads her team in offering round-the-clock support in the wake of data breaches or cybersecurity attacks. Her ability to manage the entire process from containment to recovery minimizes the impact on operations, reputation, and finances. Through her extensive experience in cybersecurity preparedness and incident response, Melissa identifies and executes the most effective strategies to protect clients' critical assets, showcasing her dedication to not just addressing immediate concerns but also fortifying her clients' defenses against future threats.

Challenges and Nuances of Cybersecurity and Privacy Law

Navigating the complexities of cybersecurity and privacy law presents a unique set of challenges, as Melissa Ventrone vividly illustrates through her experiences. A significant hurdle in the United States is the general underestimation of risks associated with data security and privacy. Melissa points out that in the United States, there is a tendency to focus on protecting specific data elements rather than considering the privacy of individuals in a more holistic manner. This narrow view fails to fully address the myriad ways in which data can be exploited, underscoring a critical gap in understanding and approach to privacy.

The advent of new privacy laws has introduced additional challenges, particularly concerning data deletion and tracking. Melissa highlights the difficulty in ensuring compliance with these laws, given the lack of technology capable of meticulously tracking where data are shared and ensuring their deletion across all platforms. This issue is compounded by emerging technologies, such as AI and ChatGPT, which bring forth new legal quandaries. A notable example Melissa discusses involves a lawsuit alleging the illegal use of collected information by these technologies, signaling the urgent need for legal frameworks that can keep pace with technological advancements.

At the heart of these challenges is the essential need for attorneys to grasp both the legal and business aspects of data management. Melissa emphasizes the importance of this dual understanding, noting that it is crucial for providing comprehensive advice that aligns with clients' operational realities and strategic goals. This approach not only aids in navigating current legal landscapes but also prepares clients for future developments in cybersecurity and privacy law.

Future of Cybersecurity and Privacy Law

Looking ahead, Melissa sees a dynamic future for the field of cybersecurity and privacy law, marked by significant growth and an expanding global focus. She underscores the importance of recognizing that the digital economy does not respect traditional borders. As data flow freely across the globe, legal professionals in this space cannot afford to have a narrow, region-specific understanding. Instead, a comprehensive grasp of international data protection laws and mechanisms becomes imperative. Melissa stresses the need for education on these global concepts, highlighting the necessity for attorneys to familiarize themselves with international data transfer mechanisms to effectively navigate the complexities of cross-border data flows.

The challenges in achieving a coherent global framework for data privacy and security are evident in the ongoing struggles to establish stable data transfer mechanisms between regions, such as the European Union and the United States. Melissa points to the repeated legal challenges and court decisions that have invalidated agreements like Privacy Shield and Safe Harbor, underscoring the fluid and often uncertain landscape of international data law. This situation, she notes, exemplifies the considerable work that lies ahead for the industry, not just in terms of crafting durable legal frameworks but also in achieving consensus among diverse regulatory environments.

This evolving landscape presents numerous opportunities for those entering the field. Melissa encourages aspiring attorneys to immerse themselves in the complexities and nuances of cybersecurity and privacy law, particularly as it becomes more intertwined with international regulations. By doing so, they position themselves at the cutting edge of a field that is not only growing but also increasingly vital to the functioning of the modern, digital world. As the industry continues to mature, the demand for skilled professionals who can navigate both the legal and technical aspects of data security and privacy on a global scale will only increase, offering a promising horizon for those with the foresight and dedication to specialize in this area.

Advice for Early Career Attorneys in Cybersecurity and Privacy Law

For those embarking on a career in cybersecurity and privacy law, Melissa offers advice drawn from her extensive experience. Central to her guidance is the importance of finding one's passion within the vast landscape of legal practice. Cybersecurity and privacy law, with its rapid evolution and critical importance to the digital economy, offers a plethora of opportunities for specialization and impact. Melissa's own satisfaction in guiding clients through the aftermath of ransomware attacks to a stronger, more secure position underscores the profound difference passionate legal professionals can make in this field.

Melissa also emphasizes the significance of staying abreast of emerging technologies. The legal challenges presented by innovations such as artificial intelligence and blockchain are vast and varied. By paying close attention to these developments, aspiring attorneys can position themselves at the forefront of the field, ready to address the novel legal questions these technologies raise. Developing a deep understanding of the industries one aims to serve is equally crucial. Melissa notes that a nuanced grasp of both the business and legal landscapes enables attorneys to provide advice that is not only legally sound but also strategically astute, aligning with clients' operational realities and goals.

Innovative Legal Practices: Exploring Nontraditional Roles, Niche Specializations, and Entrepreneurial Approaches

The legal profession stands at a crossroads, influenced by a confluence of globalization, technological advancements, and evolving client expectations. This dynamic environment presents both challenges and opportunities, compelling legal practitioners to venture beyond the confines of traditional roles and explore innovative pathways. This section delves into the realms of nontraditional legal roles, niche specializations, and entrepreneurial approaches that are redefining the contours of business law. Through this exploration, we aim to illuminate the diverse possibilities that await forward-thinking legal professionals eager to adapt, innovate, and lead in an ever-changing landscape. Whether it's embracing legaltech entrepreneurship, carving out a niche in emerging areas like fintech or cybersecurity law, or pioneering new legal service models, this section provides insights and strategies for those ready to embrace the future of legal practice.

Nontraditional Legal Roles

The legal profession is witnessing a paradigm shift, with the emergence of diverse career paths that extend beyond the traditional law firm model. These nontraditional roles, accessible to lawyers and law school graduates, capitalize on the unique skill set developed through legal education, offering avenues for innovative and impactful careers. This section explores the landscape of these emerging careers, the skills necessary for success, and strategies for transitioning into these dynamic fields, including roles that, while not requiring a law license, greatly benefit from a legal education.

Overview of Emerging Legal Careers

The expansion of legal careers into nontraditional areas has led to the creation of diverse opportunities that leverage the analytical, research, and ethical training of law school graduates. Some of these emerging careers include the following:

- **LegalTech Entrepreneurship:** The intersection of law and technology offers fertile ground for developing software and platforms that address legal needs, from document automation to legal analytics.
- **Legal Operations:** Focused on optimizing the delivery of legal services, legal operations professionals work to improve efficiency through process improvement, technology adoption, and vendor management.
- **Compliance Roles:** As regulations become more complex, the demand for compliance professionals grows. These roles involve ensuring organizational adherence to legal standards and regulatory requirements.
- **Privacy and Data Protection:** The importance of data privacy has led to roles specializing in navigating data protection laws and developing strategies to safeguard sensitive information.
- **Policy Development and Advocacy:** Working with governmental bodies or nonprofits to shape public policy and advocate for legal and regulatory changes, utilizing a deep understanding of the legislative process.
- **Legal Journalism and Media:** Reporting on legal news and analyzing high-profile cases, where a legal background enhances credibility and depth of reporting.
- **Corporate Governance and Risk Management:** Overseeing governance structures and managing risks associated with legal and regulatory challenges.

- **Human Resources and Employment Law Compliance:** Handling legal issues related to employment law, workplace policies, and labor regulations.

Skills for Success in Nontraditional Roles

Thriving in these innovative positions requires a blend of traditional legal skills and new competencies, including the following:

- **Technological Proficiency:** Essential for roles in legal tech and operations, as well as for navigating modern legal challenges.
- **Project Management:** Critical for managing initiatives in legal operations, compliance, and policy development.
- **Strategic Thinking:** Necessary for roles that require a strategic approach to legal and regulatory issues, including policy advocacy and corporate governance.
- **Adaptability and Continuous Learning:** The legal landscape is evolving rapidly, making adaptability and a commitment to continuous learning essential for success.

Transitioning to Nontraditional Roles

For lawyers and law school graduates interested in exploring nontraditional legal careers, the transition can be both exciting and challenging. Strategies to facilitate this shift include the following:

- **Leverage Legal Skills:** Highlight the transferable legal skills and knowledge you bring to the table, emphasizing how they can be applied in the specific role.
- **Expand Your Network:** Connect with professionals already working in nontraditional legal roles. Attend industry events, join relevant online communities, and engage in discussions to gain insights and advice.
- **Gain Relevant Experience:** Look for opportunities to gain experience in your desired field, even if it means starting with volunteer or part-time roles.
- **Pursue Continuous Education:** Consider additional certifications or courses that can complement your legal education and enhance your qualifications for the desired role.

The emergence of nontraditional legal roles represents a significant shift in the legal industry, offering new avenues for lawyers and law school graduates to apply their skills and passions. By understanding the landscape of these careers, developing the necessary skills, and strategically navigating the transition, legal professionals can position themselves to thrive in this evolving legal environment.

Social Entrepreneurship and Impact Innovation: A Journey with Neetal Parekh

Founder and CEO, Innov8social; Principal, Innovate Impact Media LLC

Neetal Parekh's journey into the legal profession and her subsequent pivot toward social entrepreneurship is a testament to the evolving nature of careers in law. With a foundation in international political science and business administration from UCLA, Neetal initially embarked on a path that might have led to a traditional legal career. However, her deep-seated interest in potentially doing international work propelled her toward law school, setting the stage for a career that would blend legal expertise with a passion for social impact.

Upon completing her law degree, Neetal's career trajectory took a distinctive turn toward social entrepreneurship—a field that was just beginning to gain recognition. As the Founder and CEO of Innov8social and Principal of Innovate Impact Media LLC, she has carved out a niche at the intersection of law, digital strategy, storytelling, and communications. Her work, notably through Innov8social, aims to make social entrepreneurship and impact leadership more accessible and actionable. This is achieved through a variety of mediums, including her book *51 Questions on Social Entrepreneurship*, The Impact Podcast by Innov8social, and the innovative event series, Impactathon.

Neetal's contributions to the field of social entrepreneurship and impact innovation reflect a broader trend of professionals leveraging their legal training in unconventional ways. Through her efforts, she not only champions the cause of social entrepreneurship but also serves as a role model for aspiring legal professionals and entrepreneurs alike. Her story underscores the potential of a legal education to serve as a versatile tool for those looking to make a meaningful impact beyond the traditional confines of the legal profession.

Early Career and Innov8social Beginnings

After law school, Neetal's career path took an unexpected turn. She joined an animal rights organization, a move that introduced her to the burgeoning world of social enterprise and the concept of the benefit corporation legal structure. This experience was pivotal, sparking a deep interest in how businesses could be structured to prioritize social impact alongside profit. It was a revelation that businesses didn't have to choose between doing good and doing well financially; they could aim to achieve both through innovative legal frameworks.

Motivated by this insight, Neetal launched Innov8social, initially as a blog and podcast. The platform was designed to explore the intersections of social entrepreneurship and legal structures, aiming to demystify these concepts for a broader audience. Her efforts expanded into authoring the book *51 Questions on Social Entrepreneurship*, a comprehensive guide that delves into the intricacies of launching and running a social enterprise. Recognizing the need for a more interactive approach to social entrepreneurship, Neetal also created Impactathon. These events, inspired by the hackathon model, provide a structured yet dynamic environment for individuals to collaborate on social impact projects, offering workshops and talks to guide participants from ideation to pitch stage.

Through these initiatives, Neetal has not only contributed significantly to the field of social entrepreneurship but has also established a unique niche at the intersection of law and social innovation. Her work exemplifies how legal knowledge and entrepreneurial spirit can combine to foster new ways of thinking about business and impact, setting a precedent for others in the legal profession to follow.

Advice for Law Students and Early Career Attorneys

Neetal Parekh offers advice to law students and early career attorneys, urging them to embrace their curiosity and consider using their law degrees in innovative ways. Reflecting on the changing landscape of legal education, she likens the law degree to an MBA, highlighting its versatility and the broad array of opportunities it can open up. This perspective challenges the traditional view of a law degree as solely a pathway to practicing law, suggesting instead that it equips individuals with a skill set that is highly adaptable and applicable across various sectors.

She advocates for the inclusion of rotations in different legal settings as part of the law school curriculum, drawing a parallel to the medical school model where students gain hands-on experience through rotations in various specialties. This, she believes, would better prepare law students for the diverse realities of legal practice and help them make more informed career choices. Neetal's suggestion underscores the importance of practical experience and exposure to the multifaceted nature of the legal profession.

Neetal sees significant potential for lawyers to venture into entrepreneurship or technology roles, leveraging their legal expertise to innovate and drive change. She points to the growing intersection between law and technology, particularly in the realm of legal tech, as an area ripe for exploration. Lawyers, with their deep understanding of the legal system and its intricacies, are uniquely positioned to develop tools and solutions that can democratize access to legal services and streamline the functioning of the legal industry. This shift toward entrepreneurship and tech underscores the evolving role of legal professionals in today's rapidly changing world.

Impactathons and Career Alignment

Neetal's innovative concept of Impactathons stands at the core of her mission to make social entrepreneurship more accessible. Drawing inspiration from hackathons, these events bring together individuals passionate about social impact for a weekend of collaboration and creativity. Unlike traditional hackathons that focus solely on coding and technology, Impactathons provide additional scaffolding to guide participants through the process of developing social enterprise ideas. This includes workshops on social enterprise basics, problem mapping to ensure solutions address root issues rather than symptoms, and lightning talks for varied perspectives. Through these events, participants leave not only with a viable social impact idea but also with a deeper understanding of how to use business models to create lasting change.

Neetal's advice for those seeking a career path aligned with their values emphasizes starting small and leveraging opportunities within one's current organization. For individuals in the legal field or other sectors, she suggests exploring entrepreneurship on the side or engaging with employee resource groups to find fulfillment. This approach allows for testing new ideas in a low-risk environment, providing valuable insights into one's preferences and strengths. In addition, Neetal encourages presenting constructive suggestions to leadership for making one's role more fulfilling, highlighting the potential for individual agency to effect change within an organization. ”

Entrepreneurial Approaches in Law

The legal profession, traditionally viewed as a bastion of conservatism, is now at the forefront of innovation, with entrepreneurial approaches gaining traction and becoming indispensable. Legal entrepreneurship is a multifaceted endeavor that transcends the mere establishment of law firms. It embodies the spirit of reimagining legal service delivery to meet the evolving demands of the market and clients. This expanded section delves deeper into the essence of legal entrepreneurship, exploring its diverse manifestations, the challenges and opportunities it harbors, and drawing inspiration from the journeys of pioneering legal entrepreneurs.

Legal Entrepreneurship: A Spectrum of Innovation

Legal entrepreneurship is a dynamic concept that encompasses a wide range of innovative activities:

- **Boutique and Specialized Law Firms:** Entrepreneurs are founding niche law firms that cater to specific industries or areas of law, such as environmental law, tech start-ups, or entertainment. These firms often employ flexible billing models, including flat fees or equity stakes, to align more closely with their clients' needs.
- **Legal Tech Ventures:** Visionaries are harnessing technology to revolutionize legal processes. Beyond AI and blockchain, there are ventures exploring the use of virtual reality for courtroom simulations, machine learning for predictive legal analytics, and platforms that democratize access to legal advice through crowdsourcing.
- **Legal Service Productization:** Innovators are packaging legal expertise into accessible products. This includes not just automated templates but also subscription-based legal advice services, DIY legal health checkups for businesses, and mobile apps that guide users through legal procedures.
- **Community Legal Education:** Some legal entrepreneurs focus on empowering communities through legal education platforms that offer easy-to-understand legal resources, workshops, and online courses, aiming to bridge the justice gap.

Navigating the Entrepreneurial Landscape: Challenges and Opportunities

Challenges

- **Ethical and Regulatory Navigation:** The legal industry's stringent ethical and regulatory framework poses a significant challenge, especially for models that disrupt traditional attorney–client paradigms.

- **Cultural Resistance:** Overcoming the legal profession's inherent resistance to change requires not just innovation but also persuasion, showcasing the tangible benefits of new models.
- **Financial Hurdles:** Securing investment and managing cash flow are critical challenges, particularly for start-ups aiming to disrupt well-entrenched legal practices.

Opportunities

- **Unmet Legal Needs:** The vast unmet need for legal services, especially among small businesses and underserved populations, presents a fertile ground for innovative legal solutions.
- **Interdisciplinary Collaboration:** The fusion of legal expertise with other disciplines, such as technology, design thinking, and business strategy, opens up new avenues for service delivery and problem solving.
- **Sustainability and Social Entrepreneurship:** There's a growing opportunity for legal entrepreneurs to contribute to social justice and sustainability, aligning legal practice with broader societal goals.

Legal entrepreneurship is not just about creating new businesses; it's about fostering a culture of innovation within the legal profession. By embracing the challenges and seizing the opportunities presented by the modern world, legal entrepreneurs can redefine the delivery of legal services, making them more efficient, accessible, and aligned with the needs of today's clients. As the legal landscape continues to evolve, the stories of these pioneers serve as both inspiration and a call to action for aspiring legal innovators, highlighting the profound impact that creative, entrepreneurial thinking can have on the future of law.

Innovative Legal Services for the Creative Industry: Christopher Valdheims

Founder and Partner, Counsel for Creators

Christopher Valdheims brings a distinctive blend of legal expertise and creative industry experience to his role as the Founder and Partner of Counsel for Creators. His educational journey at UCLA School of Law, where he studied under some of the nation's top-ranked practitioners in intellectual property, business law, and international law, laid a solid foundation for his legal career. While at UCLA Law, he also served as one of the two editors-in-chief of the UCLA Journal of International Law and

Foreign Affairs, further honing his legal acumen and understanding of complex legal issues.

Before embarking on his legal education, Chris had already established himself in the creative industries as a designer and software developer. This firsthand experience in the creative sector not only gives him unique insights into the challenges and needs of creative professionals but also informs his approach to providing legal services. It is this unique combination of skills and experiences that has enabled Chris to successfully navigate the intersection of law and creativity, making him a trusted advisor to those in the creative industries.

As the leader of Counsel for Creators, Chris has dedicated himself to redefining legal services for the creative community. His firm, which was started in 2013, is notable for its innovative approach to legal services, offering flat fee billing and a legal subscription membership program. This model aims to make legal services more accessible and predictable for creative professionals, aligning with the firm's mission to help more people at scale. Through his work, Chris continues to demonstrate the importance of blending legal expertise with a deep understanding of the industries one serves, establishing a new standard for legal support in the creative sector.

Redefining Legal Services for the Creative Industry

Christopher Valdheims set out to address a gap he observed in the legal market, particularly for creative professionals. This led to the establishment of Council for Creators, a law firm designed to cater specifically to the needs of the creative community. At the core of the firm's innovative approach is the implementation of flat fee billing and a legal subscription membership program. This model was developed as a response to the dissatisfaction Chris noted among creative professionals regarding traditional legal services, which often seemed inaccessible and unpredictable in terms of cost.

Chris explains that the traditional hourly billing model used by many law firms does not align well with the needs and expectations of creative professionals. Many of his clients had experienced frustration with other legal service providers, either because of unexpected high costs or because the services did not meet their needs. To address this, Council for Creators offers a more transparent and predictable pricing structure, which Chris believes is crucial for building trust and long-term relationships with clients in the creative industries.

The firm's legal subscription membership program is one of the first of its kind, aiming to provide ongoing support to clients for a fixed monthly fee. This program reflects the firm's goal to help more people at scale by making legal services more accessible. Chris emphasizes that this approach not only benefits the clients by providing them with the legal support they need when they need it but also allows the firm to work more efficiently and focus on delivering value. Through these innovative service models, Council for Creators seeks to bridge the gap between traditional law firms and online legal services, offering a middle path that combines the reliability and comprehensive support of a law firm with the ease and simplicity of online services.

The Importance of Business Acumen in Law

Chris emphasizes the significance of viewing and operating a law firm not just as a legal practice but as a business in its own right. He advises aspiring law firm founders to step into the role of business owners from the outset, underscoring the importance of gaining knowledge in various business disciplines such as marketing, sales, leadership, and finance. This comprehensive understanding, Chris argues, is crucial for the success of a law firm. By treating his own firm, Council for Creators, with the same strategic considerations as any other business, Chris has been able to navigate the firm toward innovative service models that resonate well with the creative community they serve.

Reflecting on his journey, Chris shares that his background as a designer and software developer provided him with a firsthand understanding of the creative industries, but it also highlighted the need for a business-oriented approach to running a law firm. He recognized early on that the skills necessary for business success—effective marketing to reach potential clients, sales strategies to convert interest into engagement, leadership to inspire and guide a team, and financial acumen to manage a firm's resources—were just as applicable to his legal practice. This holistic approach to business has not only contributed to the success of Council for Creators but has also allowed the firm to innovate in service delivery and pricing.

Chris points out the value of understanding the perspectives of business owners, which has been instrumental in tailoring legal services that meet their specific needs. By aligning the firm's offerings with the expectations and realities of business operations, Council for Creators has been able to establish deeper and more meaningful relationships with their clients. This client-centric approach, rooted in a solid grasp of business fundamentals, has enabled Chris and his team to provide legal services that are not only effective but also empathetic to the challenges faced by creative professionals.

Innovations in Pricing and Client Relationships

Chris is vocal about the need for innovation in the legal profession, particularly concerning pricing models. He points out the limitations of the traditional hourly billing system, noting that it often doesn't serve the best interests of either the lawyer or the client, especially for routine legal tasks. "For things like forming a company or helping someone through a trademark, there's no need for hourly billing," Chris explains. This insight led to the adoption of flat fee billing at Council for Creators, a move aimed at making costs more predictable and transparent for clients. According to Chris, this approach not only simplifies the billing process but also removes the financial unpredictability that can strain client relationships.

Chris highlights how innovations in pricing can significantly enhance the client experience. He shares that clients appreciate the predictability and transparency of flat fee billing, as it allows them to seek legal advice without the fear of an escalating bill. "The more they talk to their lawyer, the more they're going to get charged under an hourly system. It's unpredictable. They'll wonder, 'Is this going to cost me $2,000 or $8,000? I have no idea,'" he recounts. By implementing flat fee billing, Council for Creators has managed to eliminate this uncertainty, fostering a more trusting and open relationship with their clients.

These innovations extend beyond just pricing; they're about reshaping the client–lawyer relationship into one that's more collaborative and supportive. Chris and his team focus on delivering not just legal services but also on providing a sense of confidence and understanding to their clients. "Ultimately, our clients are coming to us so that they can feel confident, that they've done everything right, that they understand how to run their business," he says. This approach underscores the firm's commitment to addressing not only the legal but also the emotional needs of their clients, ensuring they feel heard, seen, and supported. Through these efforts, Council for Creators not only challenges traditional billing practices but also redefines what it means to be a legal partner to the creative industries.

Integrating Technology and Law

The intersection of technology and law is a dynamic space where innovation thrives, transforming the practice of law and enhancing the delivery of legal services. As advancements in AI, blockchain, and other emerging technologies continue to unfold, they not only create new possibilities for legal practice but also significantly improve efficiencies and access to legal services. This section explores the role of technology as a driver of innovation, outlines strategies for developing tech-savvy legal solutions, and offers insights into the future of legal technology, with a focus on creating efficiencies for lawyers and enhancing access to legal services for clients.

Technology as a Driver of Innovation

Technological advancements are revolutionizing legal practice by automating routine tasks, improving data analysis, and facilitating client engagement. Key areas of innovation include the following:

- **Artificial Intelligence and Machine Learning:** Enhancing legal research, document review, and predictive analytics, enabling lawyers to make data-driven decisions and provide more informed advice.
- **Blockchain Technology:** Offering new approaches to smart contracts, intellectual property management, and secure legal transactions, increasing transparency and trust.
- **Automation and Productivity Tools:** Streamlining administrative tasks such as document generation, billing, and client intake, allowing lawyers to focus on high-impact work.

These technologies are catalysts for rethinking traditional legal processes and developing innovative legal solutions that improve efficiency and service delivery.

Creating Efficiencies and Enhancing Access to Legal Services

Integrating technology into legal practice not only streamlines operations but also makes legal services more accessible and affordable:

- **Efficiencies for High-Impact Work:** By automating routine tasks and leveraging legal practice management software, lawyers can reallocate their time toward strategic thinking, complex case strategy, and direct client counseling. Cloud-based platforms and collaboration tools further enhance productivity and flexibility, enabling lawyers to deliver higher quality services more efficiently.

- **Democratizing Access to Legal Services:** Online legal platforms, legal aid technologies, and self-help legal resources are breaking down barriers to legal services. These tools provide affordable, convenient access to legal advice, document preparation, and legal information, empowering individuals and small businesses. Advanced e-discovery tools also make litigation more accessible by reducing the costs associated with document review.

The Future of Legal Technology

As we look to the future, the legal profession can expect continued rapid evolution in legal technology. Anticipated developments include the following:

- **Further Advancements in AI:** More sophisticated legal analytics and personalized legal services will likely emerge, offering deeper insights and enhancing client experiences.
- **Integration of the Internet of Things (IoT):** IoT technology could significantly impact evidence collection, compliance monitoring, and asset management in legal contexts.
- **Virtual and Augmented Reality Applications:** These technologies may transform legal education, trial preparation, and the visualization of complex legal scenarios, offering immersive and interactive experiences.

To prepare for and leverage these technological advancements, lawyers should:

- **Stay Informed and Engaged:** Keeping abreast of technological trends and actively participating in legal tech communities will be crucial for staying ahead of the curve.
- **Invest in Continuous Learning:** Pursuing education and training in emerging legal technologies will enhance lawyers' ability to adapt and innovate.
- **Collaborate with Tech Experts:** Building partnerships with technology experts will facilitate the co-creation of innovative legal solutions and ensure that legal practices remain at the forefront of technological innovation.

Integrating technology into law is about more than adopting new tools; it's about reimagining the practice of law in the digital age. By embracing innovation, creating efficiencies, enhancing access to legal services, and preparing for the future of legal technology, lawyers can not only improve their practice but also contribute to a more just and accessible legal system.

To thrive in this evolving environment, legal practitioners must embrace a mindset of continuous learning and adaptability. Developing tech proficiency and integrating technology into legal practice are no longer optional but essential for providing high-quality, efficient, and accessible legal services. The future of legal technology, with its promise of further advancements and innovations, calls for a proactive approach to understanding and leveraging these changes.

It is clear that the integration of technology and law holds the potential to transform not just how legal services are delivered but also how justice is administered and accessed. By embracing the opportunities presented by legal technology, legal professionals can lead the way in creating a more efficient, accessible, and equitable legal system for all. The future of legal practice is bright, and it is incumbent upon today's legal professionals to shape this future with foresight, innovation, and a commitment to the greater good.

The Evolving Landscape of the Legal Profession: Insights from Jordan Furlong

Legal Sector Analyst and Forecaster

Jordan Furlong's path in the legal profession, starting from his law studies and early practice, quickly evolved beyond traditional law roles. After graduating from law school and a brief tenure at a law firm, he discovered a passion for legal journalism. By 1996, he was deeply involved in legal media, significantly impacting as an editor for a major legal association's magazine and contributing to its national acclaim and member satisfaction. His editorial leadership extended to launching another influential legal magazine, marking his transition from law practice to a key figure in legal journalism and thought leadership.

Jordan Furlong has become a key strategic consultant and thought leader in the legal sector, known for his analysis of the evolving global legal market. Through his influential blog and newsletter, he shares deep insights on the transformation of legal services. With over two decades of experience, including roles with Edge International Consulting, Jordan advises on navigating the dynamic legal landscape, positioning him as a pivotal figure in shaping the future of the profession.

The Essence of People Law and Interpersonal Skills

Jordan emphasizes a fundamental truth about the practice of law: it's all about people. Whether working with individual clients or representing large corporations, the core of legal work involves understanding, empathizing with, and addressing the needs of people. This perspective challenges the stereotype of law as a purely intellectual or adversarial profession. Instead, Jordan highlights the indispensability of interpersonal skills such as empathy, the ability to listen effectively, and a genuine concern for the well-being of clients.

He argues that these skills are not just nice to have but essential for successful legal practice. "At its heart, law is about helping people navigate complex systems and challenges," Jordan notes. "This means that lawyers need to be more than just technically proficient. They need to be able to connect with their clients on a human level, to understand their concerns and motivations, and to communicate complex legal concepts in a way that is accessible and reassuring."

Jordan shares stories from his own experiences and observations, illustrating how lawyers who excel in these interpersonal skills can achieve better outcomes for their clients. He recounts instances where the ability to listen carefully and empathize with a client's situation led to more effective and creative legal strategies. Conversely, he also reflects on situations where a lack of these skills resulted in misunderstandings or missed opportunities.

For Jordan, developing these interpersonal skills is a continuous process that requires intentionality and practice. He encourages law students and young lawyers to seek out opportunities to hone these abilities, whether through coaching, volunteering, or simply being mindful of their interactions with others. By prioritizing empathy, listening, and genuine care in their professional development, lawyers can better serve their clients and fulfill the true potential of their role in society.

Navigating a Career in Business Law

Jordan stresses the significance of understanding the unique challenges and opportunities within business law, a field that demands not only legal acumen but also a deep understanding of the multifaceted nature of businesses and their stakeholders. For Jordan, the journey into business law begins with a critical assessment of one's career goals and the motivations driving the pursuit of this particular legal path.

He advises early career lawyers and law students to contemplate what draws them to business law, encouraging them to look beyond the surface allure of working with corporations or the potential for financial reward. Jordan points out that at the core of business law is a commitment to navigating complex organizational structures and addressing the diverse needs of stakeholders, from shareholders to employees and the broader community. This requires a lawyer to not only be adept at legal analysis but also possess strong interpersonal skills and a capacity for empathetic engagement.

The Future of Law Firms in the Age of Generative AI

Jordan predicts a significant transformation in the landscape of legal services, marked by the emergence of fewer, yet more powerful and influential law firms. This shift, according to Jordan, will not necessarily be characterized by the size of these firms in terms of personnel but rather by their profitability, revenue generation, and the volume of solutions they provide. He anticipates a clear separation in the market, where a small percentage of firms will dominate, leaving others to face considerable challenges. This prediction underscores the importance of adaptability and strategic positioning for law firms aiming to thrive in the future.

Technology, particularly generative AI, plays a central role in Jordan's forecast. He envisions a future where the platforms through which legal solutions are rendered will be markedly different from today's law firms. This technology-driven evolution will empower not only the mega firms but also small enterprises and solo practitioners, enabling them to deliver legal services more efficiently and effectively. The implication here is profound; the ability to leverage technology will become a critical determinant of success in the legal sector. Jordan's perspective suggests that law firms must embrace and integrate technological advancements not just as tools but as fundamental components of their business models.

Jordan highlights the potential for disruptive changes in the next five to seven years, driven by the end of the life spans of many classic institutions and the transformative power of generative AI. This period of turbulence and disruption presents both challenges and opportunities for law firms. On one hand, traditional revenue models based on billing for time and effort may become increasingly untenable. On the other hand, the advent of generative AI offers unprecedented possibilities for enhancing the efficiency and scope of legal services. Jordan's predictions emphasize the need for law firms to remain agile, forward-thinking, and open to reimagining their roles in a rapidly evolving legal landscape. By doing so, they can not only navigate the challenges ahead but also seize the opportunities presented by technological advancements to redefine the value they offer to their clients and society at large.

The Role of Lawyers in Human Betterment

Jordan ardently believes that the legal profession plays a crucial role in the betterment of society. He sees lawyers as agents of change, capable of making significant contributions to human welfare and justice. This perspective is especially relevant in today's world, where technology has the potential to bridge gaps in access to legal services. Jordan emphasizes the importance of lawyers understanding their role beyond the courtroom or the corporate deal table. They are, in his view, stewards of justice, with the ability to empower individuals and communities by leveraging legal knowledge and technological tools.

He encourages new lawyers to remember the reasons that drew them to law school in the first place. Many enter the legal field with a desire to make a difference, to stand up for the underrepresented, or to contribute to the rule of law. Despite the inevitable challenges and the pressures of the profession, Jordan urges lawyers to keep these ideals at the forefront of their practice. By doing so, they not only find personal fulfillment but also contribute to the overarching goal of human betterment.

Jordan's vision for the legal profession includes a strong emphasis on the use of technology to create opportunities for those who have historically been marginalized. Tools like generative AI can fundamentally change how legal services are delivered, making them more accessible and affordable. This technological shift is not just about efficiency; it's about expanding the reach of justice. Jordan sees a future where lawyers use these tools not only to enhance their practice but to open doors for people who have never had access to legal help before. In this way, lawyers can truly fulfill their role in improving the human condition, one case at a time.

Adapting the Partnership Model and Learning across Generations

Jordan is a proponent of rethinking the traditional law firm partnership model, particularly in the context of training and transitioning between generations of lawyers. He sees the current model, which often emphasizes short-term gains over long-term sustainability, as a barrier to the development of young lawyers and the healthy evolution of law firms. Jordan suggests that law firms should consider implementing an "off-ramp" for older partners. This concept involves providing senior lawyers with a structured and incentivizing pathway to gradually reduce their involvement in the firm, thereby making room for the next generation of lawyers to step into leadership roles. Such a model not only facilitates smoother transitions but also encourages the sharing of knowledge and experience across generations.

Moreover, Jordan discusses the challenges inherent in bridging the gap between different age groups within the legal profession. He acknowledges that there can be significant differences in how lawyers from various generations view the practice of law, embrace technology, and approach client service. These differences, while potentially challenging, also present opportunities for mutual learning and growth. Jordan advocates for creating environments within law firms where open dialogue and mentorship are encouraged. By doing so, firms can foster a culture of continuous learning, where younger lawyers benefit from the wisdom and experience of their older counterparts, and senior lawyers can stay abreast of new legal technologies and changing client expectations through their younger colleagues.

The key to successfully adapting the partnership model and fostering intergenerational learning, according to Jordan, lies in acknowledging and respecting the diverse perspectives and skills each generation brings to the table. He emphasizes the importance of creating mechanisms within law firms that not only recognize the contributions of senior partners but also actively support the professional development of younger lawyers. This includes providing them with meaningful opportunities to take on leadership roles, engage in high-value work, and contribute to the strategic direction of the firm. By doing so, law firms can ensure they are well positioned to adapt to the rapidly evolving legal landscape, meet the changing needs of their clients, and secure their long-term success and relevance in the legal market. ”

Conclusion

Forging Your Path in Business Law

As we conclude our journey through the evolving landscape of business law, it's important to reflect on the key insights and strategies that have been shared. From understanding the dynamic nature of the legal profession to embracing innovation and building a robust professional network, the path to success in business law is multifaceted and deeply personal.

The stories of those who have navigated their way to fulfilling careers in business law, often overcoming significant barriers, serve as a testament to the power of determination, creativity, and strategic planning. These narratives not only inspire but also provide practical blueprints for carving out your own path in this dynamic field.

As you move forward, remember that the journey to success is ongoing and ever-evolving. The legal profession will continue to change, and with it, new opportunities and challenges will arise. Staying informed, adaptable, and proactive in your career planning will be key to navigating these changes successfully.

We encourage you to take the insights and strategies discussed in this book and apply them to your own career aspirations. Reflect on your goals, strengths, and the unique value you can bring to the field of business law. Consider the next steps you can take to advance your career, whether it's pursuing further education, seeking mentorship, or exploring new areas of specialization.

Thank you for joining us on this exploration of business law. Your commitment to personal and professional growth is commendable, and we are confident that the insights gained from this book will serve you well as you forge your path in the legal profession. Remember, the future of business law is in the hands of innovative, dedicated professionals like you. We look forward to seeing the impact you will make.

Index

About the Author

Lana Manganiello, a strategist, coach, and trainer in lawyer development, specializes in equipping legal professionals with the tools and methodologies necessary for fostering growth and establishing enduring relationships. She works with lawyers to define a career or business focus that is in line with their values, interests, and goals, and to enhance their visibility and credibility among key contacts in their chosen fields.

With a career spanning nearly twenty years, she has dedicated herself to working with both new and seasoned lawyers, as well as other service professionals, to build their practices and develop their careers. She excels at integrating systems and processes that foster behaviors leading to inclusive and successful workplaces. Her comprehensive approach leverages strategic planning, data-driven decision making, and optimizing organizational performance to drive sustainable growth.

Committed to increasing equity and access to justice, she actively contributes to the legal community at a local level. She serves as President for the Counsel for Justice (CFJ) of the Los Angeles County Bar Association, a nonprofit dedicated to providing legal services to vulnerable populations in Los Angeles. In addition, she serves on the Board of Directors for the San Diego County Bar Foundation, focusing on delivering justice to the underserved in San Diego. Her commitment extends to her roles in the Legal Marketing Association, the National Association for Law Placement (NALP), and the Professional Development Consortium (PDC).

Her contributions and leadership in the areas of legal strategy, diversity, and inclusion have been widely recognized. She was recently honored as a "Global Leader in Legal Strategy and Consulting" by Lawdragon, named a "Top Diversity Professional" by the *San Diego Business Journal*, and awarded the title of "Diversity Champion" by *Consulting Magazine*.